ORIGINALITY, IMITATION, AND PLAGIARISM

DIGITALCULTUreBOOKS is a collaborative imprint of the University of Michigan Press and the University of Michigan Library dedicated to publishing innovative work about the social, cultural, and political impact of new media.

Originality, Imitation, and Plagiarism

Teaching Writing in the Digital Age

Caroline Eisner and Martha Vicinus
EDITORS

THE UNIVERSITY OF MICHIGAN PRESS AND
THE UNIVERSITY OF MICHIGAN LIBRARY
Ann Arbor

Copyright © by the University of Michigan 2008
All rights reserved
Published in the United States of America by
The University of Michigan Press
Manufactured in the United States of America
⊗ Printed on acid-free paper

2011   2010   2009   2008   4   3   2

A CIP catalog record for this book is available from the British Library.

Library of Congress Cataloging-in-Publication Data

Originality, imitation, and plagiarism : teaching writing in the
    digital age / Caroline Eisner and Martha Vicinus, editors.
      p.   cm.
    Includes bibliographical references and index.
    ISBN-13: 978-0-472-07034-3 (cloth : alk. paper)
    ISBN-10: 0-472-07034-7 (cloth : alk. paper)
    ISBN-13: 978-0-472-05034-5 (pbk. : alk. paper)
    ISBN-10: 0-472-05034-6 (pbk. : alk. paper)
      1. Plagiarism.   2. Imitation in literature.   3. Creation (Literary, artistic, etc.)
    4. Authorship—Study and teaching. I. Eisner, Caroline, 1965–   II. Vicinus,
    Martha.

    PN167.O75   2008
    808—dc22   2007036088

For
John and Susan Sweetland
Generous friends and devoted supporters

Contents

Introduction

Originality, Imitation, and Plagiarism: Teaching Writing in the Age of the Internet

Caroline Eisner and Martha Vicinus

Across university and college campuses, writing centers face questions about plagiarism. All too often these queries are framed in narrow, judgmental terms that leave little room for either the teacher or the student to understand the complexities of permission, attribution, and copyright. Teachers find themselves placed in an adversarial position in relation to students, as if all writing assignments involved the risk of plagiarism. This collection of essays addresses not only such immediate problems, but also a larger, more central, argument that academic integrity goes beyond the classroom and that any discussion of plagiarism must involve the current questions regarding "fair use" and copyright. It is no accident that public debates about plagiarism have coincided with efforts to limit access to copyrighted material. On the one hand, we face the exponential increase in readily available information from the Web, and, on the other, threats of property-rights litigation and increasingly limited access to this material. Adding to the mix, postmodern literary theory reminds us that nothing is wholly original—that we depend on remixing and reusing the past, adding to or remaking old plots, insights, and ideas. Across disciplines and fields, we find that plagiarism is not a simple wrong; a full understanding of its role in contemporary intellectual life depends on a broad approach that includes notions of what is original and what role imitation plays in the creation of new texts. As numerous contributors remind us, at no time has copyright law guaranteed complete control over an individual work.

Within the university we rightly have a profound investment in responsible, independent, intellectual work, lest we undermine the very nature of our profession. Both students and researchers can be tempted to short-circuit, via unacknowledged use of others' work, the necessary groundwork in learning; most of those who succumb do not get caught. In the past, before the Web, probably even fewer were caught. Stealing or buying the work of others, however, undermines the credibility of the written word and damages the open and free exchange of ideas. In the past few years, we have witnessed a rash of high-profile plagiarism cases, ranging from a Harvard undergraduate's plagiarized novel to fabrication of evidence in the biomedical field. How do we conserve and inculcate a tradition of ethical research and writing standards, while acknowledging and taking full advantage of the opportunities provided by new technologies? How can students be taught to evaluate sources and then to credit the authors appropriately? Why have so many experienced researchers been found guilty of stealing from others?

The essays selected for this anthology address these and other questions from different points of view. For, as its table of contents reveals, issues of authorial authority and control over writing cut across every area of study. We have organized the essays to highlight the ways in which experts across many fields, ranging from the fine arts to physics, are grappling with these issues. However different the starting point, each author shares a concern about the increasingly angry public debate for or against file sharing, fair use, and plagiarism. We have organized the essays to speak to each other about this issue, as well as about shared pedagogical concerns. We hope that both novice and experienced teachers will learn from the practical and concrete suggestions about how to fashion unique assignments, to teach about proper attribution, and to increase students' involvement in their own writing. At its core, this is an anthology for anyone interested in the process of learning. How can we encourage the free and ethical exchange of ideas? How can we encourage students, so accustomed to digital sharing, to understand citation practices, free use, and the legitimate ownership of ideas? These seemingly local concerns are nevertheless also implicated in larger national issues because access to and use of trustworthy information and writing are, of course, fundamental to public discourse in a democratic society.

Many of the authors included here allude to the groundbreaking work of Rebecca Moore Howard, who first suggested the importance of "patch writing" for learners confronted with massive amounts of new information. She argues that students frequently quote without citation material that they are still mastering, or may not understand, as an initial step in their learning process. The reasons for such lapses are not easy to come by:

students may fail to acknowledge their sources because of a failure in teaching the rules; because it is easy to forget who said what when sifting through many different sources; or because they come from countries in which quoting without citing an expert is a way of acknowledging the greatness of the expert's ideas. It may also be that intertexuality is simply fundamental to their knowledge base. Attribution seems artificial in a world saturated with references to familiar songs and popular culture. In her essay, Amy England points to yet another complication: what may be "common knowledge" to academics is rarely so for students—and vice versa. Joel Bloch and Lisa Emerson highlight the contextual nature of knowledge and the difficult cultural leaps international students must make to understand what is considered common knowledge within the context of a particular discipline.

The situation is more complicated for advanced and professional writers. Perhaps no field has had more high-profile cases of plagiarism than history; the notorious Sokolow case is only one of many possible examples (Mallon). Michael Grossberg documents a familiar tale of high-minded intentions torpedoed by timid committees, nonexistent enforcement strategies, and fears of litigation. His essay is also a salutary reminder of the difficulty of monitoring plagiarism within a single discipline, especially when confidentiality and privacy drive the process. Gordon Kane explains that in theoretical physics, by contrast, self-policing works effectively not only because it is a small field where everyone knows everyone else, but also because the Internet has enabled the rapid exchange of work and ideas. Rather than waiting several months or even years for publication, physicists often place their work online; congratulations, refinements, and rebuttals follow with equal speed. Yet Kane also acknowledges the difficulties of policing a larger, more amorphous discipline, such as medical biology, Gilbert S. Omenn's field. In science, the theft of ideas or data can be far more serious than the unacknowledged use of an author's words and argument. As Omenn makes clear, researchers worry that anonymous peer reviewing may enable established scholars to steal the ideas of applicants for grants.

When the Sweetland Writing Center sponsored a conference that placed plagiarism in dialogue with notions of originality and imitation, it was striking how few papers considered the place of imitation in training writers. Many participants asked but did not answer the question, "Why has imitation fallen out of composition studies?" Classical rhetoric from the time of Aristotle emphasized the pedagogic value of imitating famous orators and authors as the best means of learning to speak and write effec-tively. Imitation meant emulation, not perfect reproduction; indeed, it was assumed that no one could make an exact copy of the work of another speaker or writer. By close study, a novice gained appreciation of the ele-ments that make an effective oration, and could then imitate them. After sufficient practice, he would join the masters, armed with the vocabulary, style, and form deemed most effective to persuade others. These days the only element of classical teaching still widely employed is paraphrase, in which a teacher asks students to summarize as closely as possible a particu-lar passage (Corbett). Given how frequently teachers across fields complain about students' careless reading, they might do well to reconsider the ways that imitation, paraphrase, and précis writing can be used to inculcate close reading skills and also improve writing and vocabulary.

As long ago as 1900, the educational psychologist Jasper Newton Deahl remarked on teachers' failure to realize the important role that imitation played in their own education:

> The value of imitation in teaching composition is too often overlooked. This is especially clear of young teachers and strikingly manifested in those teachers who have a ready intuition and who have easily devel-oped good literary tastes. This holds not only for teachers of rhetoric and composition, but it may be observed in most teachers who readily acquired their academic training. . . . They more fully absorbed their models and consequently were not aware of imitating. They did not imitate less but more. It was, however, a higher order of imitation. The process is so natural and powerful that we are largely unconscious of it. (76)

Imitation, indeed, is the backbone of writing courses in many disciplines, enabling students to master the distinctive and defining terms and style of their specialty. For example, first-year graduate students routinely learn to write literature surveys, fellowship applications, and book reviews by look-ing closely at previously successful efforts.

Christina Pugh demonstrates the effectiveness of imitation in a creative writing class. Determined to move her students beyond the mantra "Write about what you know," she crafted a course that asks students to "write in the style of these great writers." Despite these "limitations," students found themselves becoming freer, more compelling writers. Both Christiane Donohue and Joel Bloch document the long-standing exercise of imitating classical authors in France and China. Although both the French and the

Chinese educational systems operate within well-articulated guidelines about what constitutes appropriate and inappropriate imitation, neither seems always to recognize their own pedagogic contradictions. Ironically, the French are lauded for their tradition of individualism and the Chinese are criticized for their collectivism, even though both share a respect for imitating the work of experts as an integral part of the novice's learning process.

Although it may seem the most straightforward of our three concepts, originality is in many ways the most elusive. As graduate students can attest, nothing is more daunting than writing a dissertation that claims to be "an original contribution to knowledge." Despite our best intentions as writing teachers, even first-year students often prefer to follow a formula, a formula dictated by the organization of the five-paragraph essay. Anne Berggren focuses on classroom techniques for fostering originality in novice writers; she argues that rules may build confidence in the short run, but are destructive in developing a writer's voice. Anis Bawarshi casts a critical eye on those who prioritize originality over other authorial intentions. He addresses how originality functions in different genres and social contexts. After examining the difficulties students encounter in mastering academic genres, he turns to an infamous case of the *testimonio, I, Rigoberto Menchú,* by the Nobel Prize winner who wrote within a tradition that valued mixing the personal and the collective. For some American readers, who have confused the genre of *testimonio* with a personal autobiography, Menchú was guilty of dishonest borrowing; yet she herself never claimed sole, original authorship of her *testimonio.* A clear understanding of different genres teaches readers to understand different cultural conventions, whether it be an academic setting or a faraway country.

Christopher M. Kuipers's discussion of the history of the anthology provides a striking example of how difficult it can be to define plagiarism. He demonstrates how the genre combines forms of originality, imitation, and plagiarism, and suggests that perhaps all writing partakes of this mix. But as he reminds us, anthologies are also at times far more creative than they may seem to the casual reader. If anthologies are themselves a mixture of the old and the new, the borrowed and the created, this is even truer on the World Wide Web. Amit Ray and Erhardt Graeff use the example of writing for Wikipedia, in which anyone can contribute, correct, and alter the content of an entry. As they argue, the implications of open access in the creation and editing of Web content are vast, for it turns all texts into unstable entities, and the unique role of the author disappears into a medley of voices. In the process, the concept of an individual original creation becomes moot because, in spite of fair-use laws, copyright owners insist on protecting permissions to copy. This is, not surprisingly, increasingly difficult to enforce in the digital age, and creators find themselves forced to turn over their rights to traditional intermediaries—publishers, record companies, and movie studios. While Wikis may be liberating for some, many authors feel a loss of control, and of royalties, with the present state of affairs.

Although the authors in this volume describe a confusing and contradictory system, they find opportunities for teachers and students. Lynn Z. Bloom describes two successful writing courses employing nontraditional assignments. She admits that both she and her students worked much harder on these assignments than they had thought possible, but the results were far more satisfying for everyone. Stefan Senders recounts his experience sending a plagiarizing student to his college's Committee on Standards. When he suggested that she write a defense of her behavior, the student began to take her writing seriously, so that he could teach and she could learn. But not every writing situation involves personal experience or an individual crisis. Kim Walden and Alan Peacock note the historical circumstances that have encouraged students' disengagement from their own learning, including the corporate structure of large, impersonal universities, overworked and distant faculty, and the seeming necessity of certification rather than education. In an effort to remedy this alienating situation and help students to trace their learning and writing on a topic, they devised an "i-map," in which students can document each stage of their research, thinking, and writing processes.

In their contribution, Linda Adler-Kassner, Chris M. Anson, and Rebecca Moore Howard suggest that we must reframe how we talk about the learning process, and how we define and discuss plagiarism. Like Lisa Emerson, they are doubtful of the benefits of Web-based, commercial plagiarism detection services, and emphasize the ways in which an obsession with plagiarism prevention can destroy the trust between teacher and student. Instead of policing student writing, teachers need to acknowledge the existence of "different discursive communities with different practices and activities." They urge readers to reframe the discussion of plagiarism in universities and in the media; rather than focusing on theft and morality, teachers should encourage students to understand different genres and contexts and to use academic citation practices.

The legal ramifications for writers and readers are subtly explored in our opening essay by Jessica Litman, a pioneer in the field of intellectual property law and digital media. Drawn from her book *Digital Copyright,* this essay explores recent changes in the framing of copyright. What the founding fathers described as quid pro quo, limited exclusive rights in return for immediate public dissemination, quickly became seen as a *financial bargain,* whereby copyright owners earned a reasonable profit and the public gained easy access to information. Copyright offered limited and time-bound protection to an owner, who may or may not have been an author. It never included control "over reading, or private performance, or resale of a copy legitimately owned, or learning from and talking about and writing about a work, because those were all part of what the public gained from its bargain." Litman argues that in the last thirty years we have seen a substantial, and accelerating, shift in power away from fair use and the public's right of access. She notes that copyright is no longer about providing compensation but about *control.* Even though the United States has no legal authority over the copyright laws of another country, enhanced control within the United States is framed as an effort to control the theft of intellectual property by foreigners. "Piracy" has become a favorite word to describe even legal copying of material because in the digital age the potential arises to make millions of copies easily.

Cultural and legal critics remind us that intellectual property and copyright laws do not give authors, musicians, publishers, agents, or corporations absolute control over all aspects of a work. They argue forcefully that we must fight for the free exchange of ideas and cultural artifacts, whether on the Internet or by more traditional means. In the words of Lawrence Lessig,

> A free culture supports and protects creators and innovators. It does this directly by granting intellectual property rights. But it does so by indirectly limiting the reach of those rights, to guarantee that follow-on creators and innovators remain *as free as possible* from the control of the past. A free culture is not a culture without property, just as a free market is not a market in which everything is free. (xiv)

Those like Lessig who have followed the technological revolution closely have documented the efforts of large, invested interests in preserving and even expanding traditional property rights. The clamping down on Napster and the policing of peer-to-peer music sharing are only the best-known examples of this battle. As the Google initiative works to index the contents of university libraries, including the library here at the University of Michigan, a group of authors have sued for copyright infringement, arguing that Google must first receive permission from each author indexed. Efforts are also under way to limit free access to information printed from the Web. Countering these legal efforts is our long tradition of fair use, which includes the need for creative work to build upon the work of others—to borrow, alter, allude to, and create something new and timely. Ironically, as we focus on the epidemic of student cheating, we ignore a crucial legal right: the fair use of copyrighted material. When properly citing, we have a legal right to quote and use this material. But contradictory court decisions, in addition to the increasing power of corporate ownership of copyright (as opposed to individual ownership), have complicated maintaining a "fair use" system that protects both author and user rights.

Building upon the pioneering work of Lawrence Lessig, Jessica Litman, and Siva Vaidhayanthan, Martine Courant Rife and Laura J. Murray outline the difficulties of those interested in the *noncommercial* uses of copyrighted material. Teachers, Rife and Murray argue, need both to defend the free exchange of ideas and to emphasize the requirement of correctly attributing information to its proper sources. Rife documents the contradictions in recent court decisions that make fair use difficult to understand and defend. She encourages writing teachers to educate their digitally savvy students about the legal status of information sharing and copyright. Murray describes the subtle ways in which universities, fearful of legal entanglements, may undermine legal fair use. She suggests separating the academic system of citation, which engages by right with texts and ideas, and the copyright system, which insists upon permission. Murray argues that the free use of materials under copyright is an essential public good that needs to be defended; universities should guard against creating an environment of copyright permission that trumps users' rights. If they do not do so, we risk losing the necessary free exchange of ideas that was originally written into copyright law.

While Rife and Murray analyze the ways in which the noncommercial uses of intellectual property have been hemmed in, Jeff Ward uses the example of a public artwork, Chicago's *Cloud Gate,* in order to explore the contradictions in copyright law. Concentrating on the case of a professional photographer who wished to sell photos of the massive $11.5 million sculpture, Ward explores the distinctive functions of photography in terms of reproduction, description, and depiction. What are the appropriate legal constraints for the *commercial* reproduction of a work of art? Is a photograph a copy of a work of art, or is it a separate work of art? What rights do the taxpaying citizens of Chicago have in regard to public art? Ward traces this public debate, and like Litman, argues for a broad public rethinking about what it means to make a copy in today's technological world.

The authors in this collection investigate originality, imitation, and plagiarism in and through their own disciplines and technologies. Beyond the title's grouping of these themes, we encourage readers to locate diverse views on the place and responsibilities of the author, asking who and what an author becomes in the age of wikis and the Internet. Some readers will note how many of our teacher-writers hope to create reverence for rigorous ideas. This means honoring the careful thinking of both novices and experts, and combining the assimilation of ideas with training in analytic writing skills. One of the single most difficult tasks is integrating the teaching of intellectual integrity with challenging writing assignments. Could the problems sometimes inherent in originality, imitation, and plagiarism be as simple as teaching integrity and responsibility so that students, colleagues, and peers honor the ideas that have come before? Is it as simple as recognizing creativity and originality and placing such innovation in high regard? Our undertaking as teachers, writers, and thinkers is to encourage others to work honestly and creatively, amid the challenges posed by new technologies, litigation, and the demands of teaching generations of students to think, question, discover, and invent.

Works Cited

Corbett, Edward P. J. "The Theory and Practice of Imitation in Classical Rhetoric." *College Composition and Communication* 22, no. 3 (1971): 243–50.

Deahl, Jasper Newton. *Imitation in Education: Its Nature, Scope, and Significance.* New York: Macmillan, 1900.

Howard, Rebecca Moore. "Plagiarisms, Authorships, and the Academic Death Penalty." *College English,* 57, no. 7 (1995): 788–806.

Lessig, Lawrence. *Free Culture: How Big Media Uses Technology and the Law to Lock Down Culture and Control Creativity.* New York: Penguin, 2004.

Mallon, Thomas. *Stolen Words: Forays into the Origins and Ravages of Plagiarism.* New York: Ticknor and Fields, 1989.

Originality

Choosing Metaphors

Jessica Litman

A public domain work is an orphan. No one is responsible for its life. But everyone exploits its use, until that time certain when it becomes soiled and haggard, barren of its previous virtues. Who, then, will invest the funds to renovate and nourish its future life when no one owns it? How does the consumer benefit from that scenario? The answer is, there is no benefit.

—Jack Valenti[1]

The copyright law on the books is a large aggregation of specific statutory provisions; it goes on and on for pages and pages. When most people talk about copyright, though, they don't mean the long complicated statute codified in title 17 of the U.S. Code. Most people's idea of copyright law takes the form of a collection of principles and norms. They understand that those principles are expressed, if sometimes imperfectly, in the statutory language and the case law interpreting it, but they tend to believe that the underlying principles are what count. It is, thus, unsurprising that the rhetoric used in copyright litigation and copyright lobbying is more often drawn from the principles than the provisions.

One can greatly overstate the influence that underlying principles can exercise over the enactment and interpretation of the nitty-gritty provisions of substantive law. In the ongoing negotiations among industry representatives, normative arguments about the nature of copyright show up as rhetorical flourishes, but, typically, change nobody's mind. Still, normative understandings of copyright exercise some constraints on the actual legal provisions that the lobbyists can come up with, agree on, convince Congress to pass, and persuade outsiders to comply with. The ways we have of thinking about copyright law can at least make some changes more difficult to achieve than others.

Lawyers, lobbyists, and scholars in a host of disciplines have reexamined and reformulated copyright principles over the past generation, in ways that have expanded copyright's scope and blinded many of us to the dangers that arise from protecting too much, too expansively for too long. That transformation has facilitated the expansion of copyright protection and the narrowing of copyright limitations and exceptions.

At the turn of the century, when Congress first embraced the copyright conference model that was to trouble us for the rest of the century, the predominant metaphor for copyright was the notion of a quid pro quo.[2] The public granted authors limited exclusive rights (and only if the authors fulfilled a variety of formal conditions) in return for the immediate public dissemination of the work and the eventual dedication of the work in its entirety to the public domain.[3]

As the United States got less hung up on formal prerequisites, that model evolved to a view of copyright as a bargain in which the public granted limited exclusive rights to authors as a means to advance the public interest. This model was about compensation:[4] it focused on copyright as a way to permit authors to make enough money from the works they created in order to encourage them to create the works and make them available to the public. That view of the law persisted until fairly recently.

If you read books, articles, legal briefs, and congressional testimony about copyright written by scholars and lawyers and judges fifty years ago, you find widespread agreement that copyright protection afforded only shallow and exception-ridden control over protected works. Forty, thirty, even twenty years ago, it was an article of faith that the nature of copyright required that it offer only circumscribed, porous protection to works of authorship. The balance between protection and the material that copyright left unprotected was thought to be the central animating principle of the law. Copyright was a bargain between the public and the author, whereby the public bribed the author to create new works in return for limited commercial control over the new expression the author brought to her works. The public's payoff was that, beyond the borders of the authors' defined exclusive rights, it was entitled to enjoy, consume, learn from, and reuse the works. Even the bounded copyright rights would expire after a limited term, then set at fifty-six years.

A corollary of the limited protection model was that copyright gave owners control only over particular uses of their works.[5] The copyright owner had exclusive rights to duplicate the work. Publishing and public performance were within the copyright owner's control. But copyright never gave owners any control over reading, or private performance, or resale of a copy legitimately owned, or learning from and talking about and writing about a work, because those were all part of what the public gained from its bargain. Thus, the fact that copyright protection lasted for a very long time (far longer than the protection offered by patents); the fact that copyright protection has never required a government examination for originality, creativity, or merit; and the fact that copyright protects works that have very little of any of them was defended as harmless: because copyright *never* took from the public any of the raw material it might need to use to create new works of authorship, the dangers arising from over-protection ranged from modest to trivial.

There was nearly universal agreement on these points through the mid-1970s. Copyright was seen as designed to be full of holes. The balance underlying that view of the copyright system treated the interests of owners of particular works (and often those owners were not the actual authors) as potentially in tension with the interests of the general public, including the authors of the future; the theory of the system was to adjust that balance so that each of the two sides got at least as much as it needed.[6] In economic terms, neither the author nor the public was entitled to appropriate the entire surplus generated by a new work of authorship.[7] Rather, they shared the proceeds, each entitled to claim that portion of them that would best encourage the promiscuous creation of still newer works of authorship.

If you're dissatisfied with the way the spoils are getting divided, one approach is to change the rhetoric. When you conceptualize the law as a balance between copyright owners and the public, you set up a particular dichotomy—some would argue, a false dichotomy[8]—that constrains the choices you are likely to make. If copyright law is a bargain between authors and the public, then we might ask what the public is getting from the bargain. If copyright law is about a balance between owners' control of the exploitation of their works and the robust health of the public domain, one might ask whether the system strikes the appropriate balance.[9] You can see how, at least in some quarters, this talk about bargains and balance might make trouble. Beginning in the late 1970s and early 1980s, advocates of copyright owners began to come up with different descriptions of the nature of copyright, with an eye to enabling copyright owners to capture a greater share of the value embodied in copyright-protected works.[10]

In the last thirty years, the idea of a bargain has gradually been replaced by a model drawn from the economic analysis of law, which characterizes copyright as a system of incentives.[11] Today, this is the standard economic model of copyright law, whereby copyright provides an economic incentive for the creation and distribution of original works of authorship.[12] The model derives a lot of its power from its simplicity: it posits a direct relationship between the extent of copyright protection and the amount of authorship produced and distributed—any increase in the scope or subject matter or duration of copyright will cause an increase in authorship; any reduction will cause a reduction.

The economic analysis model focuses on the effect greater or lesser copyright rights might have on incentives to create and exploit new works. It doesn't bother about stuff like balance or bargains except as they might affect the incentive structure for creating and exploiting new works. To justify copyright limitations, like fair use, under this model, you need to argue that authors and publishers need them in order to create new works of authorship,[13] rather than, say, because that's part of the public's share of the copyright bargain. The model is not rooted in compensation, and so it doesn't ask how broad a copyright would be appropriate or fair; instead it inquires whether broader, longer, or stronger copyright protection would be likely to lead to the production of more works of authorship.

The weakness in this model is that more and stronger and longer copyright protection will always, at the margin, cause more authors to create more works—that's how this sort of linear model operates. If we forget that the model is just a useful thought tool, and persuade ourselves that it straightforwardly describes the real world, then we're trapped in a construct in which there's no good reason why copyrights shouldn't cover everything and last forever.

Lately, that's what seems to have happened. Copyright legislation has recently been a one-way ratchet, and it's hard to argue that that's bad within the confines of the conventional way of thinking about copyright. In the past several years we've seen a further evolution. Copyright today is less about incentives or compensation than it is about control.[14] What ended up persuading lawmakers to adopt that model was the conversion of copyright into a trade issue: The content industries, copyright owners argued, were among the few in which the United States had a favorable balance of trade. Instead of focusing on American citizens who engaged in unlicensed uses of copyrighted works (many of them legal under U.S. law), they drew Congress's attention to people and businesses in other countries who engaged in similar uses. The United States should make it a top priority, they argued, to beef up domestic copyright law at home, and thus ensure that people in other countries paid for any use of copyrighted works abroad. U.S. copyright law does not apply beyond U.S. borders, but supporters of expanded copyright protection argued that by enacting stronger copyright laws, Congress would set a good example for our trading partners, who could then be persuaded to do the same. Proponents of enhanced protection changed the story of copyright from a story about authors and the public collaborating on a bargain to promote the progress of learning, into a story about Americans trying to protect their property from foreigners trying to steal it.

That story sold. It offered an illusion that, simply by increasing the scope and strength and duration of U.S. copyright protection, Congress could generate new wealth for America without detriment or even inconvenience to any Americans. That recasting of the copyright story persuaded Congress to "improve" copyright protection and cut back on limitations and exceptions.[15]

The upshot of the change in the way we think about copyright is that the dominant metaphor is no longer that of a bargain between authors and the public. We talk now of copyright as property that the owner is entitled to control—to sell to the public (or refuse to sell) on whatever terms the owner chooses. Copyright has been transformed into the right of a property owner to protect what is rightfully hers. (That allows us to skip right past the question of what it is, exactly, that ought to be rightfully hers.) And the current metaphor is reflected both in recent copyright amendments now on the books and in the debate over what those laws mean and whether they go too far.

One example of this trend is the piecemeal repeal of the so-called first-sale doctrine, which historically permitted the purchaser of a copy of a copyrighted work to sell, loan, lease, or display the copy without the copyright owner's permission, and is the reason why public libraries, video rental stores, and art galleries are not illegal.[16] The first sale doctrine enhanced public access to copyrighted works that some were unable to purchase. Because the first sale doctrine applies only to copies of a copyrighted work, it became increasingly irrelevant in a world in which vast numbers of works were disseminated to the public through media such as television and radio, which involved no transfer of copies. Copyright owners who did distribute copies of their works, however, lobbied for the first sale doctrine's repeal. Congress yielded to the entreaties of the recording industry to limit the first sale doctrine as it applied to records, cassette tapes, and compact discs in 1984, and enacted an amendment that made commercial record rental (but not loan or resale) illegal.[17] After the computer software industry's attempts to evade the operation of the first sale doctrine—by claiming that their distribution of software products involved licenses rather than sales[18]—received an unenthusiastic reception in court,[19] Congress partially repealed the first sale doctrine as it applied to computer programs.[20] Bills to repeal the first sale doctrine for audio/visual works were introduced in Congress,[21] but never accumulated enough support to be enacted. The actual bites these laws took out of the first sale doctrine were small ones, but in the process, the principle that the doctrine represents has been diminished.

If we no longer insist that people who own legitimate copies of works be permitted to do what they please with them, that presents an opportunity to attack a huge realm of unauthorized but not illegal use. If copyright owners can impose conditions on the act of gaining access, and back those conditions up with either technological devices, or legal prohibitions, or both, then copyright owners can license access to and use of their works on a continuing basis. Technological fences, such as passwords or encryption, offer some measure of control, and enhanced opportunities to extract value from the use of a work. The owner of the copyright in money management software, for example, could design the software to require purchasers of copies to authorize a small credit card charge each time they sought to run the program. The owner of the copyright in recorded music could release the recording in a scrambled format, and rent access to descramblers by the day. Technological controls, though, are vulnerable to technological evasion, which is where the part about legal controls comes in.

When copyright owners demanded the legal tools to restrict owners of legitimate copies of works from gaining access to them, Congress was receptive. Copyright owner interests argued that, in a digital age, anyone with access to their works could commit massive violations of their copyrights with a single keystroke by transmitting unauthorized copies all over the Internet. In order for their rights to mean anything, copyright owners insisted, they were entitled to have control over access to their works—not merely initial access, but continuing control over every subsequent act of gaining access to the content of a work.[22] Thus, to protect their property rights, the law needed to be amended to prohibit individuals from gaining unauthorized access to copyrighted works.[23]

Augmenting copyright law with legally enforceable access control could completely annul the first sale doctrine. More fundamentally, enforceable access control has the potential to redesign the copyright landscape completely. The hallmark of legal rights is that they can be carefully calibrated. Copyright law can give authors control over the initial distribution of a copy of a work, without permitting the author to exercise downstream control over who gets to see it. Copyright law can give authors control over the use of the words and pictures in their books without giving them rights to restrict the ideas and facts those words and pictures express. It can give them the ability to collect money for the preface and notes they add to a collection of Shakespeare's plays without allowing them to assert any rights in the text of those plays. It can permit them to control reproductions of their works without giving them the power to restrict consumption of their works. Leaving eye-tracks on a page has never been deemed to be copyright infringement.

Copyrighted works contain protected and unprotected elements, and access to those works may advance restricted or unrestricted uses. Access controls are not so discriminating. Once we permit copyright owners to exert continuing control over consumers' access to the contents of their works, there is no way to ensure that access controls will not prevent consumers from seeing the unprotected facts and ideas in a work. Nor can we make certain that the access controls prevent uses that the law secures to the copyright owner, while permitting access when its purpose is to facilitate a use the law permits. If the law requires that we obtain a license whenever we wish to read protected text, it encourages copyright owners to restrict the availability of licenses whenever it makes economic sense for them to do so. That, in turn, makes access to the ideas, facts, and other unprotected elements contingent on copyright holders' marketing plans, and puts the ability of consumers to engage in legal uses of the material in those texts within the copyright holders' unconstrained discretion. In essence, that's an exclusive right to use. In other words, in order to effectively protect authors' "exclusive rights" to their writings, which is to say, control, we need to give them power to permit or prevent any use that might undermine their control. What that means is that a person who buys a copy of a work may no longer have the right to read and reread it, loan it, resell it, or give it away. But the law has been moving away from that principle for years.

A second example of this trend is the campaign to contract the fair-use privilege. Fair use was once understood as the flip side of the limited scope of copyright.[24] The copyright law gave the copyright holder exclusive control over reproductions of the work, but not over all reproductions.[25] The justifications for fair use were various; a common formulation explained that reasonable appropriations of protected works were permissible when they advanced the public interest without inflicting unacceptably grave damage on the copyright owner. Fair use was appropriate in situations when the copyright owner would be likely to authorize the use but it would be a great deal of trouble to ask for permission, such as the quotation of excerpts of a novel in a favorable review or the use of selections from a scholarly article in a subsequent scholarly article building on the first author's research. Fair use was also appropriate in situations when the copyright owner would be unlikely to authorize, such as parodies and critiques, under a justification Prof. Alan Latman described as "enforced consent." The social interest in allowing uses that criticized the copyright owner's work, for example, outweighed the copyright owner's reluctance to permit them. Fair use was appropriate whenever such uses were customary, either under the implied-consent rubric or as a matter of enforced consent. Fair use was finally asserted to be the reason that a variety of uses that come within the technical boundaries of the exclusive rights in the copyright bundle, but were difficult to prevent, like private copying, would not be actionable.[26]

Recent reformulations of the fair use privilege, however, have sought to confine it to the implied-assent justification. Where copyright owners would not be likely to authorize the use free of charge, the use should no longer be fair. The uses that were permitted because they were difficult to police are claimed to be a subset of the impliedly permitted uses; should copyright owners devise a mechanism for licensing those uses, there would, similarly, no longer be any need to excuse the uses as fair.[27] In its most extreme form, this argument suggests that fair use itself is an archaic privilege with little application to the digital world: where technology permits automatic licensing, legal fictions based on "implied assent" become unnecessary.[28] Limiting fair use to an implied assent rationale, moreover, makes access controls seem more appealing. Thus, the fact that access controls would make no exception for individuals to gain access in order to make fair use of a work is said to be unproblematic. Why should fair use be a defense for the act of gaining unauthorized access?

By recasting traditional limitations on the scope of copyright as loopholes, proponents of stronger protection have managed to put the champions of limited protection on the defensive. Why, after all, should undesirable loopholes not now be plugged? Instead of being viewed as altruists seeking to assert the public's side of the copyright bargain, library organizations, for example, are said to be giving aid and comfort to pirates. Instead of being able to claim that broad prohibitions on technological devices are bad technological policy, opponents of the copyright-as-control model are painted as folks who believe that it ought to be okay to steal books rather than to buy them. And when educators have argued that everyone is losing sight of the rights that the law gives the public, they have met the response that the copyright law has never asked authors to subsidize education by donating their literary property.

Then there's the remarkable expansion of what we call piracy. Piracy used to be about folks who made and sold large numbers of counterfeit copies. Today, the term "piracy" seems to describe *any* unlicensed activity—especially if the person engaging in it is a teenager. The content industry calls some behavior piracy despite the fact that it is unquestionably legal. When a consumer makes a noncommercial recording of music by, for example, taping a CD she has purchased or borrowed from a friend, her copying comes squarely within the privilege established by the Audio Home Recording Act. The record companies persist in calling that copying piracy even though the statute deems it lawful.[29]

People on the content owners' side of this divide explain that it is technology that has changed penny-ante unauthorized users into pirates, but that's not really it at all. These "pirates" are doing the same sort of things unlicensed users have always done—making copies of things for their own personal use, sharing their copies with their friends, or reverse-engineering the works embodied on the copies to figure out how they work. What's changed is the epithet we apply to them.

If we untangle the claim that technology has turned Johnny Teenager into a pirate, what turns out to be fueling it is the idea that *if* Johnny Teenager were to decide to share his unauthorized copy with two million of his closest friends, the *effect* on a record company would be pretty similar to the effect of some counterfeit CD factory's creating two million CDs and selling them cheap. Copyright owners are worried, and with good reason. But, in response to their worry, they've succeeded in persuading a lot of people that any behavior that has the same effect as piracy must *be* piracy, and must therefore reflect the same moral turpitude we attach to piracy, even if it is the same behavior that we all called legitimate before. Worse, any behavior that *could potentially cause the same effect* as piracy, even if it doesn't, must also be piracy. Because an unauthorized digital copy of something *could* be uploaded to the Internet, where it *could* be downloaded by two million people, even making the digital copy is piracy.

Because an unauthorized digital copy of something could be used in a way that could cause all that damage, making a tool that makes it *possible* to make an unauthorized digital copy, even if nobody ever actually makes one, is itself piracy, regardless of the reasons one might have for making this tool. And what could possibly be wrong with a law designed to prevent piracy?

My argument, here, is that this evolution in metaphors conceals immense sleight of hand. We as a society never actually sat down and discussed in policy terms whether, now that we had grown from a copyright-importing nation to a copyright-exporting nation, we wanted to recreate copyright as a more expansive sort of control. Instead, by changing metaphors, we somehow got snookered into believing that copyright had always been intended to offer content owners extensive control, only, before now, we didn't have the means to enforce it.

Notes

1. *Copyright Term Extension Act: Hearing on H.R. 989 Before the Subcommittee On Courts and Intellectual Property of the House Committee on the Judicary,* 104th Cong., 1st sess. (June 1, 1995) (testimony of Jack Valenti, Motion Picture Association of America).

2. *See* Jessica Litman, *The Public Domain,* 39 Emory Law Journal 965, 977–92 (1990).

3. *See, e.g., London v. Biograph,* 231 F. 696 (1916); *Stone & McCarrick v. Dugan Piano,* 210 F. 399 (ED La 1914).

4. I'm indebted to Professor Niva Elkin-Koren for this insight. See Niva Elkin-Koren, *It's All About Control: Copyright and Market Power in the Information Society* (7/00 draft).

5. *See, e.g., U.S. Library of Congress Copyright Office, Report of the Register of Copyrights on the General Revision of the U.S. Copyright Law* 6, 21–36 (1961).

6. *See, e.g., Chaffee, Reflections on the Law of Copyright,* 45 Columbia Law Review 503 (1945); Report of the Register of Copyrights, note 5 above, at 6.

7. Economists would say that the authorship of a new work creates a benefit that exceeds the costs of authoring it. That is the reason why the public benefits when authors create new works. The excess benefit is a surplus. It falls to the law to determine how that surplus should be allocated. Classically, copyright law accorded the author a portion of the surplus thought to be necessary to provide an incentive to create the work, and reserved the remaining benefit to the public.

8. *See, e.g.,* Jane C. Ginsburg, *Authors and Users in Copyright,* 45 Journal of the Copyright Society of the USA 1 (1997).

9. *See* Benjamin Kaplan, *An Unhurried View of Copyright* 120–22 (Columbia University Press, 1967); Stephen Breyer, *The Uneasy Case for Copyright: A Study of Copyright in Books, Photocopies and Computer Programs,* 84 Harvard Law Review 281 (1970).

10. One series of writings explored the possibility of characterizing copyright as a

natural right, on the theory that works of authorship emanated from and embodied author's individual personalities. *See, e.g.,* Edward J. Damich, *The Right of Personality: A Common Law Basis for the Protection of the Moral Rights of Authors,* 23 Georgia Law Review 1 (1988); Justin Hughes, *The Philosophy of Intellectual Property,* 77 Georgetown Law Journal 287 (1988); John M. Kernochan, *Imperatives for Enforcing Authors' Rights,* 11 Columbia-VLA Journal of Law &. the Arts 587 (1987). Ignoring for the moment that, at least in the United States, the overwhelming majority of registered copyrights were corporately owned, these thinkers posited the model of author who creates all works from nothing. The parent/progeny metaphor was popular here— authors were compared with mothers or fathers; their works were their children. Therefore, the argument went, they were morally entitled to plenary control over their works as they would be over their children.

11. *See, e.g.,* Paul Goldstein, *Derivative Rights and Derivative Works in Copyright,* 30 Journal of the Copyright Society 209 (1982); Wendy J. Gordon, *Fair Use as Market Failure: A Structural and Economic Analysis of the Betamax Case and Its Predecessors,* 82 Columbia Law Review 1600 (1982); William M. Landes and Richard Posner, An *Economic Analysis of Copyright,* 18 Journal of Legal Studies 325 (1989).

12. *See, e.g.,* Dennis Karjala, *Copyright in Electronic Maps,* 35 Jurimetrics Journal 395 (1995); Alfred C. Yen, *When Authors Won't Sell: Parody, Fair Use and Efficiency in Copyright Law,* 62 University of Colorado Law Review 1173 (1991).

13. *See* Wendy J. Gordon, *Toward a Jurisprudence of Benefits: The Norms of Copyright and the Problems of Private Censorship,* 57 University of Chicago Law Review 1009, 1032–49 (1990); Litman, note 2 above, at 1007–12.

14. Again, I'm indebted to Professor Elkin-Koren for the taxonomy. *See* Elkin-Koren, note 4 above.

15. I have told that story in some detail in Jessica Litman, *Copyright and Information Policy,* 55 Law & Contemporary Problems (Spring 1992), at 185.

16. *See* 17 USCA § 109; see generally John M. Kernochan, *The Distribution Right in the United States of America: Review and Reflections,* 42 Vanderbilt Law Review 1407 (1989).

17. Record Rental Amendment of 1984, Pub. L No 98–450, 98 Stat 1727 (1984) (codified as amended at 17 USCA §§ 109, 115).

18. *See* Pamela Samuelson, *Modifying Copyrighted Software: Adjusting Copyright Doctrine to Accommodate a Technology,* 28 Jurimetrics Journal 179, 188–89 (1988).

19. In *Vault Corp. v. Quaid Software, Ltd.,* 847 F2d 255 (5th Cir 1988), the court rejected such a license and the state law purporting to enforce it because the court found it to be inconsistent with federal copyright law, which gives purchasers of copies of computer programs the rights that the shrink-wrap license attempted to withhold.

20. Computer Software Rental Amendments Act of 1990, Pub. L. No. 101–650, 104 Stat 5089, 5134 § § 801–804 (codified at 17 USC § 109). Like the Record Rental Act, the CSRA prohibits commercial software rental, but not resale, gift, or loan.

21. *See* S. 33, 98th Cong., 1st sess. (January 25, 1983), in 129 Congo Rec. 590 (January 26, 1983); H.R. 1029, 98th Cong., 1st sess. (January 26, 1983), in 129 Congo Rec. H201 (January 27, 1983); Home Video Recording, Hearing Before the Senate Committee on the Judiciary, 99th Cong, 2d sess. (1987).

22. *See* Jane C. Ginsburg, *Essay: From Having Copies to Experiencing Works: the Development of an Access Right in U.S. Copyright Law,* in Hugh Hansen, ed., *U.S. Intellectual Property: Law and Policy* (Sweet &. Maxwell, 2000).

23. As enacted, access-control amendments prohibit individuals from circumventing any technological devices designed to restrict access to a work, and make it illegal to make or distribute any tool or service designed to facilitate circumvention. *See* 17 U.S.C. § 1201. The law imposes substantial civil and criminal penalties for violations. *See* 17 U.S.C. §§ 1203, 1204.

24. *See, e.g.,* Alan Latman, *Study # 14: Fair Use 6–7* (1958), reprinted in 2 Studies on Copyright, Studies on Copyright 778, 784–85 (Arthur Fisher Memorial Edition 1963).

25. *See Folsom v. Marsh,* 9 Fed Cas. 342 (1841); H. Ball, The Law of Copyright and Literary Property 260 (Bender, 1944); L. Ray Patterson, *Understanding Fair Use,* 55 Law and Contemporary Problems (Spring 1992), at 249.

26. *See generally* Latman, note 24 above at 7–14, 2 Studies on Copyright at 785–92; Lloyd Weinreb, *Commentary: Fair's Fair: A Comment on the Fair Use Doctrine,* 105 Harvard Law Review 1137 (1990).

27. *See, e.g.,* Jane C. Ginsburg, note 8 above, at 11–20 (1997); *American Geophysical Union v. Texaco,* 60 F.3d 913 (2d Cir. 1995).

28. *See, e.g.,* Tom W. Bell, *Fared Use V. Fair Use: The Impact of Automated Rights Management on Copyright's Fair Use Doctrine,* 76 N. Carolina Law Review 101 (1998).

29. *See, e.g., Music on the Internet: Is There an Upside to Downloading? Hearing Before the Senate Judiciary Committee,* 106th Cong., 2d sess. (July 11, 2000) (remarks of Hilary Rosen, RIAA).

Works Cited

American Geophysical Union v. Texaco. 60 F.3d 913 (2d Cir. 1995).

Ball, Horace G. *The Law of Copyright and Literary Property.* New York: M. Bender, 1944.

Bell, Tom W. "Fair Use v. Fared Use: The Impact of Automated Rights Management on Copyright's Fair Use Doctrine." *North Carolina Law Review* 76 (1998): 557–619.

Breyer, Stephen. "The Uneasy Case for Copyright: A Study of Copyright in Books, Photocopies and Computer Programs." *Harvard Law Review* 84 (1970): 281–351.

Chaffee, Zechariah, Jr. "Reflections on the Law of Copyright." *Columbia Law Review* 45 (1945): 503–29, 719–38.

Computer Software Rental Amendments Act of 1990. Pub. L. No. 101–650, 104 Stat. 5089, 5134 §§ 801–804 (codified at 17 USC § 109).

Congressional Record. H.R. 1029, 98th Cong., 1st sess. January 26, 1983. In vol. 129 *Cong. Rec.* H201, January 27, 1983.

Congressional Record. S. 33, 98th Cong, 1st sess. January 25, 1983. In Vol. 129 *Cong. Rec.* 590. January 26, 1983.

Damich, Edward J. "The Right of Personality: A Common Law Basis for the Protection of the Moral Rights of Authors." *Georgia Law Review* 23 (1988): 1–96.

Elkin-Koren, Niva. "It's All about Control: Copyright and Market Power in the Information Society." In *The Commodification of Information,* ed. Niva Elkin-Koren and Neil W. Netanel, 79–106. The Hague: Kluwer Law International, 2002.

Folsom v. Marsh. 9 Fed Cas. 342 (1841).

Ginsburg, Jane C. "Authors and Users in Copyright." *Journal of the Copyright Society of the USA* 45 (1997): 1–20.

Ginsburg, Jane C. "Essay: From Having Copies to Experiencing Works: The Development of an Access Right in U.S. Copyright Law." In *U.S. Intellectual Property: Law and Policy,* ed. Hugh Hansen. Cheltenham: Sweet and Maxwell, 2000.

Goldstein, Paul. "Derivative Rights and Derivative Works in Copyright." *Journal of the Copyright Society* 30 (1983): 209–52.

Gordon, Wendy J. "Fair Use as Market Failure: A Structural and Economic Analysis of the Betamax Case and Its Predecessors." *Columbia Law Review* 82 (1982): 1600–1657.

Gordon, Wendy J. "Toward a Jurisprudence of Benefits: The Norms of Copyright and the Problems of Private Censorship." *University of Chicago Law Review* 57 (1990): 1009.

House Committee on the Judiciary. *Copyright Term Extension Act: Hearing on H.R. 989 Before the Subcommittee On Courts and Intellectual Property,* 104th Cong., 1st sess., June 1, 1995. Testimony of Jack Valenti, Motion Picture Association of America.

Hughes, Justin. "The Philosophy of Intellectual Property." *Georgetown Law Journal* 77 (1988): 287–366.

Kaplan, Benjamin. *An Unhurried View of Copyright.* New York: Columbia University Press, 1967.

Karjala, Dennis. "Copyright in Electronic Maps." *Jurimetrics Journal* 35 (1995): 395–415.

Kernochan, John M. "The Distribution Right in the United States of America: Review and Reflections." *Vanderbilt Law Review* 42 (1989): 1407–38.

Kernochan, John M. "Imperatives for Enforcing Authors' Rights." *Columbia-VLA Journal of Law & the Arts* 11 (1987): 587–99.

Landes, William M., and Richard Posner. "An Economic Analysis of Copyright." *Journal of Legal Studies* 18 (1989): 325–63..

Latman, Alan. "Study # 14: Fair Use 6–7." 1958. In *Studies on Copyright,* comp. and ed. under the supervision of the Copyright Society of U.S.A. Arthur Fisher Memorial Edition. South Hakensack, NJ: F. B. Rothman, 1963.

Litman, Jessica. "Copyright and Information Policy." *Law & Contemporary Problems* 55 (1992): 185–209.

Litman, Jessica. "The Public Domain." *Emory Law Journal.* 39 (1990): 965–1023.

London v. Biograph, 231 F. 696 (1916).

Patterson, L. Ray. "Understanding Fair Use." *Law and Contemporary Problems* 55 (Spring 1992): 249–66.

Record Rental Amendment of 1984, Pub. L No 98–450, 98 Stat 1727 (1984) (codified as amended at 17 USCA §§ 109, 115).

Samuelson, Pamela. "Modifying Copyrighted Software: Adjusting Copyright Doctrine to Accommodate a Technology." *Jurimetrics Journal* 28 (1988): 179–221.

Senate Judiciary Committee. *Home Video Recording Hearing.* 99th Cong, 2d sess. (1987).

Senate Judiciary Committee. *Music on the Internet: Is There an Upside to Downloading? Hearing.* 106th Cong., 2d sess. July 11, 2000. Remarks of Hilary Rosen, RIAA.

Stone & McCarrick v. Dugan Piano, 210 F. 399 (ED La 1914).

U.S. Library of Congress Copyright Office. *Report of the Register of Copyrights on the General Revision of the U.S. Copyright Law* 6 (1961): 21–36.

Vault Corp. v. Quaid Software, Ltd., 847 F2d 255 (5th Cir 1988).

Weinreb, Lloyd. "Commentary: Fair's Fair: A Comment on the Fair Use Doctrine." *Harvard Law Review* 105 (1990): 1137–61.

Yen, Alfred C. "When Authors Won't Sell: Parody, Fair Use and Efficiency in Copyright Law." *University of Colorado Law Review* 62 (1991): 79–108.

On Ethical Issues in Publishing in the Life Sciences

Gilbert S. Omenn

There are many complex ethical and policy issues in the diverse fields of scientific publishing. This essay deals with certain aspects of publishing in the life sciences and clinical research fields. The originality and quality of published articles and books depend ultimately on the rigor of the ideas, methods, research design, and potential impact of the findings. In biomedical research fields, journal articles carry more weight than scholarly books, partly reflecting the sense of urgency about sharing news on progress that might improve public health and medical care. Peer review is a valued feature of the publication process and is itself a complex, sometimes controversial, matter, loaded with ethical obligations.

It is instructive to examine life sciences publishing from the points of view of the scientist or group of scientists preparing the publication and choosing the target journal; the editor at the journal and the journal's peer reviewers; the research community eager for breakthrough results and yet skeptical about out-of-the-box claims; and the media and broader public seeking news about the advances of the biomedical and behavioral sciences that might have practical importance. Of course, publishing policies and practices change with time. Two current developments are new models of publishing, utilizing the Internet, and concerns that publication of certain biotechnology advances may increase the risks of bioterrorism. In the first case, the ethical issues relate to ownership of information and rights to access to information; in the second case, they concern the risks involved in providing tools that could be abused for terror or used in counterterrorism efforts, a matter sometimes called *dual-use domain*.

Author's Issues

Effective publication requires a carefully thought-through analysis by the prospective authors. They must decide how to characterize the aims of their research and determine the most important findings to be presented in the tables and figures and explained in the text. A critical decision that should orient the drafting of the paper is the choice of the most appropriate journal, both to reach the most appropriate audience for the information and to enhance the reputation of the authors. Too often authors wait until the paper is written to decide where to submit it for publication. Often authors shoot for the most prestigious journal, when the likelihood of acceptance is quite low.

Biagioli and Galison (1) highlight "the function of the author" as a standard research question in literary, legal, and gender studies, as well as in other fields. Contrasted with single-author books and scholarly works in other disciplines, scientific publications commonly have several or many coauthors, reflecting the collaborative and increasingly interdisciplinary nature of the research and the involvement at various academics levels, from students and postdoctoral fellows to principal investigators and lab directors. Who should be listed as an author, and in what order should authors be listed? The general guidance is that authorship should be limited to those who played substantial roles in the design, conduct, and analysis of the results and the writing of the manuscript. "Courtesy" coauthors, such as the head of the department or director of the laboratory, if they had no direct role in the work, and contributors of cells or reagents, are more properly acknowledged and thanked, without being made coauthors. Listed authors who played no role get unwarranted credit, and those who did the work have their roles diluted, violating ethical principles of fairness and justice. However, there is a huge zone of discretion about these credits. Several leading biomedical journals now require each coauthor to sign a statement that he or she played a significant role and to identify what that role was. The International Committee of Medical Journal Editors has issued "uniform requirements."

There is a well-developed convention in life sciences and biomedical publishing about the order of authors: The primary researcher is expected to be the first author, especially if that individual really did lead all aspects of the project from design to conduct to analysis, even with guidance and assistance at each stage. For many faculty, it is a priority to put first a graduate student or postdoctoral fellow, or even an exceptional undergraduate student, when that status has been earned. If two individuals share this lead responsibility, the lab may publish a pair of papers with a different first author on one of the two papers, or may use asterisks to identify each as "equally contributing to the work." A statistician is required for many kinds of studies to assure the credibility and quality of the quantitative inferences. The statistician, if not the primary researcher, is usually given the second position. For certain kinds of studies, especially clinical trials results, journals require that a qualified statistician be willing to put her or his name on the paper. The senior investigator or lab director generally goes last, as a means of indicating who had originally obtained the research grant. In multi-author collaborative studies, other coauthors are fit into the order, sometimes alphabetically, sometimes in subgroups by institution or role. The practice in the social sciences of presenting authors alphabetically is unknown in biomedical fields.

As might be expected, there can be disagreements within the group about who should receive the credit of being first and, when more than one senior leader is involved, who should be last. These authorship positions matter a lot, subsequently, in competing for faculty positions, in being considered for promotion, in being evaluated for grant funding, and in individual awards for research achievements. Decisions about academic advancement put a premium on "independent" research and independent grant funding. This premium is excessive, especially when many kinds of life sciences research now clearly require and benefit from a multidisciplinary team approach. Sometimes someone yields on author position just to avoid conflict, only to suffer later in individual evaluations. Sometimes the group asks a shrewd or well-connected member of the team to take on the responsibility of writing the manuscript in order to maximize the quality of the paper, the match to the target journal, and the likelihood of acceptance for publication. This tactic demonstrates the many pressures on authors— from colleagues, department chairs, technology transfer offices, and press offices; indeed, it introduces the chapter on authorship in the Office of Research Integrity document on responsible conduct of research (Steneck, *Office*).

In large collaborations involving dozens of participating investigators, papers will frequently have only the names of a few leaders of the whole collaborative group, or use a group name, and then footnote the remaining authors or participating investigators. Many journals in recent years have limited the number of coauthors listed in the bibliography to conserve space; some permit one named author with the rest covered by *et al.* Such policies make the authorship opaque until the actual article is obtained. Some journals omit titles in the bibliography in order to leave more room for authors, yet titles are helpful to the reader perusing the literature cited. The point here is that journals have tremendous discretion. For these and other reasons, the leader of a large research team should encourage side projects with ancillary analyses so that individual members or small groups of researchers can have separate publications.

Choice of Journal

A distinct hierarchy exists among journals in regard to reputation and, consequently, the presumed quality of their articles. The "citation index," based on how many subsequent articles cite the article (with adjustments for self-citation, field, and specific journals), quantifies this ranking. Journals and their publishing companies advertise their citation index ranking as a way to attract the strongest manuscripts, as well as subscribers; they use it as the basis for advertising rates in those journals that accept (and seek) paid advertising. Some journals appeal to an audience across a broad range of scientific fields, specifically *Science, Nature,* and *Proceedings of the National Academy of Sciences;* among biomedical/clinical journals, the *New England Journal of Medicine,* the *Journal of the American Medical Association, Lancet,* and the *Journal of Clinical Investigation* have the most breadth and prestige. Every field, from cell biology to surgery, has its own pecking order for more specialized journals. The choices are enormous: PubMed indexes five thousand journals! The size of the biomedical research workforce and the numbers of journals continues to increase, making it especially difficult for beginners to be heard in the marketplace of ideas.

Like first-listed author status, the quality of the journals in which individuals publish carries substantial weight in appointment, promotion, grant-funding, and research awards. Thus, scientists seek to make their manuscripts appear attractive and important for the most competitive journals, and to respond precisely and aggressively to constructive criticism from peer reviewers and editors. Properly carried out, these activities insure the publication of the highest quality work in the most prestigious journals.

The Manuscript Review Process

In the biomedical and behavioral sciences, great emphasis is placed on peer review of submitted manuscripts. The editor and editorial staff must identify appropriate reviewers for each manuscript; often several reviewers must be asked in order to find two or three willing to undertake the review in the timeframe desired by the authors and editor. Of course, busy scientists have many other duties and deadlines, and a manuscript may languish awaiting review. The peer reviewer may find that cited or uncited articles need to be read in order to make a knowledgeable and fair assessment, which can lead to delay.

Critical ethical issues arise in peer review (Steneck, *Office;* Schachman). Some journals invite the authors to submit names for one or two potential reviewers; others examine the reference citations for appropriate names. Of course, these methods may introduce bias or favoritism. Some journals protect the reviewers' anonymity to encourage candid review, while others encourage voluntary identification, perhaps believing that reviews may be more conscientious and civil. Some journals remove the names of the authors when providing the article to the reviewer, yet most reviewers can figure out the likely research group from the methods and citations. Editors recognize the ethical problems in obtaining a fair reading of new work, but no one has resolved them.

Some authors are afraid that reviewers will be highly critical of the paper, or demand extensive, time-consuming revisions. Others worry that a reviewer will misappropriate, consciously or subconsciously, new concepts or findings to advance the reviewer's own research. This potential problem has its counterpart in peer review of grant proposals for new research or as an extension of current research. Delays in publication are both a career problem and an ethical problem in an environment that places priority on being the first to publish important findings.

After receiving peer review reports, editors exercise discretion about which papers to accept, since the top journals have room for only a minority of all submitted papers rated as highly credible. The editors may be looking for something unusual or newsworthy, or may have prejudices for or against certain topics or methods of analysis. Editors compete to attract exciting papers, promising expedited review or other advantages. Conversely, reviewers and editors may be unwilling to accept papers with unconventional methods or surprising findings—which may turn out to be breakthroughs.

Not all fields rely on peer review. Gordon Kane, in this anthology, notes the sharp difference between publishing in theoretical physics and the preoccupation of the biological sciences with the peer review of journal articles. He notes that certain fields of physics reject the notion of empowering just two or three colleagues to act as quality control on papers; instead the practice of online publication encourages open publication, with the whole world immediately able to assess and criticize the report and the authors.

Conflicts of Interest

Conflicts of financial interest may arise, not just for the authors, but also among the reviewers. Medical journals now routinely ask reviewers to disclose potential conflicts of interest, but the process is for the most part voluntary. Conflicts may be particularly important with articles that show benefit or risk from medical therapies or products, affecting the pocketbook of particular companies or their competitors (Schachman). There is a mini-literature of publications demonstrating the high probability that authors supported by a pharmaceutical company will report results favorable to the product. Nearly a decade ago Deyo and colleagues published a report in the *New England Journal of Medicine* entitled "The Messenger under Attack—Intimidation of Researchers by Special Interest Groups." These groups—pharmaceutical companies, patient advocacy organizations, providers and advocates of surgical or other procedures, and plaintiff lawyers—sought to block the publication of findings that could undercut their business interests, or attempted to discredit the publication and the researchers when the paper appeared in print or was presented at a scientific meeting and highlighted in press releases from the conference. Why are editors not more suspicious? Why are authors so disingenuous?

Under federal guidelines, there exist three categories of scientific misconduct: fabrication, falsification, and plagiarism. There are quite a few celebrated cases of fabrication or falsification of data. A red flag should go up when individuals, especially in leading labs, have publication rates far above the reasonable upper end of the peer group (Claxton). The federal government established what is now called the Office of Research Integrity in 1989; they investigate some two hundred cases per year. For the year 2001 for example, ORI investigated twenty-four cases of fabrication, twenty of falsification, and four of plagiarism (Steneck, *Office*). All institutions utilizing NIH research funding are required to conduct training in "responsible conduct of research" for all trainees (Steneck, "Fostering Integrity"). Audits have shown that some individuals list articles as published or in press that do not exist, a particular form of falsification that is hardly unique to scientists.

The ORI website includes numerous educational initiatives, including "a guide to ethical writing" (Roig). The criteria for plagiarism are quite elastic, ranging from finding a certain minimal number of identical words in a sentence or phrase to substantial lifting of text or data from other published works. For example, the term "plagiarism" covers the lifting of extensive text, figures, or tables from another author without attribution; duplicate publication by the same author; and a very restrictive definition of any six consecutive identical words. In this era of electronic searches for phrases, it is simple to run a search on suspicious statements or phrases. The subset of self-plagiarism is generally frowned upon; a more serious problem is dividing one publishable set of work into numerous overlapping or redundant papers submitted to multiple journals. Whatever the definition, an inoffensive, actually desirable, use of redundant language arises from identical descriptions of experimental and analytical methods, reflecting standardized procedures. A May 19, 2005, editorial in *Nature* on plagiarism led to a flurry of letters and further articles. In general, federal requirements and university procedures are focused on fabrication and falsification of data, with much less attention to plagiarism. Universities and faculty groups chart an uneasy course between fearing adverse publicity and public and congressional stereotyping and threats of litigation from accused individuals.

The broad category of plagiarism raises numerous ethical questions about careerism versus appropriate shared standards. How much overlap in successive publications is permissible by an author? How can the sequencing of a series of publications by one research group be made more coherent? Authors have little control of the actual timing of their publications. Increasingly, authors utilize electronic listservs and appropriate websites to maintain collaborative and mutually informative relationships. Journals are putting articles on line when accepted, sometimes months before the printed journal appears. Since monographs and book chapters generally summarize and synthesize previously published work, what must authors do to avoid a potential charge of plagiarism? One approach to avoid self-plagiarism is to hold new material for peer-reviewed submissions. The reviews then could focus on the integration of published material, hopefully with fresh interpretations.

Journals could screen manuscripts for plagiarism, once criteria are agreed upon. As the editors of *Nature* have noted, arbitrary word limits for detection of plagiarism or self-plagiarism are unwise; they suggest a useful, user-friendly software tool that identified acceptable duplication (authors' websites and properly referenced quotations) and a new category of missing information—articles hidden behind subscription barriers to online search of whole text. But such tools can only go so far.

There are significant pressures on authors. Many journals have strict page limits or word limits. Editors may force authors to shorten manuscripts and publish only a portion of the data, leading to multiple smaller papers. Authors have long struggled with the obligation to present methods in sufficient detail so that another lab could repeat the experiment and expect to obtain the same results, so as to have a basis for extending the work. Withholding critical details may cause others to fail and will lead to controversy about the findings. Fortunately, the Internet now makes it feasible to publish methods and supplementary results in depth without utilizing print pages in the journal.

Editors use precious pages for commentaries by others to promote the importance of selected articles. As noted above, editors are competing for "hot" articles, offering accelerated review, releasing "embargoed" versions of upcoming journal issues to the press, a practice initiated by the *New England Journal of Medicine* decades ago. The general media have come to rely on such access, raising the stakes for the authors competing for attention for themselves and their institutions.

The "rules of the road" for responsible conduct of research include professional codes, government regulations, institutional policies, and personal commitments to the basic principles of honesty, accuracy, efficiency, and objectivity. Society trusts that the results of research reflect an honest attempt by scientists to describe the world accurately and without bias (National Academy of Sciences). The relevant literature encompasses thousands of articles and a few hundred confirmed cases of misconduct. Fabrication, falsification, and plagiarism as elements of "scientific misconduct" are more objective than earlier terminology of *deception* or *fraud,* which required demonstration of deliberate intent. The terms *research integrity* and *questionable research practices* are even broader, embracing sloppy research, inaccurate methods, excessive claims of accuracy (numerous significant figures), poor mentoring, bias, and conflict of interest (Institute of Medicine; Committee on Science, Engineering, and Public Policy; Schachman; Steneck, "Role" and "Fostering Integrity"). Journals that have given these matters particular emphasis are the *Journal of the American Medical Association, Academic Medicine,* and *Science and Engineering Ethics* (Steneck, "Institutional and Individual Responsibilities").

Scientific Publishing as Business

Library budgets are overwhelmed with high subscription charges and a proliferation of journals. During a recent ten-year period, subscription charges for journals from commercial publishing houses rose 224 percent, uncorrected for inflation (Frank). For-profit conglomerate corporations are consolidating the academic publishing industry. Conversely, many scientific societies and nonprofit organizations depend upon the revenues and prestige of their journals. Of course, peer review and scientific publishing are costly; if subscriptions and reprint charges are to be dropped, or made irrelevant through downloading from the Internet, it will be necessary to have publication fees placed on the authors and their funding agencies. Many journals already impose such charges on top of their subscription income. NIH, Howard Hughes, and Wellcome Trust have announced that they will pay such charges for their grantees. The current (and foreseeable) budget situation at NIH, however, makes the accelerated adoption of these policies and the inclusion of these costs more complicated.

Partly as a response, the open-access movement has emerged. Led by several prominent biomedical scientists, a new publishing venture called Public Library of Science (PLoS) has secured generous financial support from the Gordon and Betty Moore Foundation to publish electronic journals without fees for subscription or access. One of its arguments is that taxpayers have already paid for the conduct of the research, so ready access to the results without charge and without delay should be a public benefit.

Another impetus for open access is the frustration felt by individuals without site licenses at their universities, companies, or public libraries. In many cases, such individuals can access the abstracts for articles online via PubMed, but they cannot access the full content of the paper. Patients, patient advocates, and especially lawyers find this barrier irritating. Scientists seeking to confirm findings in a long list of potential reference citations likewise are irritated by a barrier that offers access, however briefly, to the text only with payment of between $19 and $29 per article. Journals, while trying to protect their subscription base, have begun to make all text available online after a period of twelve months or less. NIH has issued guidance that calls on journals to do so within twelve months of publication and urges authors to make articles available informally through websites. There is pressure on the NIH, including from interested members of Congress, to accelerate this process. NIH guidance, moreover, has caused some confusion about whether the submitted manuscript, the accepted manuscript, or the final edited published manuscript will be made available, at least initially.

PLoS publishes *PLoS Biology, PLoS Medicine, PLoS Computational Biology, PLoS Genetics,* and *PLoS Pathogens.* These are rapidly becoming highly cited journals. BioMedCentral has created more than one hundred open-access journals in the past two years, with more than four thousand original articles. Many established journals now use websites to make available extensive datasets, tables, figures, and detailed methods for which the journal does not provide space in the print version. BioMedCentral has such online features as the provenance of the paper—the original submission, peer reviewers' comments, authors' responses to the reviews, the revised manuscript and reviews, and citations after online publication. It is likely that these online open-access journals will continue to grow. Established journals, like *Science,* will very likely continue to sell print and electronic subscriptions, since readers highly value the "News and Comment" and other features of the journal, besides the original research articles. (Author disclosure: I am currently chairman of the board of the American Association for the Advancement of Science [AAAS] that publishes *Science.*) But, clearly, there is ferment in the scientific publishing world. The view that "knowledge is a public resource" is gaining traction. The AAAS position is, "We welcome experiments and assessments, and expect change." While it is unlikely that biomedical research will move completely to online publication, following the model of theoretical physics, clearly online access will become increasingly important, for it includes not only the fuller versions of articles, but also important unfiltered access to work.

Scientific Research and Bio-Security

In this era of renewed concern about bioterrorism, homeland security experts, the media, and the general public fear that new biotechnology methods and open publication of life sciences research on infectious agents may serve the interests of terrorists. Articles describing how to assemble poliovirus or reconstitute the 1918 influenza virus have caused consternation. Introducing highly infectious organisms into the food supply through livestock or crops could be hugely disruptive to our society. The line between defensive and offensive biological research is "perilously thin," resting on the intent and perception of different parties (Allison). Many reports have been published on this matter, and national and international agencies are trying to balance the value of new knowledge and methods—including the value for counterterrorism—against the risk of deliberate misuse. This dilemma derives from what are known as "dual-use" technologies, long a matter of restrictive regulation in the computer sciences and other fields directly utilized in military systems. Now, in addition to Cold War antagonists and "rogue nations," we must anticipate the intentions and actions of terrorist groups.

For those interested in these matters, a series of major reports from the National Research Council can be recommended. *Biotechnology Research in an Age of Terrorism* (the Fink Report) (Committee on Research Standards) urged expansion of existing regulations alongside reliance on self-governance by scientists and editors. Governments were advised to trust scientists and journals to screen their papers for security risks. Seven types of risky studies were identified as requiring advance approval by Institutional Biosafety Committees—such studies as making an infectious agent more lethal or rendering vaccines powerless. In response, the Department of Health and Human Services became the lead agency for implementation of the National Science Advisory Board for Biosecurity, with twenty-four members outside the government and fifteen agency ex-officio members. This committee is quite active. Another committee addressed "Pathogens, Open Access, and Genome Databases" (Committee on Genomics, *Seeking Security*). NRC published *Globalization, Biosecurity, and the Future of the Life Sciences* (Committee on Advances in Technology), touting cutting-edge scientific developments like nanobiotechnology and synthetic biology, and calling for vigilance internationally and in the intelligence agencies, while relying on self-governance in the research community. Instances of misconduct or misuse could make this whole scheme open to charges of inadequate safeguards.

Scientific publishing is a complex process with many public and professional benefits and responsibilities for all parties. Explicit attention to the pressures on researchers and journals, high standards for research integrity, and respect for the public's interest will benefit all parties.

Works Cited

Allison, Graham. "Implications for Public Policy of the Threat from Bioterrorism." Discussion Paper 2003–11, Belfer Center for Science and International Affairs, Harvard University, November 2003.

Biagioli, Mario, and Peter Galison, eds. *Scientific Authorship: Credit and Intellectual Property in Science.* New York: Routledge/Taylor and Francis Books, 2003.

Claxton, Larry D. "Scientific Authorship." *Mutation Research* 589 (2005): 17–30.

Committee on Advances in Technology and the Prevention of Their Application to Next Generation Biowarfare Threats, National Research Council. *Globalization, Biosecurity, and the Future of the Life Sciences.* Washington, DC: National Academy Press, 2006.

Committee on Genomics Databases for Bioterrorism Threat Agents, National Research Council. *Seeking Security: Pathogens, Open Access, and Genome Databases.* Washington, DC: National Academy Press, 2004.

Committee on Research Standards and Practices to Prevent the Destructive Application of Biotechnology, Development, Security, and Cooperation, National Research Council. *Biotechnology Research in an Age of Terrorism.* Washington, DC: National Academy Press, 2004.

Committee on Science, Engineering, and Public Policy, National Academy of Sciences, National Academy of Engineering, Institute of Medicine. *Responsible Science: Ensuring the Integrity of the Research Process.* Washington, DC: National Academy Press, 1992.

Deyo, Richard A., Bruce M. Psaty, Gregory Simon, Edward H. Wagner, and Gilbert S. Omenn. "The Messenger under Attack: Intimidation of Researchers by Special Interest Groups." *New England Journal of Medicine* 336 (1997): 1176–80.

Frank, Martin. "Access to the Scientific Literature." *New England Journal of Medicine* 354 (2006): 1552–55.

Institute of Medicine. "The Responsible Conduct of Research in the Health Sciences." Washington, DC: National Academy Press, 1989.

International Committee of Medical Journal Editors. "Uniform Requirements for Manuscripts Submitted to Biomedical Journals." Updated February 2006. www.icmje.org. Consulted July 5, 2007.

National Academy of Sciences, Committee on the Conduct of Science. *On Being a Scientist: Responsible Conduct of Research.* 2nd ed. Washington, DC: National Academy Press, 1995.

"Policing Integrity." Editorial. *Nature* 435 (May 19, 2005): 248.

Roig, Miguel. *Avoiding Plagiarism, Self-Plagiarism, and Other Questionable Writing Practices: A Guide to Ethical Writing.* Office of Research Integrity, Dept. of Health and Human Services. http://ori.hhs.gov/education/products/roig_st_johns/, consulted July 5, 2007.

Schachman, Howard K. "From 'Publish or Perish' to 'Patent and Prosper.'" *Journal of Biological Chemistry* 281 (2006): 6889–6903. http://www.jbc.org/cgi/doi/10.1074/jbc.X600002200, consulted July 5, 2007.

Steneck, Nicholas H. "Fostering Integrity in Research: Definitions, Current Knowledge, and Future Directions." *Science and Engineering Ethics* 12 (2006): 53–74.

Steneck, Nicholas H. "Institutional and Individual Responsibilities for Integrity in Research." *American Journal of Bioethics* 2 (2002): 51–53.

Steneck, Nicholas H. *Office of Research Integrity Introduction to the Responsible Conduct of Research.* Washington, DC: Department of Health and Human Services, 2004.

Steneck, Nicholas H. "The Role of Professional Societies in Promoting Integrity in Research." *American Journal of Health Behavior* 27, Suppl. 3 (2003): S239–S247.

Reviewing the Author-Function in the Age of Wikipedia

Amit Ray and Erhardt Graeff

Introduction: Wikis, Authorship, and Authority

As social computing practices transform how cultural texts can be generated and circulated, written communities fostered by wikis offer some insight into the possibilities and pitfalls of dynamic, group-"authored" content production. Wikis are server-side software programs that allow anyone to create and edit web pages with only an Internet connection and a web browser. Quite simply and literally, wikis are a collaborative software tool. The inventor of wikis, Ward Cunningham, describes his software as "the simplest online database that could possibly work." Cunningham borrowed the Hawaiian word *wiki,* or *wikiwiki,* meaning fast or quick, alluding to the ability of a wiki user to quickly change the content of a page.[1]

The ability for users to edit web pages has profound implications for the development and distribution of knowledge. By de-emphasizing the central role of individual authorship in the production of texts, wikis offer a dynamic, multiauthored approach to their composition. In the last decade, wikis have emerged as a prominent and intriguing component in the production, modification, and dissemination of information and knowledge via the Internet.

Wiki users can be registered on a wiki system, and in some cases they can participate without naming themselves—they are known only by an IP address. The ability of a user to edit the content is the most striking feature of wikis. Open access has profound implications for the creation and editing of content insofar as it exposes texts' inherent instability. Unlike fixed media, wikis display the dynamic and inherently social nature of language and meaning as described in theoretical models of language and epistemology. In an unprecedented way, wikis allow discourse to emerge that is continually negotiated and articulated through a community of users—sometimes thousands of interlocutors. The properties of texts generated through active collaboration test the boundaries of established avenues of knowledge production and modern institutions of knowledge and authority. And while changes to a wiki page can be made by anyone, such changes are ultimately archived as part of the wiki. Therefore, the wiki also functions as a digital palimpsest.

Wikis invoke a multitude of the theoretical issues regarding authorship raised in late structuralist and poststructuralist thought. For many in the humanities and social sciences, the decentering of authorship in favor of discursive and systemic methodologies more attuned to power, historicity, and a dynamic "field" of representation has led to novel methods for critical interpretation and evaluation. However, such models have not become a significant component in how communication is understood within the public sphere. The singular author is very much the model that governs the expectations of most readers. By complicating traditional notions of authorship, wikis affect associated issues of authority, originality, and value.

Authorship, the Author-Function, and Literary Studies

The romantic "author," whose genius and originality bring "newness" into the world, has been increasingly problematized by literary theorists and cultural historians over the course of the last forty years. Martha Woodmansee's historical work on the development of authorship vis-à-vis Romanticism and property has played an influential role in relating market logic with aesthetic rationale. While not reducing individualized authorship and the uniqueness of the literary work to a function of market economics and legal theory, Woodmansee's 1994 study, *The Author, Art, and the Market: Rereading the History of Aesthetics,* provides a detailed analysis of how changing market conditions in the eighteenth century facilitated the development of a romantic view of authorship.[2] Such detailed historical and cultural analysis has demonstrated that views of authorship are contingent upon a number of factors: historical moment, geographical location, and prior cultural practice. Not only is the individual author a relatively recent historical phenomenon, but the birth of the author as a solitary entity has marginalized writing practices in which the individual does not solely develop a work. Only in the last forty years have literary and cultural studies mounted a sustained examination of the "author" as a contingent figure.

The debate over authorship came to the fore during the mid-1960s when structuralism was being critiqued based on deconstructive insights into the relativity of language acts. In his seminal 1968 essay, "The Death of the Author," Roland Barthes implores his readers to acknowledge the death of the author in order to liberate the reader.[3] Using structuralist insights on language as a system, Barthes posits that the act of writing "is that neutral, composite, oblique space where our subject slips away, the negative where all identity is lost, starting with the very identity of the body writing" (142). He argues that by falling back upon the concept of an idealized, corporeal, and totalizable author, we lose the ability to appreciate how texts function. Barthes is laying the foundation of an argument that he would develop over the course of his career: the movement away from autonomous literary work to contingent cultural text. Replacing the author, he posits a modern scriptor that would emerge "simultaneously with the text," never "preceding or exceeding the writing" (146).

Barthes makes the case that any analysis of iteration and representation must consider the social, interactive, and communicative function of language, and not just the biography, psychology, and intentionality of the author (or, parallel with the "author," an idealized "work" of the sort posited by some formalists, such as the New Critics). He writes, "A text is made of multiple writings, drawn from many cultures and entering into mutual relations of dialogue, parody, contestation, but there is one place where this multiplicity is focused and that place is the reader, not, as was hitherto said, the author" (148). In order to recognize Barthes's insight, it is important to note the intellectual relevance of authorship to virtually every facet of humanistic scholarly inquiry. During the modern era, the humanistic traditions of literature, philosophy, and history all developed in conjunction with, and were reinforced by, the concept of individualized authorship. Thus, Barthes was responding to both academic and popular representations of authorship with his polemical essay, concluding with his now famous dictum, "The birth of the Reader must be at the cost of the death of the Author" (148).

The following year, Foucault responded to Barthes with "What Is an Author?" which develops the concept of the author-function.[4] The notion of the corporeal author is reviewed as part of the discursive regimens that link the author to the work. Foucault heuristically deploys the question, adapted from Samuel Beckett's *Texts for Nothing*, "What does it matter who is speaking?" to develop a new set of parameters to interrogate authorship, textuality, and the types of authority that relate to conceptions of authorship.[5] Much of the essay involves a careful explication of how we might conceive of the author-function. Importantly, Foucault is careful to note its variability. Authorship exists within different discourses, defining characteristics such as originality, authority, and property that vary according to the particular discourse. But Foucault does not want simply to replace the concept of the author with the author-function. In trying to read authorship as a contingent affair, he shows that the author-function does not affect discourse in a "universal and constant way" (149). Here Foucault the historian analyzes different types of authorship at different historical moments, noting the variable and at times contradictory function of the author under different conditions of discourse.

For example, Foucault looks at the inversion of the author-function as it relates to discourses we now call "scientific" and "literary." During the Middle Ages, only those scientific texts marked by authorship could be accepted as having authority. Yet literary works were circulated and valorized without any consideration of authorship. He notes that in the seventeenth and eighteenth centuries, this situation reversed and the author-function became more prominent in literature and less influential in science. This observation, on the variability of the author-function, serves two purposes. It shows how authorship can vary both among different discourses and within them as well. Thus, the question of authorship becomes a contingent affair, no longer to be projected upon a corporeal figure, but subject to specific, if variable, forces. Reorienting the reception and analysis of texts toward an author-function would enable us to ask different kinds of questions than those we had grown accustomed to asking: that is, "Who really spoke? Is it really he and not someone else? With what authenticity or originality? And what part of his deepest sense did he express in his discourse?" (157).

Foucault's aim in undertaking this critique of the author, not unlike Barthes's, is to query naturalized conceptions relating author with work. But Foucault goes beyond Barthes's own romanticization of the reader to a model in which the author-function is variable and reconfigurable according to the tenets of the juridical, political, and social institutions that shape all discourses and thereby frame how knowledge and authority come to be understood. While he suggests that the author-function may one day disappear, discourse requires that other forms of restriction and delimitation emerge in its absence. In wikis, such order arises from what Foucault forecasts as a new mode of "experience" (160), embodied by the engagement with a specific burgeoning and palimpsestic medium.

Wiki Technology and the Wiki Writing Process:
The Case of Wikipedia

The "About" page on Wikipedia.org (as of January 30, 2006 at 4:33 p.m.) begins, "Welcome to Wikipedia, the communal encyclopedia that anyone can edit. The content of Wikipedia is free, written collaboratively by people from all around the world. This website is a wiki, which means that anyone with access to an Internet-connected computer can edit entries simply by clicking on the "edit this page" link.

If you wanted, you could change the introduction on the "About" page without creating an account or typing a password. Similarly, you could view the "Discussion" or "Talk" page—another editable record used to track dialogue between users editing the main content page. Here you can see content in the process of refinement toward a publishable state—with discrepancies being hashed out among users, or the ever scrutinized neutral point of view (NPOV) of the article being debated (wikipedia.org/wiki/WP:NPOV). There is significant authorial power available by entering into the online discourse at any point on any page—this is the ability to leave one's mark via content or style on the wiki's dynamic history. In fact, your last option, to view the "History" of the page, is a time-stamped record of all edits made to a page. The trifold set of article, discussion, and history—each possessing separate but interrelated purposes—together completes a single wiki article.

The structure of the wiki's interface—specifically the MediaWiki software used by Wikipedia—in both presentation and editing views enables a transparent connection/interrelation between author, reader, and editor. These seemingly separate roles are represented by the interconnected Wikipedia community as a whole and, as we shall later suggest, can be consolidated into a single online entity. This facilitation of a synthesis of writing roles within the grander scope of a comprising community allows wikis to transcend even the superficial definition as a transparent tool or simple piece of software.

A wiki is—beyond the digital bits of software application code—the technological support structure for what we will call the *wiki writing process*. This process incorporates the aforementioned standard roles in writing and facilitates a new paradigm of collaboration on a massively distributed scale. Where there may once have been a one-to-one or one-to-many relationship between the separated roles, there now exist many-to-many relationships among wiki *users* as they interact with and within the community.

These relationships persist beyond any singular or even traditionally serialized publication. In fact, the only way to define the publication of wiki content is in the sense of "Serial Collaborations," a term used by Peter Jaszi (40). These collaborations are pieces of writing that are, or can be, infinitely edited over time by the users. There is a persisting dialogue between the users as they assume the various roles of reader, writer, and editor, which forces the actual wiki writing process into the loose category of "discursive practice," as put forth by Foucault. The collaborative and iterative aspect of wikis serves, then, to magnify this idea and gives the process its inherent strength, as well as its inherent weakness in regard to traditional definitions of authority.

Essentially, Wikipedia provides an example of poststructuralist principles operating online—an idea impressively illustrated by the "history flow visualizations" of Wikipedia article revisions generated by Fernanda B. Viégas, Martin Wattenberg, and Kushal Dave. The original analysis of Wikipedia article evolution by the team "revealed complex patterns of cooperation and conflict" (575). These stem from the community-enabling editing capabilities built in to the "Talk" and "History" article pages, as well as the "Watch List" option available to registered users, providing an alert system for vigilant writer-editors to defend the integrity of specific articles. The goal of these discursive provisions is informal oversight of content, which can be subject to "malicious editing"[6]—one of the strongest criticisms against Wikipedia. The history flow visualizations mapped three categories of wiki article revisions: (1) editing of content on average, (2) a malicious mass deletion of content, and (3) a mass deletion replaced by obscene content. The median survival time of the first category was 90.4 minutes, which broke down to 21 percent of edits reducing page size, 6 percent reducing it by no more than fifty characters.[7] Such numbers primarily indicate tightened prose and the elimination of irrelevant information (579, 581). Of course this dynamism is what makes citing Wikipedia problematic. This downside—most apparent when trying to perceive Wikipedia in the vein of a traditional encyclopedia—is balanced by the fact that new content is quickly and easily added to articles as events unfold. For instance, the study refers to how within a week of the invasion of Iraq in 2003 an entry devoted to the topic was written, and had tripled in size in a few weeks (581). The fast-responding character of the Wikipedia *user community* also catches and repairs mass deletions at a median delay of 2.8 minutes— 1.7 minutes for those involving obscenities (579). The data produced indicates, to at least those versed in poststructuralist insights on language, that

Wikipedia's neoteric authorial/editorial community is attempting to maximize the radical functionality/medium of wiki technology—publishing, editing, and republishing content (with self-governing oversight) at a frequency unimaginable in other media.

The aforementioned famous last line of Barthes's "The Death of the Author" is meant to undermine the authorial identity ascribed to a given text, devaluing what was once the author-genius into a mean "scriptor." This serves as preparation for new media, rather than a total destruction of previous cultural regimes. When we examine the wiki writing process, we find that the distinctions between author and reader have been blurred. Though individual "readers" will come across wiki pages, they are empowered to edit the very content they are consuming—to superannuate the traditionally bilateral division of reader/author, or the earlier mentioned trilateral division of reader/writer/editor. The reader and author are birthed in unison as the wiki "users." In this moment the author-genius subordinates itself to the community that comprises these superempowered users.[8]

In Foucault's inquisitive response to Barthes, the analysis of the semantic tangles of a dying author suggest the potential capacity for wikis to act as an evolved species of literature, employing the communitarian army of users on hand. Digital phenomena are seemingly fragile and fraught with change, but wikis provide a dynamically collaborative (edit), continuous (discussion), and constant (history) space. And we see this digital palimpsest harnessing an Internet of multifunctional users. As such, our wiki—the new media institution for the wiki writing process—forms the instance of an authorial framework that Foucault's critique of Barthes anticipates.

Notes

1. Cunningham developed wiki software in the mid-1990s. His WikiWikiWeb, the first wiki, has been running since 1995 and facilitates specialized programming.

2. Woodmansee, along with legal scholar Peter Jaszi, under the auspices of the Society for Critical Exchange (SCE), convened a large interdisciplinary group of scholars to address the state of "author" studies in the early nineties. This meeting resulted in a diverse array of essays published in 1994 as *The Construction of Authorship: Textual Appropriation in Law and Literature*. In 2006, SCE held a follow-up conference, Con/texts of Invention, which reexamined these issues in light of the previous decade's work and the emergence of pervasive digitality.

3. Barthes's essay originally appears as "La mort de l'auteur" in *Manteia* 5 (1968): 12–17.

4. Foucault's response originally appears as "Qu'est-ce qu'un auteur?" in *Bulletin de la Société Française de Philosophie: Séance du Samedi* February 22, 1969, 73–104.

5. Foucault invokes a passage from Beckett's *Texts for Nothing*, which he slightly modifies from the original, "What matter who's speaking, someone said what matter who's speaking" (16).

6. *Malicious* edits are analogous to "vandalism" of wiki article content (Viégas, Wattenberg, and Dave 578). This vandalism can take the form of mass deletions or additions of obscene or injurious content.

7. Viégas, Wattenberg, and Dave define *median survival time* as "the total time that these edits remained on the site" (579).

8. Not all wikis function exactly like Wikipedia. Many wiki programs, including the open-source Media-Wiki platform upon which Wikipedia is based, can be configured to provide different levels of access. For example, in a classroom environment, the wiki's administrator might restrict writing/editing access only to class participants. Despite such variability, the basic principle of providing access to shared documents remains intact irrespective of the specific wiki platform. The ability to read, compose, and edit content, whatever the constitution of the group, allows for a very different form of written expression to take shape. In the classroom, this results in a composition process that is more explicitly social. Communication need no longer take place solely between student and instructor, writer and reader, but among a community of interlocutors. Thus, acts of composition are not conducted solely in isolation and require continual linguistic and communicative negotiations with active participants.

Works Cited

Barthes, Roland. "The Death of the Author." In *Image Music Text*, trans. Stephen Heath, 142–48. New York: Hill and Wang, 1978.

Beckett, Samuel. *Texts for Nothing.* Trans. Samuel Beckett. London: Calder and Boyers, 1974.

Cunningham, Ward. "What Is Wiki?" Edited June 27, 2002. http://wiki.org/wiki.cgi?WhatIsWiki, consulted May 30, 2005.

Foucault, Michel. "What Is an Author?" In *Textual Strategies,* trans. and ed. Josué Harari, 141–60. London: Methuen, 1978.

Jaszi, Peter. "On the Author Effect: Contemporary Copyright and Collective Creativity." In *The Construction of Authorship: Textual Appropriation in Law and Literature,* ed. Martha Woodmansee and Peter Jaszi, 29–56. Durham, NC: Duke University Press, 1994.

Viégas, Fernanda B., Martin Wattenberg, and Kushal Dave. "Studying Cooperation and Conflict between Authors with *History Flow* Visualizations." Conference on Human Factors in Computing, Vienna, April 24–29, 2004. http://opensource.mit.edu/ papers/viegaswattenbergdave.pdf, consulted June 24, 2005.

"Wikipedia: About." *Wikipedia.* January 30, 2006, 2:16 UTC. http://en.wikipedia.org/w/index.php?title=Wikipedia:About&oldid=37298037, consulted January 30, 2006.

"WP:NPOV." *Wikipedia.* January 30, 2006, 2:21 UTC. http://en.wikipedia.org/w/index.php?title=Wikipedia:Neutral_point_of_view&oldid=37298596, consulted January 30, 2006..

Woodmansee, Martha. *The Author, Art, and the Market.* New York: Columbia University Press, 1994.

Internet and Open-Access Publishing in Physics Research

Gordon Kane

Publication of research in most areas of physics has changed dramatically in the past decade, with nearly all research now being published on the Internet. To appreciate how this has happened, why it is here to stay, and how it is likely to spread to other areas, it is necessary to understand that publication in physics is essentially done via papers, usually rather narrowly focused short papers on a single topic. The few books that physicists have written are mainly pedagogical. In my field, theoretical physics, papers typically have one to four authors. In most areas of physics the order of authors on a paper is always alphabetical. The changes in how research is published, which I will describe below, have in turn significantly modified how research is done. Most research is still (also) published in journals, but their purpose is now largely archival: I and most physicists no longer subscribe to or read journals.

Every day anyone anywhere who finishes a paper posts it on the Internet, at www.arxiv.org. The next day anyone anywhere with Internet access can visit that site, read the title and author(s) of all the papers posted that day, click and read the abstracts if they wish, and then click and bring up any paper on their screen, click and print it. The arXiv (as it is named) was started by Paul Ginsparg in 1991 for theoretical particle physics, and has now expanded to most areas of physics as well as such theoretical fields of science as mathematics, quantitative biology, and so on. To help keep the system always accessible and responsive, and fast even for large information transfers, there are currently seventeen mirror sites worldwide, including three in the United States, five in Europe, and four in Asia. Currently the arXiv is supported mainly by Cornell University and the National Science Foundation. The costs are small, on the order of 2 percent of that of the main U.S. physics journal, *Physical Review*. The arXiv manifesto is "ArXiv is an openly accessible, moderated repository for scholarly papers in specific scientific disciplines. Material submitted to arXiv is expected to be of interest, relevance, and value to those disciplines. ArXiv was developed to be, and remains, a means for specific communities to exchange information" (www.arXiv.org). Note that the criteria do not directly include some that one might expect to find on the list, such as "correct." Originally anyone could post papers, with essentially no content control or peer review. That has evolved to mild control—basically once one has posted something, one can then post anything in that and related areas. First-time authors need "endorsement" from someone who has posted something.

An unintended consequence of the existence of the arXiv with daily posting is that it has hugely accelerated the rate of research, and subtly shaped the form papers take. Research has shifted toward being a dialogue, or better, multilogue. Communication has always been very important for research in theoretical physics. In the past one might work on a topic for some months without much interaction with others. Now as one is working, relevant papers are appearing, so one integrates their results, and work moves rapidly.

Journal publication is still used for archival purposes, and for evaluations by committees, chairs, deans, and so on. The posted arXiv papers are not peer reviewed. If an active researcher cannot tell whether something is valid, it is his or her problem. It is pretty clear to experts what work is relevant. There are strong inhibitions against posting low-quality or wrong work because of the resulting damage to one's reputation. For two reasons this system is probably relatively easy to implement in theoretical physics compared to other areas, such as biology. First, in physics results are normally right or wrong, relevant or irrelevant, and it is not very hard to tell which. Second, most people who have been in the field for a while are acquainted with or at least aware of nearly all the others in the field, and with their work and biases and how likely they are to be correct.

In theoretical physics this open-access Internet publishing is an unqualified success. Will it spread to all areas of science and even more broadly? At the institutional level there is movement toward making this happen. As one example, the Abdus Salam International Centre for Theoretical Physics (based in Trieste) has very recently organized an open-access archive that allows the scientific work of any scientist from any country to be posted free of charge. Authors may upload preprints, reprints, conference papers, prepublication book chapters, and so on. Acceptable subjects include science areas such as physics, mathematics, biology, earth sciences, computer sciences; technology areas such as computer software and networking, environmental technology; education areas; science policy areas; and more.

CERN, the European particle physics center, in December 2005, hosted an international meeting, attended by about eighty representatives of major publishers, learned societies, funding agencies, and authors from Europe and the United States. Its goal was to promote open-access publishing. In March 2007, a task force recommended establishing a sponsoring consortium for open-access publishing in particle physics (SCOAP), in which a "global network of funding agencies, research laboratories, and libraries will contribute the necessary funding" ("Proposal"). Contributors will recover their payments by cancelling paper subscriptions; payments will be based on the number of scientific publications from a country or laboratory over a specified time period. It seems rather clear that in essentially all areas of quantitative theoretical science open-access publishing will be increasingly important. The American Association for the Advancement of Science (publisher of *Science*) has recently done a study on open access, available at www.alpsp.org (though it focuses on open-access journal publishing rather than independent posting such as the arXiv).

Moving to open-access publication will be more difficult in biology for several reasons. Evaluating the validity of reported results is considerably more difficult in biological areas and particularly in biomedical ones, where many more variables and considerations can affect the outcome of experiments and analyses. Science in these areas is less theoretical than in physics. There are far more practitioners, so it is much less likely that the people and their reputations are known to nearly everyone. It is harder to tell who actually did the work. The top journals (e.g., *Science* and *Nature*) currently refuse to publish a paper if it is first posted on the arXiv. Coming to terms with these issues, and finding a productive level of open-access publishing for areas other than theoretical science, will receive increasing attention in the near future.

The arXiv (and presumably open-access publishing in general) will keep evolving. Recently the arXiv added a new feature whose value and use level are not yet known. A qualified physicist with a blog can write a comment about a particular paper. Using a new protocol called Track-Backs, the blogger's website notifies the arXiv, which then provides a link to the blog next to the abstract of the paper. Anyone who looks at a paper can then click and read what others have written about it. Only those qualified to post on arXiv can comment, and TrackBacks from anonymous sites are not allowed.

Finally I will comment briefly on some of the themes of this anthology, plagiarism and scientific fraud. They provide further perspective on why open-access publishing has been and will be easier to implement in theoretical science than in other areas. Basically, plagiarism of writing and fraud are not important issues in theoretical science, whatever one might read from experts in these areas or in the media. First, the fraction of workers who might do these things is probably smaller than in other areas, partly because workers mostly are trained by example not to do it, and more importantly, because they are aware that they are highly likely to be caught. The results of science can be trusted, with high probability in the short term, and with very high probability in the longer term. That is not because every scientist is honest—not all are—but because if a paper or a result is interesting then knowledgeable people will quickly see it, read it, and try to reproduce the result. Copying and fraud will be spotted, and not ignored. Reproducing results can take longer if detailed calculations or lab measurements are involved, but they will be done. These mechanisms have operated effectively in all the well-publicized cases, with scientists catching the fraud about as quickly as possible, given the time needed for checking the results, despite current media and "ethics expert's" hype. The integrity of science is functioning just as it should and protecting the public as well as is possible. It is extremely difficult to fool scientists into thinking a false result is true (and, of course, the results of science are compared to a real world, so truth is not socially constructed).

Plagiarism of ideas is a somewhat larger problem, but not a significant one. The period from having an idea to showing the idea is not inconsistent with existing data and theory, and figuring out feasible tests of the idea can take weeks to months and can only be done by qualified scientists. Theoretical science is a communication-intensive area, so scientists mostly know what everyone in the world in their area is doing, and who has what ideas. Top research universities and labs have one to two seminars a week in each research area (theoretical particle physics, astrophysics, etc.), mostly from outside visitors, usually about recent or unfinished work. ArXiv posting settles literal priority (journal publication dates are no longer relevant). Plagiarism of ideas may occur, but is unlikely to go undetected; the subsequent damage to the reputation of those doing it acts as a deterrent.

Theoretical physicists and theoretical scientists in general are very happy with the arXiv and with open-access publishing. There seems to be a nearly ideal match with how research should be done in these areas. Some modifications will be needed for open-access publishing to spread to other areas of science, and beyond science, but I am confident that will probably happen.

Work Cited

"The arXiv Endorsement System." www.arXiv.org/help/endorsement, consulted May 8, 2007.
"Proposal to Establish a Sponsoring Consortium for Open Access Publishing in Particle Physics." http://doc.cern.ch/archive/electronic/cern/preprints/open/open 2007-009.pdf. Consulted July 26, 2007.

Do Thesis Statements Short-Circuit Originality in Students' Writing?

Anne Berggren

I decided to take on the issue of thesis statements when I failed a test. It was a test on essay introductions in Diana Hacker's online exercises, and the example that pushed my buttons posed these two possible beginnings and asked which was better:[1]

> *Soft money* is the term used for campaign contributions that sidestep laws governing the amount of contributions candidates can get from any one source. Many election campaigns are financed largely with soft money, whether it is raised by the candidates themselves or by their party organizations. Soft money pays for items such as television ads that endorse a political issue rather than a candidate.

> Every election year, political parties and candidates raise millions of dollars in soft money, contributions that sidestep laws limiting the amount of money a candidate can receive from any one source. Because unregulated soft money can make winning candidates feel indebted to wealthy donors such as unions and corporations, we must close the undemocratic loopholes in our current campaign finance laws.

I saw more potential in the first beginning. While the second seemed to require more information between the first and final sentence, the first led coherently and specifically into the subject, and I felt a distinct "but" at the end of the passage, implying that in the upcoming paragraph the writer would turn from definition to problem. However, when I selected the first passage I received this rebuke:

> Sorry. The opening sentence defines a term instead of engaging the reader's attention. More important, the introduction goes nowhere: It does not assert a thesis to be developed in the rest of the paper.[2]

53

An introduction to an essay—academic or otherwise—should indeed engage the reader and set the stage for the intellectual work the writer intends to do. But only in student writing is the writer expected to place at the end of the first paragraph a one-sentence statement of the conclusion the writer is aiming for and then, as students often put it, "prove" that point. Today, students are taught as early as elementary school to use thesis statements, and can arrive at college with several years of practice in mechanical beginnings that encapsulate the argument and often forecast the three or four pieces of evidence that will follow. I wonder, then: Does requiring a thesis at the end of the first paragraph undercut efforts to teach students to try different techniques, to let form follow content, to be creative, even original?

My favorite beginnings do not involve thesis statements. Peter Elbow, for example, in "Reflections on Academic Discourse: How It Relates to Freshmen and Colleagues," characteristically starts off with a question:

> I love what's in academic discourse: learning, intelligence, sophistica-
> tion—even mere facts and naked summaries of articles and books; I love
> reasoning, inference and evidence; I love theory. But I hate academic
> discourse. What follows is my attempt to work my way out of this
> dilemma. In doing so I will assume an ostensive definition of academic
> discourse: it is the discourse that academics use when they publish for
> other academics. And what characterizes that discourse? This is the
> question I will pursue here. (135)

Harriet McBryde Johnson, in "Unspeakable Conversations Or How I Spent One Day as a Token Cripple at Princeton University," her *New York Times Magazine* essay about her discourse with pragmatist philosopher Peter Singer, starts with humor—and provocation:

> He insists he doesn't want to kill me. He simply thinks it would have
> been better, all things considered, to have given my parents the option
> of killing the baby I once was, and to let other parents kill similar babies
> as they come along and thereby avoid the suffering that comes with
> lives like mine and satisfy the reasonable preferences of parents for a dif-
> ferent kind of child. It has nothing to do with me. I should not feel
> threatened.
>
> Whenever I try to wrap my head around his tight string of syllogisms,
> my brain gets so fried it's . . . almost fun. Mercy! It's like *Alice in Won-
> derland*. (50)

Indeed, professional writers can consider many options when they are casting around for beginnings: contrasting quotations, personal anecdotes, description of a problem, dialogue, narrative, and so forth. They use these options to produce introductions that identify the subject and direction of an essay without giving away the plot. What students might call the thesis statement (the professional writer might call it the argument) may even be saved until the conclusion, after readers have been prepared by the evidence to accept that position as reasonable.

Perhaps full disclosure of my bias is appropriate here: I didn't learn about thesis statements in college or graduate school or while teaching high school English and history in the 1960s. The term was never mentioned when I wrote for newspapers and did editing for a publishing company and a department of surgery in the 1970s or when I worked for a law firm in the 1980s. And so, in the 1990s, when I began to study composition theory and pedagogy and encountered thesis statements, I didn't find them useful. I attempted to ignore them.

But students today, and their writing teachers, will find it difficult to ignore thesis statements. Every handbook and almost every textbook that I have examined assumes that a thesis statement at the end of the first paragraph is the standard form in college writing.[3] At the University of Michigan's Sweetland Writing Center, where I've worked since 1998, approximately a third of students visiting the center check a form saying they want help formulating thesis statements. Most students who have appointments with me assume they must have a thesis statement at the end of the first paragraph—and if I mention that they have other options, they look bewildered.

Further, when I Googled *thesis statement* I got 186,000 hits, including a site for fifth graders (W. W. Norton) that advised them that the thesis statement "The fat content of school lunches is excessive for children" was better than "School lunches suck." (I would have chosen the wrong beginning here, too.) Narrowing my search to *thesis statement and college,* I got 61,500 sites, and most of the first 50 were websites of university writing centers, including those of Indiana, Purdue, North Carolina, Richmond, Wisconsin, Kentucky, Rutgers, Penn, Penn State, Ohio, Harvard, Colorado State, SUNY, and Temple. These sites, too, treat thesis sentences as the default mode in college writing. Indiana University's website notes that "almost all of us . . . look early in an essay for a one- or two-sentence condensation of the argument that is to follow. We refer to that condensation as a thesis statement." The University of Illinois advises students that "everything you write should develop around a *clear central thesis. . . .* It should appear in the first paragraph."[4] The University of North Carolina advises students, "Always assume that your instructors expect you to . . . [argue] a position that you set out in a thesis statement" and that "a single sentence somewhere in your first paragraph should present your thesis to the reader."

Why has the thesis sentence become a required element in college writing? Why, when we stress preparing students for any writing contingencies that may come up in jobs or in life, do we confine them to one way, and one way only, of beginning a piece of writing? Where did the thesis statement come from and what accounts for its present popularity?

To seek the origin of thesis statements, I turned to antiquity, since so many categories and methods in the teaching of writing derive from Aristotle and come to us by way of the Roman rhetorician Quintilian, who wrote copiously about teaching rhetoric. Looking up *thesis* in the index of *The Rhetorical Tradition* led me straight to Quintilian's *Institutes of Oratory,* book 2. Back then, however, thesis had a different meaning. *Theses* meant "general questions," in contrast to *hypotheses,* which dealt with specific instances. The *thesis* was an assignment given to young writers on an abstract, either/or topic. Quintilian recommends four: Whether it is better to live in the city or the country; whether a lawyer or a soldier has more merit; whether a man should marry; and whether a man should seek political office. These questions were abstract in the sense that students were to practice pure reasoning rather than attach significance to particular persons, places, or situations (298, 304–5). It struck me that a writer need not have a particular passion for either side in these exercises. He can answer yes or no and simply assemble some evidence in favor of his point. The project is thus a training exercise, what the British refer to as a *dummy run.*

If this ancient precedent is the model for today's thesis statement, one might suspect that today's thesis-driven paper is, at best, a test, a carefully circumscribed way of assessing skills useful in writing, skills such as using evidence, quoting from sources, or synthesizing information. At worst, the model suggests that education is largely ceremonial, and that students are required to enact the ceremony, just as their teachers did before them. In his introduction to Paul Heilker's *The Essay: Theory and Pedagogy for an Active Form,* Derek Owens makes a similar point, arguing that the school paper is not meant to further the student's knowledge, or further the knowledge of anyone else in the field, or convince a wider audience. As he puts it, "The research paper, the exam question, the master's thesis, the dissertation, the professional article, the scholarly book—these are almost never expected to be catalysts for real change. They are primarily icons" (xi).

Given that Quintilian required theses, I expected to find more of a history for the term.[5] But I could not find any mention of the word *thesis*, much less *thesis statement*, in my research on the teaching of writing in the eighteenth century, when the textbooks of George Campbell and Hugh Blair ruled the field (Berlin 19–34), and I found the word in only one of the nineteenth-century textbooks and handbooks I actually examined. The one exception was Elias J. MacEwan's *The Essentials of Argumentation* (1899), which defines a thesis as either "a proposition put forward to be supported by argument" or "an argumentative composition embodying the results of original research" (401). Several other nineteenth-century texts use the term *proposition*. Richard Whately, in his 1828 *Elements of Rhetoric*, advises students to state a "proposition or propositions to be maintained" (Berlin 30). Charles William Bardeen, in *A System of Rhetoric* (1884), advises "boys" to begin by indicating their area of interest and proceed to a proposition that can guide their organization. Robert Palfrey Utter, who taught at Amherst, told students in *A Guide to Good English* (1914) that in argument you need a "main proposition," a "definite assertion" or a question—something debatable. The introduction should lead to the "determination of the special issue" (114). I wondered if a proposition was merely an earlier version of a thesis statement, but Utter defines it as any "definite assertion or question" and indicates that it is a step in logic:

> Proposition: x is y.
>   Definition: y is a, b, and c.
>   If, then, x is a, b, and c, x is y.
> Special issue: The question then becomes, is x a, b, and c? (113)

Although none of the above authors specified that the proposition be included in the essay, some early textbook writers did urge students to write out a summary of the argument they intended to make. Thus, James Morgan Hart from Cornell advised in *A Handbook of English Composition* (1895): "*Formulate your subject in a complete and clearly-worded sentence, before you begin to write.* [You] need not insert [this sentence in the] composition" (451). Frances M. Perry of Wellesley, in *An Introductory Course in Exposition* (1908), asks students to summarize their arguments before they begin writing to insure that they have "a comprehensive view . . . of the subject as [they] intend to treat it" (52). But Charles Sears Baldwin, in his 1906 manual *How to Write,* warned that because an essay "deals with the outside only in order to reveal the inside" (55), its meaning "cannot so often be summed up in a single sentence" (63). Later in the manual, he advised that a "formal opening promises a cold and dry going on" (72).

Rosaline Masson describes two methods of writing an essay in her *Use and Abuse of English: A Hand Book of Composition* (1900). In the didactic method, she says, you would "begin by stating your conclusion and then justifying and illustrating it" (99); in the analytical method, you would "gradually lead the way to [a] conclusion, by giving reason after reason and fact after fact, until you have prepared the mind of the reader to receive . . . the conclusion to which all your arguments have tended" (99). Clarence Dewitt Thorpe of the University of Michigan favors the second of these two options in his 1929 text *College Composition.* "The wrong way to build an argument," Thorpe says, "is to form a conclusion and then look for facts and reasons to support this conclusion" (418).

The first appearance I have found of the term *thesis* as it is used today occurs in two textbooks published in 1943. John Crowe Ransom states in *A College Primer of Writing* that in argument, "the writer defends or opposes some 'thesis' or proposition" (82), and Argus Tresidder, Leland Schubert, and Charles W. Jones, in *Writing and Speaking,* claim that "first, in all argument a thesis must be presented" (381). The idea of presenting a thesis must not have been firmly established, however; Cleanth Brooks, in *Fundamentals of Good Writing: A Handbook of Modern Rhetoric,* published in 1950, never mentions a thesis and advises that an introduction should "state the precise question with which the discussion is to be concerned" (23).

If the idea that students' papers should present a thesis began in the 1940s, and if thesis statements became the default mode for college writing by, say, the 1980s, my attempt to account for the popularity of thesis statements must focus on what, during those years, would have made this mechanism valuable. Fueled by the GI Bill and the growing number of women seeking higher education, more students, from more varied backgrounds, poured into colleges. To teach these students, colleges turned to adjunct faculty and graduate students, many of whom were not trained in rhetoric. One can imagine that these new teachers needed specific, aptly named, easy-to-teach principles that would help them teach writing. To add support to this notion, Robert J. Connors, in *Composition-Rhetoric: Backgrounds, Theory, and Pedagogy,* points out that somewhere between the 1930s and 1950s, textbooks on writing began to focus on one "master idea" about writing that "should control the way that students learn to write"

(250) and to subordinate the textbook's pedagogical material to that idea. During that same time frame, science rather than the humanities became the dominant influence in the academy, and a more scientific, formulaic approach to writing—one that made students' writing seem more objective and less personal—may have had particular appeal for English departments.

In an e-mail message to the author on September 27, 2005, Margaret Proctor, author of the handbook *Writer's Choice* and coordinator of writing support at the University of Toronto, suggested that standardized tests such as the SATs popularized the use of thesis statements.[6] "For Canadians," she explained, "the idea of a thesis statement appears only in the 1980s, when universities here started asking for TOEFL scores and sometimes also imposed post-admission writing tests using the convenient form of the 5-paragraph essay." If the SATs precipitated a need in the United States for a form of writing that could be easily assessed, the thesis statement/support form would certainly have benefited both teachers who taught to the test and those who graded it. Furthermore, the thesis limits the discussion, and the more limited the discussion, the more quickly the teacher can judge whether the student made her case.[7]

Beyond these practicalities, however, I think the notion of a "master idea," a thesis statement—one of our most popular handouts speaks of "the Magic Thesis Sentence"—must have a certain resonance in the world today. While writing this essay, I read a *New York Times Magazine* article about George Lakoff's efforts to teach the Democrats to frame their messages using simple unified slogans like the Republicans did in the last election (Bai 2005). Did the Republicans win in 2004 because they disregarded nuance and relied on thesis statements? Asking myself that question, I recalled my students' difficulty in summarizing arguments from the *New York Times Magazine, Harper's,* the *New Yorker,* and the *Atlantic Monthly,* as well as guest editorials and op-ed pieces. Students often complain that assigned articles are too hard to understand. They want professional writers to state in the introduction exactly what they are arguing. In other words, if the argument is implied by the preponderance of evidence rather than stated succinctly at the end of the first paragraph, students can't figure out what it is. I began to wonder whether the course of history is now being changed because a generation of citizens has internalized the school ideal that all good writing begins with a thesis statement.

But while I was thinking about unified messages, it occurred to me that corporate memos and e-mails probably benefit from thesis statements that simplify the message: We need to buy more Burger King stock; I recommend Ramsey for the job. Three points of support for the assertion would undoubtedly follow. Perhaps fads in the teaching of writing—and I like to think of the thesis statement as a fad—happen because a significant technology profits from them.

I'll end with three objections to thesis statements and the thesis/support form:

1. The form makes it too easy for students to do perfunctory work that requires no engagement, creativity, or thought. One student told me he could write a thesis essay in two hours flat and get an A every time. In an article in the *Michigan Daily,* law student Dustin Lee makes a similar claim.[8]

> You can write an A-quality essay without any substantive knowledge of the reading. . . . [W]hen it comes time to write a paper, skim the reading material for a few quotes that could reasonably be suggestive of some underlying liberal theme—for example, that *The Red Badge of Courage* is actually about lesbianism—and use these quotes as evidence of the underlying theme. Make sure you emphasize in your paper that "although this topic is not explicitly addressed in the text" your excerpted quotes can reasonably be suggestive of whatever generalized theme you chose. (4)

I do see the practicality of being able to go on automatic pilot, so to speak, to write a paper. While teachers, textbooks, and handbooks may urge students to choose the thesis statement last, after significant research, students are as constrained by time as the rest of us and will opt for efficiency and fit the paper to the thesis if they can.

2. The thesis statement is not a neutral device. It affects content because it controls what you are able to say as well as how you can say it. It assumes a view of knowledge as external and somehow "provable." This view of knowledge relieves the student of any necessity for generating and reflecting on new ideas, exploring and testing her beliefs, or experimenting with different schemes of arrangement to find an organizational strategy that best suits her project. Her only question becomes, What can I say that I can support?

Isn't the above process profoundly anti-intellectual? Don't we in academia value our willingness to question everything, to suspend belief and seek new possibilities, to recognize that facts change and writers can be seduced by clichés and assumptions?

Heilker, in his book on the essay, proposes a more personal, introspective form as a substitute for the thesis paper because of three qualities summed up by Owens in the introduction:

- The author doubts easy answers and doesn't accept on faith anything that's been said about the subject before;
- The author is willing to venture into unknown territory, rejecting academic answers if necessary; and
- The author is willing to experiment, to trust "chrono-logic" rather than any established form, to let the ideas unfold as they may. (xiii–xiv)

3. Many teachers, including Nancy Sommers,[9] believe that learning to use thesis statements and provide support is a necessary developmental phase in the training of a young writer. But the work of elementary school teachers such as Lucy Calkins and Robert Graves, middle school teachers such as Nancy Atwell, and many of the teachers associated with the National Writers Project surely shows that students can do quite well without that phase. Certainly, in college, students should have available to them all the techniques and strategies that professional writers are able to use. We, as writing teachers, should encourage them to take advantage of all those door-opening, inquiry-producing, generative tools—in the hope they'll learn to say something deeply reflective, and perhaps original.

Notes

1. Diana Hacker, who died in 2004, was the author of *A Writer's Reference* and *A Pocket Style Manual*, both popular college handbooks published by Bedford/St. Martin's.

2. My session at the website for Diana Hacker's *A Writer's Reference* took place October 5, 2002. The current site, for the sixth edition, is at http://bcs.bedfordst martins.com/writersref6e/Player/Pages/Main.aspx, consulted July 7, 2007.

3. See for example Aaron 17; Hairston et al. 30; Hacker 13; Hodges et al. 50–51; and Faigley 51.

4. Googling the first sentence of this passage brings up forty university and commercial sites that use this exact sentence.

5. Erika Lindemann claims that "we can discover similarities between the five-paragraph theme . . . and formulas the classical rhetoricians proposed for structuring arguments" (38). However, she does not provide examples and I have not been able to establish this relationship.

6. I am grateful to Margaret Proctor for attending my conference session and later

suggesting several new sources. She is directly interested in this topic, having written a book chapter on academic essays, "The Essay as a Literary and Academic Form."

7. When I gave an earlier version of this paper at the Michigan College English Association Conference, respondents told me that ease in grading was their strongest motive for requiring thesis statements. If the thesis sets out a template, the grader needs only to judge how well the paper follows the template.

8. Lee's argument in the article is that University of Michigan teachers shut out conservative views but consider any liberal opinion intelligent. I disagree.

9. Nancy Sommers explained this view in answer to a question I asked during a Sweetland Writing Center workshop at the University of Michigan on October 13, 2000.

Works Cited

Aaron, Jane E. *The Little, Brown Compact Handbook.* 4th ed. New York: Longman, 2001.

Bai, Matt. "The Framing Wars." *New York Times Magazine,* July 17, 2005, 38–50.

Baker, George Pierce. *The Principles of Argumentation.* Boston: Ginn and Company, 1925.

Baldwin, Charles Sears. *How to Write.* New York: Macmillan, 1906.

Bardeen, Charles William. *A System of Rhetoric.* 1884; Ann Arbor: Scholars' Facsimiles & Reprints, 2002.

Berlin, James A. *Writing Instruction in Nineteenth-Century American Colleges.* Carbondale: Southern Illinois University Press, 1984.

Brooks, Cleanth. *Fundamentals of Good Writing: A Handbook of Modern Rhetoric.* New York: Harcourt, Brace and World, 1950.

Connors, Robert J. *Composition-Rhetoric: Backgrounds, Theory, and Pedagogy.* Pittsburgh: University of Pittsburgh Press, 1997.

Elbow, Peter. "Reflections on Academic Discourse: How It Relates to Freshmen and Colleagues." *College English* 53, no. 2 (1991): 135–55.

Faigley, Lester. *The Penguin Handbook.* New York: Pearson/Longman, 2005.

Hacker, Diana. *A Writer's Reference.* 5th ed. Boston: Bedford/St. Martin's, 2003.

Hairston, Maxine, et al. *The Scott, Foresman Handbook for Writers.* 5th ed. New York: Longman, 1999.

Hart, James Morgan. *A Handbook of English Composition.* 1895. In *The Origins of Composition Studies in the American College, 1875–1925: A Documentary History,* ed. John C. Brereton, 451–55. Pittsburgh: University of Pittsburgh Press, 1995.

Heilker, Paul. *The Essay: Theory and Pedagogy for an Active Form.* Urbana, IL: National Council of Teachers of English, 1996.

Hodges, John C., et al. *The Writer's Harbrace Handbook.* Fort Worth: Harcourt, 2001.

Indiana University Writing Tutorial Services. "How to Write a Thesis Statement." April 27, 2004. http://www.indiana.edu/~wts/pamphlets/thesis_statement.shtml, consulted September 10, 2004.

Johnson, Harriet McBryde. "Unspeakable Conversations, or How I Spent One Day as a Token Cripple at Princeton University." *New York Times Magazine,* February 16, 2003, 50–55+.

Lee, D. C. "Five Simple Steps for Increasing Your GPA." *Michigan Daily*, February 4, 2003, 4.

Lindemann, Erika. *A Rhetoric for Writing Teachers*. 2nd ed. New York: Oxford University Press, 1987.

MacEwan, Elias J. *The Essentials of Argumentation*. Boston: D. C. Heath, 1899.

Masson, Rosaline. *Use and Abuse of English: A Hand Book of Composition*. Edinburgh: James Thin, 1900.

Owens, Derek. Introduction to *The Essay: Theory and Pedagogy for an Active Form*, by Paul Heilker, ix–xx. Urbana, IL: National Council of Teachers of English, 1996.

Perry, Frances M. *An Introductory Course in Exposition*. New York: American Book Company, 1908.

Proctor, Margaret. "The Essay as a Literary and Academic Form: Closed Gate or Open Door." In *Literacy, Narrative, and Culture*, ed. Jens Brockmeier, Min Wang, and David R. Olson, 170–83. London: Curzon, 2002.

Quintilian. *Institutes of Oratory, Book II*. In *The Rhetorical Tradition*, ed. Patricia Bizzell and Bruce Herzberg, 297–334. Boston: Bedford, 1990.

Ransom, John Crowe. *A College Primer of Writing*. New York: Henry Holt, 1943.

Thorpe, Clarence Dewitt. *College Composition*. 3rd ed. New York: Harper and Brothers, 1939.

Tresidder, Argus, Leland Schubert, and Charles W. Jones. *Writing and Speaking*. New York: Ronald Press Company, 1943.

University of Illinois at Urbana-Champaign. "Developing a Thesis Statement." Writing Workshop. http://www.english.uiuc.edu/cws/wworkshop/advice/developing_a_thesis.htm, consulted September 10, 2004.

University of North Carolina Writing Center. "Constructing Thesis Statements." October 17, 2000. http://staff.agu.edu.vn/tathong/Writing/UNCWritingCenter Handout ConstructingThesisStatements.htm, consulted September 10, 2004.

Utter, Robert Palfrey. *A Guide to Good English*. New York: Harper and Brothers, 1914.

W. W. Norton. "Thesis Statement Review." *Ace Writing Home Page*. http://www.geocities.com/fifth_grade_tpes/thesis.html, consulted September 10, 2004.

Cloud Gate

Challenging Reproducibility

Jeff Ward

Jessica Litman argues that the basic reproductive unit of U.S. copyright law, the copy, "no longer serves our needs, and we should jettison it completely" (180). The challenge posed by modern technologies is central to her argument. Computers routinely produce "copies" of program code and data in use. Litman suggests that *use*—distinguished as commercial or noncommercial—would be a better way of organizing copyright legislation. But *use* is a complex and nuanced term, especially when applied to one ubiquitous reproductive technology, photography.

Photography can be described as a group of technologies with multiple uses. Reproduction, in the sense of making copies, is only one aspect. For the average snapshooter, a photograph of a relative is not used to "copy" them, but rather to *depict* a likeness as a trigger for memories. Industrial uses of photography are different. Large-scale integrated circuits are fabricated using photographic technologies. Dark and light areas in a negative detect if a resistant mask should be deposited; the negative presents a mapped *description* of circuit pathways. Much like the copies found in computer program code, reproduction occurs without recognizable depiction. The photographic functions of reproduction, depiction, and detection are separate (Maynard, *Engine* and "Talbot's Techonologies"). I agree with Litman's contention that the term *copy* has lost its utility, not merely because of digital technology, but because of technology in the broadest sense. Distinguishing between *description* and *depiction* differentiates between the "copies" computers use and copies as *reproductions*. The transitory "copies" of data present in digital technology are sets of instructions *describing* a tangible or ephemeral object—music, pictures, and words. Like the photographic negatives used to manufacture integrated circuits or circuit boards, the copied data tells machines how to reproduce objects. It neither depicts, nor reproduces them.

These subtle distinctions are present in U.S. copyright law, but only in regard to architecture. Descriptions of buildings, in the form of plans, can be copyrighted.[1] However, 17 U.S.C. §120(a) provides for a *right of depiction:*

> (a) Pictorial Representations Permitted.—The copyright in an architectural work that has been constructed does not include the right to prevent the making, distributing, or public display of pictures, paintings, photographs, or other pictorial representations of the work, if the building in which the work is embodied is located in or ordinarily visible from a public place.

This right only extends to architecture; no other category in copyright law offers similar exclusions. The statute uses the term "representation" rather than depiction and only concerns pictorial representations. Nonetheless, U.S.C. 17 §120(a) differentiates between representation and reproduction and classifies photography among representative technologies.

Photography's *depictive* power is often conflated with the descriptiveness of its reproductions. Its ability to *describe* physical objects into two-dimensional projections is unparalleled. Photographs "tell" us things about the subject, but also provide raw material for imagination. A photograph is not a "copy" of its subject. I am sympathetic to Kendall L. Walton's controversial assertion that depictive photographs are essentially *fictions* facilitating imagination. "To be a depiction is to have the function of serving as a prop in visual games of make believe" (Walton, *Mimesis* 296). A depiction does more than "copy" reality. Nonetheless, because of the power of its descriptions, photography is more suspect than painting or sketching. A person sketching a public landmark is less likely to be interrogated than a person with a camera. The right to photograph in public does not exist by statute, except in the case of architecture.

Following a 2005 controversy regarding Anish Kapoor's sculpture *Cloud Gate,* this chapter revisits the concept of reproducibility in art. Kapoor's sculpture captured the imagination of Internet users who warned of a new prohibition of photography taking hold. Though Walter Benjamin's "The Work of Art in the Age of Mechanical Reproduction" loses some of its prophetic luster in the aftermath of *Cloud Gate,* most of the mechanisms involved remain relevant. As a monument to capitalism and a "copyrightable" property, the sculpture provides a locus for discussing the right to photograph in public spaces and the *use* of media, both new and old.

Cloud Gate

Anish Kapoor's *Cloud Gate* is a publicly visible sculpture located in Millennium Park, Chicago. The park was proposed in 1996 to occupy a twenty-four-acre site, with a budget of $150 million. Originally slated to open in 2000, the park debuted in mid-2004. Changes in the project necessitated the formation of a nonprofit corporation, Millennium Park Inc., headed by former Sara Lee CEO John Bryan. With corporate support, the budget grew to $475 million, received from public and private contributions.[2] *Cloud Gate* was made possible by an $11.5 million-dollar grant from SBC Telecommunications, and was incomplete when the park opened. Composed of 168 stainless steel plates, its welds had not been polished. Although the opening was premature, Kapoor remarked: "At least it's there on the opening day, if only as a semi-finished object. One gets a sense of what it's going to be" (Nance 64). Citizens and the media in Chicago designated the structure as "the bean" before it was properly titled. Kapoor was not amused:

> I'd just as happily do without a title, actually, except that it suggests a possibility of interpretation. In this case, the work is clearly reflecting what's around it, picking up the Chicago horizon, the Chicago skyline—bringing it into itself, in a way. And it is a gate—a gate to Chicago, a poetic idea about the city it reflects. To call it something else damages the potential for a different way of thinking about the piece. (Nance 64)

Titles, according to Kapoor, focus our thoughts on what the sculpture might depict. Measuring sixty-six feet long, thirty-three feet tall, and weighing 110 tons, *Cloud Gate* has a certain gravitas undercut by the diminutive title of "bean." This early controversy makes it easier to differentiate between a descriptive label such as "the bean" and its depictive one, *Cloud Gate*. There is nothing aside from respect to prevent false labeling of the sculpture. There is no law against it. Richard Rezac, a sculptor and professor at the Art Institute of Chicago, remarked about the nickname: "I think it's a trivialization of his efforts, his ideas and his basic intention." Further, Rezac elaborates on an important aspect of the work: "The fact that it's reflective, that it functions as a mirror, is the whole essence of the work" (Nance 64). Control over what depictions of *Cloud Gate* reflect has been a problem for both the sculptor and the City of Chicago.

On January 27, 2005, the blog *New (sub)Urbanism* reported on an emerging story: professional photographer Warren Wimmer was stopped by a security guard from photographing *Cloud Gate*. Ben Joravsky's article "The

Bean Police" in the *Chicago Reader* was ground zero. Depictions of this event on the Internet caused a stir. *BoingBoing* picked up the story on February 6, and links multiplied. The City of Chicago vowed to drop its permit fee for professional photographers in Millennium Park on February 17. A follow-up article by Joravsky seemed to settle the issue on February 11. Another article in the *Christian Science Monitor* on March 30 went largely unnoticed by bloggers (Kleiman). The issues raised in this interface of media, technology, and public space deserve careful unpacking

Reaction by the media had nothing to do with *Cloud Gate* as a work of art. "The Bean Police" discovered that professional photography in Millennium Park requires a permit. Wimmer, to avoid purchasing this permit, bribed a security guard. He was also warned not to sell any photographs of *Cloud Gate.* Joravsky's research made it clear that the restrictions on photography in public parks applied not only to *Cloud Gate,* but to all professional photography in any city park. But his selective subtitle read: "The city's charging some photographers hundreds of dollars to take pictures in Millennium Park," highlighting Chicago's newest attraction. Titling the follow-up article "Pork in the Park," Joravsky declared a narrow field of interest. But the article details two distinct modes of regulation. First, "professional" photography requires a permit in public spaces. Second, photographs could not be sold without explicit permission. There was no mention of casual photography, and the ambiguous "some" of Joravsky's initial subtitle promotes misreading.

As the story proliferated on the Internet, the depiction of *professional* regulation was minimized. Instead, the focus was the threat of public space itself being copyrighted. The central commercial/noncommercial distinction was ignored. The City of Chicago attempted to differentiate between amateur and professional by identifying the type of equipment. Security guards were instructed to look for tripods and "professional looking" equipment or tripods. The purpose of both is to make more "exact" copies of a scene. The threat of exact copies of Kapoor's sculpture might be a divisive point, but public reaction accentuated the *power to prohibit,* rather than the separation of commercial and noncommercial behaviors. David Bollier expressed this imagined crisis by comparing the chain of events surrounding *Cloud Gate* to an earlier controversy blogged by Lawrence Lessig—a prohibition on photography in Starbucks Cafés. While the response on the Internet is analogous, the core situations are not. The interior of a Starbucks franchise is arguably a *private* space regulated through the policies of the franchise or the owner.[3] Casinos in Las Vegas regulate public photography. The overriding issue is an assumed privacy right for their patrons. Family-oriented casinos encourage photography, while more upscale venues discourage it.

Millennium Park is a *public* space. Nonetheless, there are statutory rights that control representations of "public" presences—be they buildings, sculptures, or images of people in public places. There is no general statutory right to photograph in public; these rights are derived from common-law precedents. Lessig has argued elsewhere that these precedents accentuate the relationship between freedom from regulation and technological innovation (345). However, the right of the public to represent, reproduce, or transmit iconic presences is shaky. Icons like *Cloud Gate* reflect cultural values, and regulating the ability of culture to reproduce itself has far-reaching implications beyond technological innovation. Lessig and others have also argued that excessive regulation of cultural products might mean the death of culture. But such regulations grow from copyright's first mandate—to promote progress in the useful arts. According to Lessig, Starbucks prohibits photography on the grounds that it reproduces their floor plan in a transmissible form, promoting infringement of their *copyrights*. The casino example is not a matter of copyright at all; photography can be prohibited because it infringes on *privacy rights*. In matters of public space, multiple rights are involved.

In response to Starbucks' prohibition, Lessig encouraged his readers to practice civil disobedience—hundreds of readers responded by posting photographs taken in Starbucks. Cory Doctorow of *BoingBoing* responded in kind to the "crisis" of *Cloud Gate* by urging readers to take photographs of *Cloud Gate* and upload them. The response was disappointing. New photographs of the sculpture were impossible; *Cloud Gate* was draped in a tent in late January to polish its seams. Moreover, amateur photography was never prohibited, and the presence of photographs of the sculpture online was a nonissue. A webcam operated by US Equity has been gradually accumulating a public Internet archive of photos of the sculpture and adjoining restaurant since March 5, 2004.[4] The transformation of *Cloud Gate* from a work of art into a politicized work of art negotiates the boundaries of both legal and aesthetic discourse.

These boundaries were more specifically addressed by the *Christian Science Monitor* story "Who Owns Public Art?" Bob Horsch, who had been selling postcards and calendars of the sculpture from his gallery, was warned by city representatives to cease selling these "copies." Horsch was shocked: "We've been representing Chicago for 32 years. We've put up with the dirt for six years and now we can't take a picture of what's across the street?" (Kleiman 15). What emerges from this mainstream article is a more accurate depiction. The prohibition the City of Chicago seeks to enforce is the commercial exploitation of its properties through "copies." The copyrights of the objects in Millennium Park have been transferred to the City of Chicago, which claims an exclusive right to commercial exploitation. Photography by the general public, considered to fall within the realm of "fair use," is exempt. What is at stake for Horsch is the ability to exploit public landmarks for financial gain.

The complexity of the situation is obscured by fear of the prohibition of photography in public spaces. Can objects be photographed freely in public space? The answer is generally yes. Can these photographs be reproduced openly for profit? The answer to that question is frequently no. Walter Benjamin observed:

> The increasing proletarianization of modern man and the increasing formation of masses are two sides of the same process. Fascism attempts to organize the newly proletarianized masses while leaving intact the property relations which they strive to abolish. It sees its salvation in granting expression to the masses—but on no account granting them rights. (120–21)

Cloud Gate deserves deeper contemplation as an object that challenges the "copy" as a measure of value. A work of art escapes being classed as a useful article—unlike buildings, the prohibition of salable photographic reproductions of public sculpture rests on solid ground. Expression of the sculpture's presence in the form of casual snapshots is granted, but a viewer has no right to profit.

Reproducibility

Are copies of *Cloud Gate* even possible? Kapoor's sculpture seems to embody Benjamin's concept of the irreproducible aura. "The Work of Art in the Age of Mechanical Reproduction," first available in English translation in the 1968 compilation *Illuminations,* has enjoyed critical success as a reflection on the importance of art in dangerous political times. Recent translations suggest that the original title is incorrect. An alternate title, "The Work of Art in the Age of Its Technological Reproducibility," is a better fit. Rather than the immutable "work of art" thrust into an age of reproduction, the possessive pronoun more accurately reflects the presence of art in an age where it is not only *subject* to reproduction, but *designed for repro-ducibility*. The benchmark "new" art medium for Benjamin was film; the classic "old" medium was sculpture. Benjamin predicted that sculpture would inevitably decline in the age of composite arts like film, because they forcefully renounce all concept of eternal value in favor of the potential for endless improvement. The effect of "eternal value" is aura, "a strange tissue of space and time: the apparition of a distance, however near it may be" (105). The social reason for aura's decay is "the desire of the masses to 'get closer' to things spatially and humanly, and their equally passionate concern for overcoming each thing's uniqueness by assimilating it as a reproduction" (105). When Millennium Park opened, no officially sanctioned reproductions were available. Bob Horsch capitalized on the desire to possess reproductions by providing calendars, refrigerator magnets, and posters.[5] Sales were only moderate, perhaps because *Cloud Gate* proved uniquely resistant to assimilation.

Cloud Gate distorts the skyline of Chicago, rendering it strange and distant while reflecting the city and its spectators. The initial public response to the sculpture was a rush to touch it and to confront their reflections in it. The "strange tissue of space and time" that Benjamin connects with the aura of a unique work of art is an essential, if not literal, aspect of Kapoor's work. As Blair Kamin described it, "The sculpture grabs you with its funhouse distortion game, then holds you, mystifies you, and eventually delights you with its sophisticated play of opposites" (10). Its monumental presence is deeply symbolic. Kapoor sees his work as an intersection between sculpture and architecture:

> My inspiration as an artist from as early as I can remember has been symbolic architecture. Perhaps some of the most deeply, philosophically coherent objects of all time are buildings. . . . Whether it's the Jantar Mantar in India, or early mosques like the one at Samara, Iraq, or the pyramids—there are two things that come together. One is the ritual procession that those structures seem to describe, evoke and even prescribe. And the other is that they define themselves with a certain self-evident gestalt. What they seem to say is that if you look at the object from here, or if you look at the object from there, it's the same object. (Ellias 1)

Cloud Gate invites a ritual procession, while granting spectators a unique view of themselves reflected inside the work. Kapoor's work illuminates, retrospectively, the blindness and insight in "The Work of Art in the Age of Its Technological Reproducibility." Although Benjamin failed to grant continuing relevance to sculptures, he acknowledged the importance of architecture as the oldest and most fundamental of the arts: "Its history is longer than that of any other art, and its effect must be recognized in any attempt to account for the relationship of the masses to a work of art" (120). Monuments rest in an uneasy space between sculpture and architecture.

Nonetheless, Benjamin's essay gives the preeminent position to film. Distribution of film is *enforced,* because without such distribution the costs of production would be prohibitive. The countervailing impulses of private enterprise and public consumption require careful negotiations. Film came of age during depressions affecting the global economy. Benjamin observes:

> The same disorders which lead, in the world at large, to an attempt to maintain existing property relations by brute force induced film capital, under the threats of crisis, to speed up the development of sound films. The introduction brought temporary relief, not only because sound film attracted the masses back into the cinema but also because it attracted new capital from the electricity industry with that of film. Thus, considered from the outside, sound film promoted national interests; but seen from the inside, it helped internationalize film production even more than before. (123)

The historic situation facing film reflects the recurrent paradox of public art. Public art requires the acquisition of capital, either through appeal to profit or the support of a nation/state. *Cloud Gate* was funded by a grant from a telecommunications company, but the line between nation/state and corporate support is thin. The city seeks to recover the cost of continued maintenance of the park through *use* and parking fees. On one level concerns are local to the city/state—maintenance of their property. But the dramatic result created through an *international* collaboration with an Indian sculptor forces us to reevaluate our perception of public art.

It is not surprising that those who funded the project have an interest in maintaining conventional property relations to recover their investment. It is also not surprising that taxpayers feel a sense of "ownership" of public works. Unlike a film, a public sculpture has a tangible presence. It has value not only in its exhibition, but also in its possession. The question of who owns *Cloud Gate*—the people of Chicago, the development corporation, or the sculptor who created it—is complex. The federal government denies copyright protection to works created by government employees, but copyright protection is granted to works created on contract, that is, "works for hire." States vary in their position on works for hire, so although a public nonprofit development corporation contracted it, it is not automatically "public property." The power to grant copyright to public works is divided state by state. The rights associated with Millennium Park are hopelessly fractured among multiple contractors with exploitation rights, state and city governments, as well as the creative rights of the artists themselves.

Benjamin's benchmark of democratic art, film, highlights a shift from *cult value,* the value of ritual possession, to that of *exhibition value.* Generally speaking, the City of Chicago proposes to pay for construction and upkeep of the park through fees, including permits for professional photography, parking fees, and event fees. These fees rely on a cultish attraction to the site. The photographer's *use* fees that triggered the *Cloud Gate* controversy perhaps reflect its cult value, but more importantly they signal utility. *Useful articles* cannot be protected under U.S. copyright.

As a work of art that weighs 110 tons produced at a cost of $11.5 million, *Cloud Gate* is not easily copied. But exhibition rights—the right to reproduce *reproductions*—are separate. Sculpture, though it is one of the oldest reproducible art forms, cannot be reproduced without permission of the creators or their assigns under U.S. copyright law. However, because of its relationship to architectural monuments and its visibility in public space, the status of *Cloud Gate* is complex.

Rights and Responsibilities

Photographing in public spaces always balances public and private rights and responsibilities. Subject matter is generally the litmus test for reproducibility. For example, individuals are assumed to have rights of privacy that supersede rights of publicity. The level of protection afforded individuals differs with their status as public or private figures. Because celebrities are deemed *newsworthy,* their rights diminish. A general right to photograph people in public spaces is assumed, but there is no right to exploit their images commercially. However, newsworthy images can be exploited as *fair use.*[6] Significantly, this assumed fair use includes the right to reproduce and sell photographs with newsworthy content for profit. Due to the reflective nature of *Cloud Gate,* if the skyline of Chicago is identified as newsworthy, photographs of the sculpture (which automatically reproduce the skyline) might be distributed under fair use. Entrepreneurs like Horsch would merely be distributing newsworthy content.

However, the case most applicable to *Cloud Gate* is *Hart v. Sampley* (1992). It centers on Fredrick E. Hart's sculpture *The Three Servicemen*, part of the Vietnam Veterans Memorial in Washington D.C. The defendants sold T-shirts and photographs of the sculpture without authorization. In court they argued that the sculpture constituted a *useful article* "that cannot be separated from the functional purpose of honoring Vietnam Veterans." Under this lens, all monumental works of art would be exempt. The court did not agree. Their reasoning was sound—if *use* were defined in this manner, most works of art might be termed exempt. The next argument was that the sculpture was located "in an ordinarily visible and public place," referencing 17 U.S. Code, Section 120(a), which exempts pictorial representation of architectural works. This was rejected on technical grounds, not because *The Three Serviceman* is not a work of architecture, but because of timing. The sculpture was unveiled on November 9, 1984, and Section 120(a) did not take effect until December 1, 1990. The defendants were prohibited from reproducing the sculpture for profit.

The invocation of Section 120(a) is suggestive—consideration of monumental works as architecture rather than sculpture seems consistent with their public use. Because it was created after 1991, a suit regarding the sale of photographs of *Cloud Gate* would clarify the rights and responsibilities regarding public monuments. As Melissa L. Mathis suggests:

> While the utilitarian nature of architectural structures was the historical justification for a denial of copyright protection, this rationale does not apply to nonfunctional monumental works. Nonetheless, monuments are perhaps our most cherished works of public art. There is a unique reciprocity in such works that is absent from the other fine arts: they exist for the public and by the public. This relationship is one that must be recognized by our copyright law. It is also, however, one that must be understood by the authors of such works. (628)

The status of professional (for profit) photographs of *Cloud Gate* can be established as fair use, but there are alternatives.

Reproductions of copyrighted works can also be treated as "derivative works." A pair of recent cases suggests dubious stature for photographs. In *Ets-Hokin v. Sky Spirits, Inc,* 225 F.3d 1068 (9th Cir. 2000), the court held that a commercial photograph created for an advertisement was not derivative of its subject. However, in this case, the subject—a vodka bottle—was not a copyrightable work. In a later case involving the photography of ornamental picture frames for a catalogue, *SHL Imaging, Inc, v. Artisan*

House, Inc., 117 F. Supp. 2d 301 (S.D.N.Y 2000), the court sought to push this ruling further:

> While the *Ets-Hokin* court correctly noted that a derivative work must be based on a "preexisting work," and that the term "work" refers to a "work of authorship" as set forth in 17 U.S.C. §102(a), it failed to appreciate that any derivative work must recast, transform or adopt [*sic*] the authorship contained in the preexisting work. A photograph of Jeff Koon's "Puppy" sculpture in Manhattan's Rockefeller Center, merely depicts that sculpture; it does not recast, transform, or adapt Koons' sculptural authorship. In short, the authorship of the photographic work is entirely different and separate from the authorship of the sculpture. (Cohen 114)

In the language chosen by the court, a photograph *merely depicts* rather than copies preexisting work. Approached as the allocation of authorial rights, this ruling suggests that photographing a sculpture embedded in public surroundings creates a new work. Photographs are neither "copies" nor derivative works.

What *use* do photographs of public monuments serve? For Bob Horsch, they provide a substantial part of his income. Nevertheless, while his photographs of Wrigley Field and other Chicago landmarks sold briskly, photographs of *Cloud Gate* had to be marked down. A few moments observing in Millennium Park provide an answer. Visitors prefer to photograph their own reflections, to image and imagine themselves in *Cloud Gate.*

Notes

1. Architecture, classed as a useful article, has received limited protection under U.S. copyright law. Protection for architectural plans was only added with the 1976 Copyright Act, and §120 was added in 1990 to increase U.S. compliance with the Berne Convention.

2. For discussion of the background, see Hubbard; Jones; and Kamin.

3. Curiously, however, Starbucks would be considered a *public* space if copyrighted music or videotapes were played. When determining the criteria for public performance §101(1) declares that "any place where a substantial number of persons outside a normal circle of family and its social acquaintants" might hear is "public."

4. Accessible at http://www.usequities.com/MPark.htm.

5. Bob Horsch, personal interview, September 24, 2005.

6. A 2004 case regarding photographs of Barbra Streisand's home on the California coast is instructive. Though 17 U.S.C. §120 grants the right to photograph architecture visible from public locations, Streisand's suit against photographer Kenneth

Adelman argued that his aerial photographs from public airspace were an invasion of privacy. The suit was summarily dismissed on the grounds that the photographs, freely sold on the Internet, were *newsworthy* and therefore fair use. The news interest was not in Streisand's house, but the coastline underneath it. Full court transcripts and press coverage are available at California Coastal Records Project, http://www .californiacoastline.org/streisand/lawsuit.html.

Works Cited

Benjamin, Walter. "The Work of Art in the Age of Its Technological Reproducibility Second Version." *Selected Writings,* vol. 3, ed. Howard Eilend and Michael W. Jennings, 101–33. Cambridge: Belknap Press of Harvard University Press, 1996.

Bollier, David. "No Joke: Copyright Fees Required for Taking Photos in Chicago Parks." *OnTheCommons.org,* February 4, 2005. http://onthecommons.org/node/ 499, consulted May 2, 2005.

California Coastal Records Project. "Barbra Streisand Sues to Suppress Free Speech Protection for Widely Acclaimed Website." *California Coastal Records Project,* May 29, 2004. http://www.californiacoastline.org/streisand/lawsuit.html, consulted May 2, 2005.

Cohen, Julie E. *Copyright in a Global Information Economy.* New York: Aspen Law and Business, 2002.

Doctorow, Cory. "Chicago's Public Sculpture Can't Be Photographed by the Public." *BoingBoing,* February 6, 2005. http://www.boingboing.net/2005/02/06/chica gos_public_scul.html, consulted May 2, 2005.

Doctorow, Cory. "Please Add Photos of Chicago's Ridiculous Millennium Park Private Sculpture." *BoingBoing,* February 7, 2005. http://www.boingboing.net/ 2005/02/07/please_add_photos_of.html, consulted May 2, 2005.

Ellias, Bina Sarkar. "Being and Nothingness—Anish Kapoor Explores In-between." *British Council,* April 2005. http://www.britishcouncil.org/india-connecting- south-april-2005-anish-kapoor.htm, consulted May 2, 2005.

Harrison, Jeffery L. "Rationalizing the Allocative/Distributive Relationship in Copyright." *Hofstra Law Review* 32 (2003–4): 853–905.

Hubbard, Sue. "Architecture: The American Dream, Finally; Chicago's Millennium Park May Be Four Years Late, but It Boasts a Stunning Pavilion by Frank Gehry and an Imposing Anish Kapoor Sculpture." *The Independent,* August 4, 2004, 12–13.

Jones, Chris. "At Last; the City That Makes No Small Plans Unveils Millennium Park, Its Biggest, Boldest Outdoor Cultural Project in More Than a Century." *Chicago Tribune,* July 15, 2004, 1.

Joravsky, Ben. "The Bean Police." *Chicago Reader,* January 28, 2005, final ed., sec. 1, p. 7.

Joravsky, Ben. "Pork in the Park." *Chicago Reader,* February 11, 2005, final ed., sec. 1, p. 8.

Kamin, Blair. "'Cloud Gate' ; ****; SBC Plaza, between Washington and Madison Streets; Anish Kapoor, London." *Chicago Tribune,* July 18, 2004, 10.

Kamin, Blair. "John Bryan: Millennium Park's Moneyman." *Chicago Tribune*, December 26, 2004, 3.

Kleiman, Kelly. "Who Owns Public Art?" *Christian Science Monitor*, March 30, 2005, 15.

Lessig, Lawrence. "Dear Starbucks, Say It Ain't True?" *Lawrence Lessig*, May 23, 2003. http://www.lessig.org/blog/archives/2003_05.shtml#001223, consulted May 2, 2005.

Lessig, Lawrence. *Free Culture : How Big Media Uses Technology and the Law to Lock Down Culture and Control Creativity*. New York: Penguin, 2004.

Litman, Jessica. *Digital Copyright : Protecting Intellectual Property on the Internet.* Amherst, NY: Prometheus Books, 2001.

Mathis, Melissa M. "Function, Nonfunction, and Monumental Works of Architecture: An Interpretive Lens in Copyright Law." *Cardoza Law Review* 22 (2000): 595–628.

Maynard, Patrick. *The Engine of Visualization : Thinking through Photography*. Ithaca, NY: Cornell University Press, 1997.

Maynard, Patrick. "Talbot's Technologies: Photographic Depiction, Detection, and Reproduction." *Journal of Aesthetics and Art Criticism* 47, no. 3 (1989): 263–76.

Nance, Kevin. "The Bean's Bone of Contention; What's in a Name? Disagreements Swirl around Kapoor Piece in Millennium Park." *Chicago Sun-Times*, July 14, 2004, 64.

Peerless, Andrew. "Millennium Park: The Official Scoop." *Chicagoist*. February 17, 2005. http://www.chicagoist.com/archives/2005/02/17/millennium_park_photography_the_official_sco op.php, consulted May 2, 2005.

Urbanist. "The Copyrighting of Public Space." *New (sub)Urbanism*, January 25, 2005. http://newurbanist.blogspot.com/2005/01/copyrighting-of-public-space.html, consulted May 2, 2005.

Walton, Kendall L. *Mimesis as Make-Believe : On the Foundations of the Representational Arts*. Cambridge: Harvard University Press, 1990.

Walton, Kendall L. "Transparent Pictures: On the Nature of Photographic Realism." *Nous* 18, no. 1 (1984): 67–72.

Imitation

Genres as Forms of In(ter)vention

Anis Bawarshi

In his chapter in this volume, "History and the Disciplining of Plagiarism," Michael Grossberg suggests that plagiarism should be differentiated, in part, according to the different spheres of activity in which it takes place. This suggests that plagiarism is not just an issue of intellectual integrity, or lack thereof, but also an issue of disciplinarity. Indeed, in their longitudinal study of first-year writing at Harvard University, Nancy Sommers and Laura Saltz describe how first-year students struggle to negotiate the "push and pull" of the novice and expert roles they variously occupy as they learn to write with authority about subjects and methods new to them. Apprentice writers struggle, in particular, to make nuanced, disciplinary-based distinctions about what is significant, what can be assumed, and what must be cited about a given subject (Sommers and Saltz 132). Part of the acquisition of disciplinary knowledge involves acquiring these nuanced distinctions, which can neither be learned once and for all across disciplines nor, when misused, legislated only through plagiarism policies and concerns about intellectual integrity.[1] These distinctions, I argue, have less to do with questions of intellectual integrity than with how we understand the nature of imitation, particularly the complex interaction between imitation and invention that informs our disciplinary knowledge of what to imitate, in what way, and for how long, as well as when to reappropriate or transform what is imitated as our own invention. To understand these complex transactions between imitation and invention, we need to look at the spheres of activity in which they are differentiated, because it is within such spheres that participants make crucial distinctions between what is commonplace knowledge and what must be cited, between what is known and what is new. One important sphere of activity in which this interaction takes place is genre.

In this chapter, I examine the complex relationship between imitation and invention, arguing that imitation and invention exist on a genre-defined continuum and thereby have a variable relationship that we must acknowledge if we want to understand imitation's inventive power—that genre-differentiated point of transformation where imitation becomes invention. To do this, I will turn to the concept of "uptake" as it has been described in recent genre scholarship. I hope to show that every imitation involves an uptake, and it is in the space of this uptake that we can gain insight into the nature of invention. At the same time, the space between imitation and invention also provides the opportunity for intervening in and resisting normalized uptakes. As I hope to show, genres are integral to this process of in(ter)vention, since they coordinate specific relations between imitation and invention. I will first explain what I mean by uptake as the space between imitation and invention, and then I will present two examples, one from research I have already done on writing prompts and student essays, and the other from the case of *I, Rigoberta Menchú: An Indian Woman in Guatemala* and the controversy it stirred.[2]

Within speech act theory, uptake traditionally refers to how an illocutionary act (saying, for example, "It is hot in here") gets taken up as a perlocutionary effect (someone subsequently opening a window) under certain conditions. Recently, Anne Freadman has brought uptake to bear on relations between genres, arguing that genres are defined, in part, by the uptakes they coordinate and sanction within systems of genre and activity: for example, how a call for papers gets taken up as proposals, or, as in Freadman's more consequential example, how a court sentence during a trial gets taken up as an execution. Uptake helps us understand how systematic, normalized relations between genres coordinate complex forms of social action—how and why genres take up other genres and how and why they are taken up within a system of activity, such as, say, a trial or a classroom. Together, these inter- and intrageneric relations maintain the complex, textured conditions within which individuals identify, situate, and interact with one another in relations of power, and perform meaningful, consequential social actions—or are, conversely, excluded from them.

Uptakes, then, can be understood as the ideological interstices that configure, normalize, and activate relations and meanings within and between systems of genres. In her work on *kairos* (defined in classical rhetoric as timing and appropriateness), Carolyn Miller describes rhetorical timing as "the dynamic interplay between . . . opportunity as discerned and opportunity as defined" (312). Uptake coordinates typified relations between opportunities discerned and opportunities defined. These relations are typified because they are *learned recognitions of opportunity* that over time and in particular contexts become habitual. As Freadman has argued, uptakes have memories—knowledge of uptake is what helps us select, define, and recontextualize one genre in bidirectional relation to another so that one genre becomes a normalized response to another (40). As such, we can think of uptake as defining a horizon of possibility or opportunity that configures a specific relationship between imitation and invention. Knowledge of uptake is knowledge of what to take up, how, and when: when and why to use a genre, how to select an appropriate genre in relation to another, how to execute uptakes strategically and when to resist expected uptakes, how some genres explicitly cite other genres in their uptake while some do so only implicitly, and so on. In short, uptake constitutes a specific relation between the known and the new, repetition and divergence. What's important to note here is that the relation between imitation and invention defined by uptake is not absolute or learned once and for all; rather, it is a *genre-specific* relation that involves recognizing when and how much to imitate; to what extent explicitly and to what extent implicitly; what must be acknowledged and what can be assumed as known; when to reappropriate or recontextualize (in short, *transform*) what's imitated as one's own invention; and whether something is worthy of being imitated in the first place. Such knowledge is often tacitly acquired and ideologically and disciplinarily consequential, especially when it is misused in ways identified as plagiarism.

To illustrate how uptake reveals and maintains particular genred relations between imitation and invention, I will turn to the example of assignment prompts and student essays, two genres related chronologically and kairotically.[3] Chronologically, the writing prompt assigns a specific time sequence for the production of the student essay, often delimiting what is due at what time and when. At the same time, the writing prompt also establishes a kairotic relationship by providing the student essay with a timeliness and an opportunity that authorizes it. Participating within this kairotic interplay between two genres, the student must discern the opportunity granted by the prompt and then write an essay that defines its own opportunity in relation to the prompt. In so doing, students negotiate a complex relationship between imitation and invention, in which they are expected to take up the opportunity discerned in the writing prompt without acknowledging its presence explicitly in their essay. This uptake between the opportunity discerned in one genre and the opportunity defined or appropriated by students in another genre appears most visibly in the introductions of student essays.

In one particular case, students had read and discussed Clifford Geertz's essay "Deep Play: Notes on the Balinese Cockfight." They had been assigned to take on the "role of cultural anthropologist"; had conducted some field observations for research; and were then prompted to write, "in the vein of Geertz in 'Deep Play,'" a

> claim-driven essay about the "focused gathering" [a term that Geertz uses] you observed. Your essay should be focused on and centered around what you find to be most significant and worth writing about in terms of the "focused gathering" you observed. . . . Some issues you might want to attend to include: How does the event define the community taking part in it? What does the event express about the beliefs of the community? What does the event say about the larger society?[4]

As they take up this prompt, we can see how students negotiate the possible range of relationships, to various degrees of success, between imitation and invention as defined between these two genres.

In those examples where students seemingly work on the periphery of the desired relationship between imitation and invention, the writing prompt can be discerned a little too explicitly in their essays. For example, one student writes the following:

> Cultural events are focused gatherings that give observers insights to that certain culture. Geertz observes the Balinese culture and gains insights on how significant cockfighting is to the Balinese: including issues of disquieting and the symbolic meaning behind the cockfights. My observations at a bubble tea shop in the International District also have similarities with Geertz's observations of the Balinese cockfight on the cultural aspect.

The phrases "cultural events" and "focused gatherings" locate the language of the prompt in the essay, but the first sentence simply imitates the language of the prompt rather than invents or recontextualizes it as part of the essay's own constructed exigency. Similarly, in the second sentence, the only way to understand the relevance of the transition into Geertz is to know the prompt, which makes that connection. By the time the student describes her own observations in the third sentence, too much of the prompt's background knowledge is assumed, so that, for the logic of these opening sentences to work, a reader needs the prompt as context. The student has not imitated the prompt in ways expected in this uptake, although if this were an answer to an exam question, the uptake might have been more appropriate.

Compare the opening sentences of the above essay to the opening sentences of the following essay:

> When you want to know more about a certain society or culture what is the first thing that you need to do? You need to make and analyze detailed observations of that particular society or culture in its natural environment. From there you should be able to come up with a rough idea of "why" that particular culture or society operates the way it does. That's exactly what Clifford Geertz did. He went to Bali to study the Balinese culture as an observer.

As in the earlier example, this excerpt borrows the language of the prompt, but this time, it reappropriates that language as it imitates it. Accordingly, the reader meets Geertz on the essay's terms, after the student has provided a context for why Geertz would have done what he did. Basic as it might be, the question that begins the essay performs the transaction I described earlier, in which the student recontextualizes the question the prompt asks of him and asks it of his readers as if this is the question *he* desires to ask.

In the next example, the student begins her essay by describing underground hip-hop music and the function it serves for its listeners, and then poses the question: "Is music created from culture, or is culture created from music?" The second paragraph begins to compare hip-hop to symphonies:

> On a different note, a symphonic band concert creates a congregation of different status people uniting to listen to a type of music they all enjoy. "Erving Goffman has called *this* a type of 'focused gathering'—a set of persons engrossed in a common flow of activity and relating to one another in terms of that flow" (Geertz 405). This type of "focused gathering" is an example of music created from culture.

By posing the question, "Is music created from culture, or is culture created from music?" the student invents an opportunity for her essay based in the opportunity presented in the prompt. This is the question the *student* is asking. In this excerpt, the student does not rely on the prompt's authority to justify the claim that "a symphonic band concert creates a congregation of different status people uniting to listen to a type of music they all enjoy." Instead, she appropriates the authority the prompt grants her to assert this claim. Only in the context of her authority does Geertz then figure into the essay. The student uses the quotation from Geertz to make it appear as though Geertz's description of a "focused gathering" was meant to define her focused gathering, the symphonic band concert. The determiner "this" no longer modifies the cockfight as Geertz meant it to; instead, it refers back to the concert. In a way, this move creates the impression that the student found Geertz rather than having been assigned to use Geertz, thereby deftly managing the relation between imitation and invention that is expected when students take up the prompt in their essays. The above examples indicate how the transaction between imitation and invention is differentiated, learned, and reproduced as part of genre knowledge—in this case, knowledge of assignment prompts and student essays, and their uptake profiles.[5]

The next case allows us to examine how uptake can be a site of intervention when it exceeds a genre's normalized relation between imitation and invention. I will briefly outline the case of Rigoberta Menchú and the book *I, Rigoberta Menchú: An Indian Woman in Guatemala,* which both won her the Nobel Peace Prize in 1992 and generated a controversy that would play itself out in the popular press and within academic circles to this day. After providing some context for the book and controversy, I will examine both from the perspective of genre and uptake.

First published in 1983 and then translated from Spanish into English in 1984, *I, Rigoberta Menchú* narrates the testimony of Rigoberta Menchú, as told by Menchú to anthropologist Elizabeth Burgos-Debray, who transcribed, edited, and published Menchú's testimony. In the book, Menchú, then twenty-three years old, recounts her struggle as a Mayan peasant growing up in war-torn Guatemala, including her community's traditions and the destruction of the Quiche-Maya way of life; the horrific working conditions on the country's coffee plantations, which led to the death of two of her brothers; the kidnapping, torture, and murder of her mother and another brother; her father's battles with oppressive Ladino landlords; the death of her father when Guatemalan security forces set fire to the Spanish embassy in Guatemala City, which her father and other activists had occupied to protest human rights abuses; and the peasants' attempts at resistance by joining forces with guerrilla movements. The power of Menchú's *testimonio* drew the world's attention to the suffering of the indigenous peoples in Guatemala and won her acclaim as a human rights advocate. The book became an international best seller as well as required reading in many university courses, and, in 1992, won Menchú the Nobel

Peace Prize. More significantly, by bringing international attention to the suffering of indigenous Guatemalans, Menchú's book helped pressure the Guatemalan government to sign a peace agreement with the Guatemalan National Revolutionary Union in 1996.

I, Rigoberta Menchú fulfills the genre conventions of a testimonio, in which a witness is moved (by conditions of war, repression, struggle, subalternity) to narrate his or her testimony, often to an interlocutor who records that testimony (Beverley 32). The act of testimony, of bearing witness to the events the narrator recounts, is one of the defining features of the genre, which emerged in the 1960s and developed in close relation to movements of national liberation and revolutionary activism, especially in Latin America—in fact, *I, Rigoberta Menchú* was first published by Cuba's Casa de las Américas, which began awarding a prize for testimonios in 1970 (Beverley 31–32). Indeed as John Beverley has defined it, testimonio is a representation and form of subaltern agency that brings an alternative voice and politics into the public sphere and its dominant genres (19). In the voice it gave to Menchú and the solidarity it brought to the resistance movement in Guatemala, *I, Rigoberta Menchú* fulfilled the genre's function.

In 1999, anthropologist David Stoll published *Rigoberta Menchú and the Story of All Poor Guatemalans,* which argued that Menchú could not have been an eyewitness to some of what she recounts having seen, especially the torture and killing of her brother along with twenty-three guerrillas, and that some of what she describes either did not actually happen the way she claims or has been exaggerated for effect. For example, Stoll questioned Menchú's claims about her lack of education and disputed her version of the conflict over land ownership and the relationship between the indigenous Indians and the guerrilla movement, which Stoll claims Menchú framed in ways that supported her revolutionary agenda. Stoll is careful to note that the human rights violations Menchú describes did occur: "that a dictatorship massacred thousands of indigenous peasants, that the victims included half of [Menchú's] immediate family, that she fled to Mexico to save her life, and that she joined a revolutionary movement to liberate her country" (viii). Nonetheless, some of these events did not happen in the versions she tells them and not always to her or her family, leading Stoll to describe Menchú's testimony as "mythic inflation" (232). Since Stoll's findings, Menchú has conceded that in some instances, she grafted other people's experiences into her own (Beverley 109 n. 24).

When a *New York Times* reporter verified (and, Menchú supporters argue, simplified) Stoll's research, the findings ignited a controversy that was played out academically and publicly. The resulting controversy saw some critics calling the book a "piece of communist propaganda" and Menchú a liar.[6] Some called for the removal of the book from college courses (Operation Remove Rigoberta), and bemoaned it as an example of the problems with political correctness and postmodernism, while others, like David Horowitz, called it a "monstrous hoax," "a destructive little book," and "one of the greatest hoaxes of the 20th century." At the same time, political and academic supporters hailed the book for its literary strength, for its ability to give voice to the voiceless, and for its ability to create change in the world (see Arias; Beverley).

How can we account for the passion and ferocity of these critiques and the responses to them (for example, see the rebuttals of Arias; Beverley; Eakin; Robin)? On one level, one could argue that Menchú's testimonio pushed the notion of "witness" beyond its genre-expected uptake profile. If I, Rigoberta Menchú were a novel, for example, it would not be an issue whether or not Menchú actually witnessed the events she narrates. In pushing the boundaries of uptake beyond those expected of a testimonio, however, Menchú seems to have challenged that genre's relationship between imitation and invention, imitating the genre's form of individual witnessing but reappropriating or reinventing it, perhaps excessively, as collective witnessing. In this way, she could be said to have intervened in the relationship between imitation and invention in a way that resisted the genre's normalized uptake, granted her power to speak, challenged the dominant social order, and brought on charges of deception.

But by many scholarly accounts, I, Rigoberta Menchú does not, in fact, exceed its genre that much. Scholars such as Beverley and Carey-Webb, for example, point out that testimonios often offer one's experiences as representative of collective memory and identity, thus displacing the "master subject" of modernist narrative and stressing "the personal as reflective of a larger collective" (Beverley 34–35, 64; Carey-Webb 6–7). In fact, Menchú announces this at the very beginning of her narrative:

> My name is Rigoberta Menchú. I am 23 years old. This is my testimony. I didn't learn it from a book, and I didn't learn it alone. I'd like to stress that it's not only my life, it's also the testimony of my people. It's hard for me to remember everything that has happened to me in my life. . . . The important thing is that what has happened to me has happened to many other people too: My story is the story of all poor Guatemalans. My personal experience is the reality of a whole people. (1)

If *I, Rigoberta Menchú* did not exceed its genre (both in terms of its notion of witness and in its political agenda), then we need to look, not at how Menchú *took up* the genre, but rather at how her book was *taken up* by readers, especially in the United States, where it had such resonance. I argue that the book achieved the circulation and attention it did, and had the impact it did, in part, because it was generally read as an autobiography, a genre that holds powerful cultural capital in North America. (References to it as autobiography, especially among opponents like Horowitz, abound to this day.)[7] Autobiographies not only hail a certain readership; they also fulfill certain desires for life-writing and the assumptions embedded in and elicited by these desires. These include a view of self as unambiguous, coherent, and interiorized subject; an understanding of memory and experience as individual and private; and a juridical understanding of testimony as something accorded to an "eyewitness." In fact, John Beverley has argued that, as the expression of public achievement and bourgeois notions of self, autobiography affirms social order and one's place in it, a trajectory quite different from testimonio's political project of reappropriating the power to define reality and enact social change (40–41).

In being taken up and figured as autobiography, *I, Rigoberta Menchú* hailed a readership expecting these desires to be fulfilled, a readership that re-presented Menchú's testimony in a form of dominance that it was seeking to dismantle.[8] At the same time, however, in being taken up as autobiography, it may have gained a readership and an influence it would not otherwise have had, and in so doing, challenged the very assumptions about subjectivity and testimony that had granted it circulation and attention in the first place. (Throughout her testimonio, Menchú describes how her community used cultural forms of power such as the Spanish language or the Bible against those who imposed these forms on them.) This recontextualization of uptake from one genre to another, I argue, in part helps to explain the assault that some readers felt when they learned that Menchú had elided or misrepresented her narrative, because it reconstituted the relationship between imitation and invention from one expected in testimonio to one expected in autobiography. But such reconstituting of the expected transaction between imitation and invention is also what allowed *I, Rigoberta Menchú* to intervene the way it did.

The two examples I have presented reveal that uptake is a site of both invention and intervention, a site of transformation guided by genre knowledge. When students take up the writing prompt as their essay, they are negotiating a complex, normalized transaction between imitation and invention. Likewise, when *I, Rigoberta Menchú* intervenes in normalized uptakes (in how it is taken up), it enables a form of resistance. Imitation always involves an uptake, a learned (and genred) recognition of opportunity that informs what we take up, why, and how. By making these choice points, these points of transformation, analytically visible to students, we enable them to participate more critically and effectively as readers and writers, because it is within uptake that the opportunity for in(ter)vention abounds.

Notes

1. Rebecca Moore Howard makes an important distinction between plagiarism as fraud (submitting a purchased paper as one's own, for example) and plagiarism as misuse of sources. While the former involves much more clearly issues of intellectual integrity, and can be legislated, the latter strikes me as having much more to do with issues of disciplinary knowledge, and must be addressed within various spheres of activity.

2. I offer a more in-depth analysis of the writing prompt–student essay relationship and other classroom genres in chapter 5 of *Genre and the Invention of the Writer*.

3. Yates and Orlikowski's work on the function of *chronos* and *kairos* in communicative interaction describes how, within communities, related genres choreograph interactions among participants and activities chronologically (by way of measurable, quantifiable, "objective" time) and kairotically (by way of constructing a sense of timeliness and opportunity in specific situations).

4. This prompt was assigned to students in a first-year composition course at the University of Washington in 2002. I have reprinted it with permission of the instructor.

5. I am grateful to John Webster, my colleague at the University of Washington, for suggesting "uptake profile" to describe a genre's normalized horizon of expectation.

6. For more on the controversy from various perspectives, see Arias.

7. In *Scandals and Scoundrels,* for example, Ron Robin refers to *I, Rigoberta Menchú* as autobiography. This question of naming, I argue, is not merely a semantic difference, as the genre we use to identify the text informs how we take it up.

8. It is important to acknowledge the role that Menchú's interlocutor and editor, Elizabeth Burgos-Debray, played in how *I, Rigoberta Menchú* was taken up. In transcribing Menchú's testimony, Burgos-Debray reordered the transcripts to render them in consumable form. As she explains to David Stoll: "Rigoberta's narrative was anything but chronological. It had to be put in order. . . . I had to reorder a lot to give the text a thread, to give it a sense of a life, to make it a story, so that it could reach the general public" (Stoll 185). As an intermediary between Menchú's testimony and how it would appear in published form, Burgos-Debray thus contributed to how and why metropolitan readers would take it up as many of them did. In part, one could argue that readers took up *I, Rigoberta Menchú* in ways that Burgos-Debray initially took it up.

Works Cited

Arias, Arturo, ed. *The Rigoberta Menchú Controversy*. Minneapolis : University of Minnesota Press, 2001.

Bawarshi, Anis. *Genre and the Invention of the Writer: Reconsidering the Place of Invention in Composition*. Logan: Utah State University Press, 2003.

Beverley, John. *Testimonio: On the Politics of Truth*. Minneapolis: University of Minnesota Press, 2004.

Carey-Webb, Allen. "Transformative Voices." In *Teaching and Testimony: Rigoberta Menchú and the North American Classroom,* ed. Allen Carey-Webb and Stephen Connely Benz, 3–18. New York: State University of New York Press, 1996.

Eakin, Paul John. *The Ethics of Life Writing*. Ithaca, NY: Cornell University Press, 2004.

Freadman, Anne. "Uptake." In *The Rhetoric and Ideology of Genre,* ed. Richard Coe, Lorelei Lingard, and Tatiana Teslenko, 39–53. Cresskill, NJ: Hampton Press, 2002.

Grossberg, Michael. "History and the Disciplining of Plagiarism." Paper presented at Originality, Imitation, and Plagiarism: A Cross-Disciplinary Conference on Writing, Sweetland Writing Center, University of Michigan, Ann Arbor, September 23–25, 2005.

Horowitz, David. "I, Rigoberta Menchú, Liar." Salon.com, January 11, 1999. http://www.salon.com/col/horo/1999/01/11horo.html, consulted July 8, 2007.

Howard, Rebecca Moore. "Representations of Plagiarism in Mainstream Media and on Campus." Paper presented at Originality, Imitation, and Plagiarism: A Cross-Disciplinary Conference on Writing, Sweetland Writing Center, University of Michigan, Ann Arbor, September 23–25, 2005.

Menchú, Rigoberta. *I, Rigoberta Menchú*. Ed. Elizabeth Burgos-Debray. Trans. Anne Wright. New York: Verso, 1996.

Miller, Carolyn R. "Kairos in the Rhetoric of Science." In *A Rhetoric of Doing: Essays on Written Discourse in Honor of James L. Kinneavy,* ed. Stephen Witte, Neil Nakadate, and Roger Cherry, 310–27. Carbondale: Southern Illinois University Press, 1992.

"Operation Remove Rigoberta." *Front Page Magazine,* May 12, 1999, http:www.front pagemag.com/campaign/rigobertacampaign.htm. Consulted January 30, 2001.

Robin, Ron. *Scandals and Scoundrels: Seven Cases That Shook the Academy*. Berkeley and Los Angeles: University of California Press, 2004.

Sommers, Nancy, and Laura Saltz. "The Novice as Expert: Writing the Freshman Year." *College Composition and Communication* 56, no. 1 (2004): 124–49.

Stoll, David. *Rigoberta Menchú and the Story of All Poor Guatemalans*. Boulder, CO: Westview Press, 1999.

Yates, JoAnne, and Wanda Orlikowski. "Genre Systems: Chronos and Kairos in Communicative Interaction." In *The Rhetoric and Ideology of Genre,* ed. Richard Coe, Lorelei Lingard, and Tatiana Teslenko, 103–21. Cresskill, NJ: Hampton Press, 2002.

When Copying Is Not Copying
Plagiarism and French Composition Scholarship

Christiane Donahue

The past fifteen years have seen an explosion of research about higher-education language activity—reading, speaking, and writing—in France. A key focus of this research has been students' interaction with other sources, with the *discours d'autrui* (the discourse of others), in particular through discussion of paraphrase, quoting, citing, and student authority in academic writing. It is clear from this research that fascination with plagiarism is far from universal. French education does not emphasize avoiding plagiarism as we know it; in fact, some French writing and teaching practices can even encourage it. Informal interviews with French teachers and students give a preliminary sense of the French understanding of plagiarism. "What is that?" say students. Secondary-school faculty tell us that discussing plagiarism is not part of the curriculum. A few university faculty mention occasional trouble with students who buy papers, but most are quick to point out that undergraduate grades and diplomas are primarily awarded based on exams—taken in person, handwritten, graded blind.[1] This perspective on plagiarism intrigues, in an era when teachers, administrators, and scholars in the world of U.S. composition studies struggle daily with a wide variety of plagiarism issues, generally lumped together under the one term and evoked with disdain, anger, or even a sense of personal injury.

Composition theories and pedagogies in France have always treated reading and writing as an integral whole; authority and ease in inhabiting others' discourses is valued over "originality" in school writing, at least until advanced postsecondary studies. France's complicated relationship with source use and textual authority begins in the relationship students are invited to develop with source texts early in their schooling. Paraphrase, however, is not a welcomed tool in that textual relationship; secondary and postsecondary students are taught an entrenched aversion to it.

After a brief overview of French teaching practices as related to source use, I will present a few textual movements in French students' writing in order to suggest alternative cultural understandings of the textual authority students might inhabit. I will propose that French students are taught to enter into relationships of equality and play with other texts, and that this leads them to a different understanding of the already-said. This does not necessarily ease their transition into advanced research writing in their fields, but does strikingly shift emphasis away from issues of plagiarism. Finally, I will offer a theoretical linguistic frame for describing this relationship with the term *reprise-modification,* adapted from French linguistic theory. I believe this frame will help to complicate the often reductive U.S. understanding of plagiarism, while encouraging a rethinking of French practices as related to paraphrase.

French Practices: Writing and Source Use Instruction, Secondary and Postsecondary

In French secondary schooling, writing is taught in all disciplines; it is always taught in relationship to reading and speaking; and writing instruction is extensively theorized with a mix of education, linguistics, and literary theory.[2] This instruction lays the groundwork for both the abilities students acquire and the problems students face in higher education. Practically speaking, the end of French secondary school is considered the beginning of postsecondary education; the final exam, the *baccalauréat,* is *le premier grade universitaire* (the first university degree) and the student who passes it is guaranteed a university seat. That weeklong exam is writing-intensive. University Writing or University Methods has always been a course in postsecondary technical fields such as engineering. Work on writing has equally been an intense part of the curriculum in elite school tracks (*écoles préparatoires* and *grandes écoles*). Since the late 1980s, the government has required one-credit first-year courses in research, thinking, and writing of all entering students in traditional university cycles; these courses have quickly become, in some settings, writing-in-the-disciplines courses, although in other settings the mandate has been ignored.

As students work on writing across their secondary or postsecondary curriculum, paraphrase, citation, quoting, and other explicit text interactions are treated differently at different grade levels, as well as in the study of literature versus the study of nonliterary texts.[3] Officially, paraphrase is a secondary and early postsecondary education concern related to writing about literature, while citing and quoting are more advanced undergraduate or even graduate study concerns, reserved for writing in particular fields.

The roots of the French perspective on student writing, paraphrase, and literary texts are in the French relationship with the aesthetic. In the ancient and medieval rhetorical traditions, the paraphraser was initially considered on par with the original author when providing reformulations of sacred texts (Daunay 72). Bertrand Daunay suggests that a paraphrase was seen as similar to a translation: a reformulation respecting the enunciative system of the source, a form of quasi- or shared authorship through ownership of the language manipulation. The paraphraser changed the expressions but traced his text on the original (73). Paraphrase was also originally a way to teach text production through the heuristic action of reformulating others' texts. By the Renaissance, it had evolved into a commentary and an explication, not just a rendering (75). It was not until the 1800s that paraphrase became the object of academic criticism and disdain.[4]

Avoiding paraphrase is today the subject of extensive explicit commentary in French textbooks and the *Instructions Officielles,* the state-mandated secondary school curriculum. Any paraphrase of literary texts read for assignments is discouraged, even punished. In a way reminiscent of our admonitions to avoid "just summarizing" (the plot, the story line, the chronology . . .), both faculty and textbooks in France warn students to avoid paraphrasing literary works, generally classified among the least sophisticated or least successful forms of literary commentary. "Run from paraphrase," one textbook says, "which repeats the text while diluting it and transposes its original phrasing into ordinary prose, in order to explain 'what it means'" (Daunay 21).[5] To explain a literary work's meaning by rephrasing it into "ordinary" language removes its aesthetic value, and thus its true meaning. Daunay cites another textbook that admonishes, "Repeating the text in another form . . . only gives rise to paraphrase, inevitably deforming because the signifier always changes the signified, imperceptibly if one is talented, but generally enough that the text becomes unrecognizable in its paraphrased translation" (13). In this version the challenge for students is even more complicated—either copy outright or develop original thoughts, but do not reformulate, no matter how sophisticated the paraphrase might be. The term *copying* reflects a complex concept that we cannot afford to take for granted in cross-cultural discussion. Both of its most obvious meanings—the actual re-production of objects or signs versus the act of doing the same kind of thing—play out in students' experiences working with text. French practitioners do not use the word *copying* but in effect encourage it in both forms: reproducing precise phrases and frames on the one hand, and "doing the same" on the other. The latter is not a case of "imitating" in the creative or rhetorical tradition, but of taking on the discursive role and position of academics, without necessarily inhabiting them at first.

Paraphrase is also treated, indirectly, in reference to students' work with texts that are not strictly "literary" (essays, news articles, memoirs, documents, editorials, and so on). Students are asked to respond to these texts, and are taught to *summarize* nonliterary texts quite radically—they learn to reduce texts to precisely one-quarter their length, maintaining the original message, maintaining key phrases, while shortening and condensing the text overall. This ability is a cornerstone to academic writing activity, and a rigorous way to learn to manipulate (in the positive sense) ideas, words, meanings, and concepts—without citing, quoting borrowed phrases, or recognizing in some other way the author of the original text. Quoting and citing are not even mentioned in most school course manuals and textbooks until late undergraduate or master's-level documents. In any analysis of nonliterary texts, up until roughly the end of undergraduate studies, students copy many of the ideas and even phrases from assigned texts with no citations or quotation marks. They build on ideas from texts read in class or for an exam, rephrasing them (barely), occasionally mentioning the author, and then providing additional examples or ideas of their own. The kernel of an idea and the actual phrasing are recast but are not credited. Students thus speak with and through the text or texts themselves, inhabiting voices, often appropriating even the style, tone, or voice of the pieces to which they respond (for examples, see appendix). Students also take up the language of assignment prompts. This is qualitatively different. If we can say that normally we would not expect a student to cite the language of the assignment, this is not so much a case of uncited words as a reusing of the assignment language that shadows the reusing of excerpts read in class, and so is considered acceptable in the same way.

When students reach later undergraduate and graduate writing work, they are required to write in a discipline and to authoritatively reflect on what they read, understand it in context, critique it if need be, represent it accurately, and position themselves with respect to it. After a first round of writing that still relies on abilities developed in secondary studies, most students move into researched writing or writing that synthesizes multiple sources read for class or read in addition to class. This is the first time students will work with abstract theoretical discourse in the discipline they have chosen. Because writing is often not taught at these later stages, or is taught in optional "methodology of research" writing courses, the references are found primarily in commercial guides sold in bookstores or in locally produced university pamphlets for students working on senior theses and other end-stage academic projects. Students struggle with parts of this new challenge of managing the *discours d'autrui,* but in response French scholarship reflects a nurturing paradigm (or an exasperated one) rather than a punitive one.

Michel Guigue and Jacques Crinon tell us that acceptable processes and practices in drafting include

- using explicit quotes in earlier drafts that act as a well of material and ideas to draw from (the later draft still has some quotes as quotes but has other ideas left in the draft in paraphrase or summary form with no reference or citation);
- including earlier short actual cited quotes that later become longer close paraphrase, cited or not;
- borrowing detailed observations from a source without citing them in what scholars consider the later, improved version. This borrowing would typically be considered a form of plagiarism in a U.S. classroom, but here is considered a successfully thorough "appropriation" of the text and the material, showing that the student has become comfortable with his or her status as a member of the disciplinary community in question. (83–86; see examples, appendix)

Copying, Close Paraphrase, and Polyphony: The Scholarly Perspective

While plagiarism has not become the focus of scholarly discussion in France, students' management of multiple voices in their essays has. Scholarship on the subject is clearly interested in understanding students' complex relationships with text and supporting students' integration into the discourse of a field without judging them for overly close work with sources.[6] French writing research thus extensively explores university students' work with other texts, with a focus on *la polyphonie énonciative,* literally the "multivoiced uttering" of students' speaking or writing or even reading at the university, a work with language that is understood in a Bakhtinian frame: "Someone who apprehends the utterances of others is not mute, silenced; on the contrary, he or she is a being full of interiorized words" (qtd. in Guibert 29).

Scholars study students' actual primary research in many cases, with requisite secondary research (literature reviews, for example) or secondary research that includes use of texts studied for class and use of class notes and professors' lectures. Consistent with practice, most of their explanations point to paraphrase as a "poor reintroduction of the original" rather than an effective interpretation of a source, and explore troubles students have with reformulation or quoting. The aesthetic judgment being made about the effective language of an original source versus the always-otherwise rephrasing of it appears to carry more weight than the judgment about "borrowing/not borrowing" language or crediting a source.

While the French method described earlier for secondary writing education builds students' ability to work in a textual frame and to inhabit academic discourse, it does not produce a uniform ability to work effectively with texts once students arrive at the university. French students clearly have trouble managing polyphonic writing (in 2002 an entire conference was dedicated to the problem). The difference often surfaces when students start working with the discourse of others, in particular the *theoretical discourse* of others in researched writing (Reuter 14). Yves Reuter focuses in particular on the problem of "patchworks," accumulations of quotes and juxtaposition of quoted material that dominate some students' essays. French research identifies students' need to learn how to get their voices into the "academic concert" (9) and to have the opportunity to "feel their way." This "feeling their way" perspective is part of the backdrop for the relative flexibility in university acceptance of forms of plagiarism like missing citations, close paraphrase, word-for-word borrowing, or other forms of "copying," including stylistic copying.

Students' earlier textual work responding to essays has clearly helped to create some of the difficulties identified by scholars. Marie Christine Pollet and Valérie Piette lament students' deference to authority, a deference that appears, to the outside observer, to arise naturally from their earlier years of exactly this kind of writing. They also explore students' trouble with effective quote integration (167), including dropping in quotes without fully understanding them (173), and citing insignificant details (173). Here, Pollet and Piette give the example, with dismay, of a student who quotes and cites a *definition,* and, to boot, one "that the professor surely knew" (173). The professor-as-audience and the context of school-based writing dominate.

Voice is another complication that has attracted French scholars' attention. Françoise Boch and Francis Grossman describe in detail the overlap of voices, the smudged distinctions, the difficulty of telling who is speaking in the student's text, all considered to be signs of a lack of polyphonic mastery (91). Pollet and Piette comment on the erasure of students' authorial voices; Rozenn Guibert describes one aspect of this complication as "voice confusion," the awkward situation of a student writer who literally loses track of a source text and begins to take on the attitude, persona, and perspectives of an author from whom he or she is working (38). This can also lead to mismanagement of meaning: "Certain students . . . generalize excessively, erasing nuances and modalizations present in the source document: 'certain doctors' becomes 'doctors'; 'some historians affirm that . . .' becomes 'historians agree that . . .'" (Pollet and Piette 175). Boch and Grossman point to other entrenched problems: not recognizing the different value of sources, not knowing why a particular source point is being introduced or cited, and tending to drop in information dogmatically, "not because the student does not know how to cite but because the student does not know how to 'own' the text being cited" (9).

Theorizing the writing and the teaching of writing that works with other texts certainly implies for French researchers an occasional discussion of formal citation work. But this discussion serves to get at questions of identity: what are the relationships between the one voice and the many? Between the writer and the reference? What subject positioning is encouraged, enabled, or prevented? What power structures are at play, how is the self-defined status of the student-subject presented, which utterance modes are used, what is the play of references in interaction with each other? What points of view, what ways of treating others' voices can we identify (distance, modulation, appreciation . . .), and what genres can be analyzed? Much of the focus is on identifying features that might help the novice writer-researcher to understand the stakes, the history, the existing structures and paradigms into which he or she is integrating written work; to resist or further the agenda of a field; and to develop hypotheses that matter and are relevant to these issues. Isabelle Delcambre includes issues of student unfamiliarity with the literature and culture of a particular discipline as part of the problem (personal interview, May 30, 2006).

The problems evoked are rarely considered plagiarism. When they are, it is just disappointing, even described as an immature concern. Plagiarism as such is mentioned only once in the recent special issue of the journal referenced here, *Apprendre à Citer le Discours d'Autrui*. Boch and Grossmann cite the following two postsecondary textbooks as childish, even infantile in their perspectives on plagiarism: "A principle of scientific work concerns referencing material: when borrowing a text from an author, mention the source. It would be serious to be accused of plagiarism. Someone who copies an author's work and attributes passages of the work to himself has plagiarized" (95). "It is not only a question of intellectual honesty, you will make yourself guilty of plagiarism, which will be sanctioned by the examination committee" (95). They conclude that plagiarism should be avoided because peers in the scientific community have no respect for plagiarized work and would, in fact, reject an article or a book that provided neither correct citation nor references to the history of preceding publications (96), rather than be treated as an object of moralizing discourse.

Pollet and Piette point to a student sample in which a citation for some specific information appears to be missing and immediately reject the idea that it might be plagiarism, quoting Elisabeth Nonnon:

> This kind of trouble is inevitable in an activity in which reading and writing are inextricably linked; one reads to nourish the reflection for one's essay, one writes to synthesize and integrate borrowings that one has made during the process of developing knowledge. Learning to situate effectively one's own discourse in relation to different discourses of others, marking out the transitions between sources. . . , all of this plays out partly in a working out of the utterance indicators one chooses. (173)

Effective quoting and citing are treated, in the scholarship, as an art; the goal is working from an author-based world (an author's text, words, ideas) toward one's own. "We can distance ourselves from the theme of plagiarism," insist Boch and Grossman, "and push for the importance instead of understanding "polyphonic management . . . *it does not matter* whether enunciative interference is from bad faith actions or clumsiness. The result, in fact, is the same from the point of view of written communication—and this point of view is the one that we feel should be highlighted" (101; emphasis added).[7] Scholars and teachers feel that the different forms of quoting, citing, and paraphrasing acceptable for different fields add to the complications for students. The university is not always clear with students about the best approach to take: "The anthropologist who cites his informants, the compiler who uses the 'method of massive excerpts,' and the journalist who references sources in passing. None of these approaches seems right to us. But what exactly do we expect of our students?" (Guibert 42).

Recasting the Issues: Paraphrase, Plagiarism, Originality, and the *discours d'autrui*

While the French practices and positions take a more nuanced view of plagiarism, they seem to miss the boat on paraphrase as a necessary language act. Students find themselves in a real bind, as they cannot accomplish the requisite close readings of literary texts without paraphrasing, an unavoidable textual movement that both renders and interprets.[8] The French understanding of paraphrase is theoretically in a bind as well: in spite of itself, it supports the Bakhtinian understanding of every utterance as simultaneously new and already said: "There can be neither a first nor a last meaning; [anything that can be understood] always exists among other meanings as a link in the chain of meaning, which in its totality is the only thing that can be real. In historical life this chain continues infinitely, and therefore each individual link in it is renewed again and again, as though it were being reborn" (Bakhtin 146). Notice that for Bakhtin, this reformulation is not only rich and positive but unavoidable; the language, as Bakhtin argues, has been completely taken over,

> shot through with intentions and accents. . . . All words have a "taste" of a profession, a genre, a tendency, a party, a particular work, a particular person, a generation, an age group, a day and hour. Each word tastes of the context and contexts in which it has lived its socially charged life. . . . Language is not a neutral medium that passes freely and easily into the private property of the speaker's intentions; it is populated, overpopulated—with the intentions of others. (273–74)

Building from Bakhtin, the French linguist Frédéric François offers us the concept of "reprise-modification," an essential textual movement, the simultaneous appropriation and modification that every new utterance, even direct and credited quoting, involves: an always-dynamic-taking-up-and-modifying, past-present-future in degrees of concert. This dynamic act is not a single act but a broad sweep of sorts of discursive modification: reaccentuations, mixtures, paraphrases, transpositions, forced changes of background, and so on (correspondence, 2006). The concept of reprise-modification might allow both French and U.S. writing specialists to move into new dialogue about paraphrase, plagiarism, and source use in our students' work. We might begin by reconsidering copying and paraphrasing as forms of reprise-modification. Copying's long and honored history in many fields is seen as a mode of learning, an apprenticeship method: art, music, writing, technology.

Considered from the frames of both translation theory and linguistics, copying is multilayered and multinatured. Translation theory encourages us to think about language not only in its "naming" relationship, as it creates equivalents, and "copying" into another language, but also in the way it develops understanding, interprets, through the "this *is like* this" relationship that reminds us of the very nature of originality in its literary iterations. To learn to speak, or write, is to learn to translate (Paz, cited in Barnstone 23). Some translation theories today pose the translator as author, as original text worker, suggesting that this textual work is no different from other reuses of available language, a perspective that recalls the early understandings of manuscript copying as authorship. If translators are authors and we posit the essential discursive movement in all language use as reprise-modification, then the act of reading is clearly part of the language production relationship. Translators necessarily see the fabric of discourse as heteroglossic, a reprise of the already-said, a complex working through of existing language in perpetually new forms, even when they are copied word for word or rendered equivalent through translation.

In students' writing, the voices in a draft—the multiple student voices, peers' voices, teachers' voices, voices from texts read—are the polyphonic utterances to be managed, inhabited self-consciously, orchestrated. Writers *reprennent-modifient* the thematic, macrostructural, rhetorical, linguistic, syntactic, and microstructural elements of already-existing discourse—copying that is not copying but a complex and culturally defined intellectual action, Bakhtinian to the core. As I have argued elsewhere, we can think about copying as one strategy along a continuum of strategies of reprise-modification: "reproducing, quoting, tracing, imitating, shadowing, miming, paraphrasing, summarizing, referring to, linking outward from a single word, indirectly suggesting, referring to through connection to a cultural commonplace, echoing through association, stylistic allure, or implied assumption, and so on" (Donahue 95). Nothing is ever clearly exact copying or wildly loose translation or paraphrase. Every one of these language acts is intertwined with the others, and all are necessary steps in text construction. What's more, the *same actions* can exist as different forms along that continuum, functioning in local versions, with differing intents, with differing receptions at different points in time or location. Summary in one instance is read or received as interpretation in another;

an imitation in one era is read as a poor copy in another. Claiming plagiarism, from this point of view, becomes quite difficult.

Concluding Thoughts

In French essays, the nature of the student's relationship with the text he or she has been assigned to read is qualitatively and specifically different. In secondary school writing, literary texts are revered aesthetic objects, and nonliterary texts are objects of appropriation. In school essays, the text's authority is equal to the student's as he or she speaks with and through the original essay. The French strategy of working closely with nonliterary text seems to provide an authority quite different from, for example, the expressive authority provided through narrative writing. Both existential and discursive positions are woven through a student's text. In university students' writing, the nature of this relationship shifts; students are asked to work with theoretical discourse and to more clearly demarcate their own voices and ideas from those they are studying. But the essential understanding of students' work as polyphonic reprise-modification leads both teachers and scholars to focus on the nature of the management and the discursive development of the new members of a discipline, rather than the moralistic, legalistic, or otherwise shame-filled act we like to call plagiarism.

APPENDIX: EXAMPLES OF STUDENT WORK
I offer here a few specific examples excerpted from studies of French students' essays, representative of what I have found in larger samples. The first text was written in first year of university studies, in a required writing class. It is a response to an assignment that specifically asks students to work with an excerpt of a text by Joël de Rosnay.[9] The second and third examples come from Guigue and Crinon.

EXAMPLE I

de Rosnay	Student
What a <u>long path</u> to follow . . . as <u>not everyone has the same chances</u> or the same talents.	This <u>long work</u> of analysis is <u>not permitted to everyone</u>.
Signs, also, of a <u>"flight" from a society</u> that has become <u>competitive, aggressive, and violent</u> . . .	This tendency translates the need for renewal and for <u>flight from a system</u> that, more and more, <u>harms individuals.</u>

We also see close paraphrase of the assignment itself.

Assignment	Student
<u>What does the author mean when he writes,</u> "<u>managing one's life</u> means accessing a certain form of liberty, of autonomy"? Do you think this *concept is desirable and possible*?	What does this management of our life mean? We will see <u>whether this concept is desirable and possible</u> . . .

EXAMPLE 2

Table 1

Draft 3	Draft 7 (final)
First of all, as P. Meirieu observes in *Apprendre, Oui, mais Comment?* that children do not know the <u>specificity of the spoken word that resides in the fact that speech is a continuous flow of words</u> not split up into sentences, . . . This is equally underscored by the work document of December 1996 refined by M. A. Morel and L. Danon-Boileu.	We observe first of all that <u>the specificity of speech resides in the fact that it is a continuous flow of words that only vocal pauses split up</u>. . . . This property is equally highlighted by <u>M. A. Morel and L. Danon-Boileu.</u>

Source: Guigue and Crinon 83

EXAMPLE 3

Table 2

Draft 2	Final Improved Draft
In conclusion, I will cite Barré de Miniac: "<u>Becoming</u> the subject of one's writing, <u>the author of one's texts</u>, is being able to establish conscious strategies, to <u>analyze the expectations of the reader</u>, the stakes of the situation."	In addition, as Barré de Miniac points out, <u>becoming the author of one's texts</u> means being able to take into account the knowledge that one shares with a future reader, <u>analyzing the expectations of the reader</u>.

Source: Guigue and Crinon 86.

Notes

1. This is a problem that is rapidly spreading in French-speaking countries. See, for example, "Plagiat: Les cas augmentent à l'Université," http://www.tsr.ch/tsr/index .html?siteSect=200001&sid=6427564.

2. See, for example, the conference proceedings of the Association Internationale de Recherches en Didactique du Français (International Association of Research in the Theory and Teaching of French) and the publications of multiple research laboratories in France, in particular the Université de Lille III research group, THEODILE, the Université Stendahl-Grenoble research group LIDILEM, and the Université de

Bordeaux II research group Psychologie de l'Education et du Développement. More information about these French research groups and activities can be found at http://comppile.tamucc.edu/wiki/CompFAQsInternational/InternationalWrit ingStudies.

3. I will not enter here into the grand debate about arbitrary dichotomies such as literary-nonliterary. I use the distinction here only because that is the distinction that has tended to dominate French education. In recent years, the dichotomy has been melting away as "literary" texts are studied for their construction of arguments, and "nonliterary" texts for their literary style. The category of creative nonfiction has also been introduced.

4. For a full discussion of this complicated process, see Daunay.

5. I find this commentary particularly telling. We often speak with disdain of the old-fashioned perspective that the idea can come before the writing and the writing simply expresses transparently that idea. The French rejection of the possibility of paraphrasing literary work makes me wonder whether we understand the degree of complexity of the act we ask students to perform in their research, reading, and writing.

6. How do we determine at what point something is "owned"? French scholars O. Dezutter and F. Thirion suggest that there is not that much difference at the university between appropriating another's speech (say, a lecture) and appropriating another's writing (109). Students come to learn and we want them to appropriate knowledge and be comfortable in the discourse of the field; at what point does something—class discussion, a professor's discourse—no longer get cited?

7. There is less flexibility for experts. Boch and Grossman say that experts know both the implicit and the explicit rules and are likely using deliberate strategies when they mask quoted material or erase frontiers between source material, paraphrase, and their own words (102). This is a fascinating reversal.

8. Daunay is, to my knowledge, the only French scholar to focus on restoring paraphrase to a recognized and positive place in textual analysis and writing instruction in France.

9. This student's text is treated in detail in Donahue, "Lycée to University."

Works Cited

Bakhtin, M. M. *Speech Genres and Other Late Essays.* Trans. V. W. McKee. Austin: University of Texas Press, 1986.

Barnstone, Willis. *The Poetics of Translation.* New Haven: Yale University Press, 1993.

Boch, Françoise, and Francis Grossman. "De l'usage des citations dans le discours théorique." *Apprendre à Citer le Discours d'Autrui* 24 (2001): 91–112.

Daunay, Bertrand. *Eloge de la paraphrase.* Versailles: Presses Universitaires de Versailles, 2002.

Delcambre, Isabelle. "Formes diverses d'articulation entre discours d'autrui et discours propre." *Apprendre à Citer le Discours d'Autrui* 24 (2001): 135–66.

Delcambre, Isabelle. Interview with author. May 30, 2006.

Dezutter, Olivier, and Francine Thirion. "Comment les etudiants entrants s'approprient-ils les discours universitaires?" *Spirale* 29 (2002): 109–22.

Donahue, Christiane. "The Lycée to University Progression in French Students' Development as Writers." In *Writing and Learning in Crossnational Perspective,* ed. David Russell and David Foster, 134–91. Urbana, IL: National Council of Teachers of English Press, 2002.

Donahue, Christiane. "Student Writing as Negotiation: Fundamental Movements between the Common and the Specific in French Essays." In *Writing in Context(s): Textual Practices and Learning Processes in Sociocultural Settings,* ed. Fillia Kostouli, 137–64. Amsterdam: Kluwer Academic Publishers, 2004.

François, Frédéric. *Le discours et ses entours.* Paris: l'Harmattan, 1998.

Guibert, Rozenn. ""Citer et se situer." *Apprendre à Citer le Discours d'Autrui* 24 (2001): 29–48.

Guigue, Michèle, and Jacques Crinon. "L'usage des lectures dans l'elaboration et l'exposition des mémoires professionnels d'IUFM." *Apprendre à Citer le Discours d'Autrui* 24 (2001): 71–90.

Pollet, Marie-Christine, and Valérie Piette. "Citations, reformulations du discours d'autrui: Une clef pour enseigner l'ecriture de recherche?" *Spirale* 29 (2002): 165–80.

Reuter, Yves. "Je suis comme un autrui qui doute." *Apprendre à Citer le Discours d'Autrui* 24 (2001): 13–28.

The Dynamic Nature of Common Knowledge

Amy England

When teachers discuss source citation with their students, inevitably the subject of common knowledge comes up. Students struggle to understand which information they should cite and which their audience will consider common knowledge. In response to this struggle, teachers tend to define common knowledge in terms of form (is it a fact?) or availability (how many sources have the same information?). Unfortunately, these limited definitions do not take into account the dynamic nature of common knowledge and discourse communities. In addition, teachers who consult professional literature in an effort to solve this dilemma will find virtually no discussions about the nature of common knowledge in composition studies. With the availability of information increasing daily, the diversity of the college student population, and the growing popularity of pedagogical strategies such as theme courses, our current approach to common knowledge is inadequate for our students' needs. In this essay, I argue for a more dynamic definition of common knowledge and suggest pedagogical strategies to enact this new approach. My purpose is to expand our current definition of common knowledge by analyzing the assumptions underlying this definition and by applying theories of discourse communities. My goal is to encourage teachers to move beyond believing that common knowledge is a stable entity that remains consistent regardless of rhetorical concerns and toward a new conception of common knowledge that takes into account the evolutionary nature of literacy and knowing.

While conducting research on how teachers represent source use and plagiarism to their students, I had the opportunity to read dozens of student essays from two first-year composition classes and one junior-level literature class and became intrigued by the idea of common knowledge. In order to code the students' essays to determine incidences of patch-written or plagiarized material from secondary sources, I first had to eliminate common knowledge information, a time consuming and sometimes difficult process. This elimination process was further complicated by the fact that both of the first-year composition classes were organized around themes; as such, the students spent most of the semester discussing a specialized area of knowledge. In one section, the class discussions and readings focused on work, while the other section's theme was memory and erasure. Because the classes focused on these themes, the students developed a common field of knowledge that they often displayed in their essays. As the semester progressed and the students grew in their understanding of the class theme, the amount of uncited common knowledge material in their essays increased.

The popularity among students of researching via the Internet further complicates common knowledge. Just as it is often defined based on the type of information, common knowledge is often defined by the availability of information. I will discuss some of these definitions in more detail in a moment, but for example, one popular rule of thumb is that if the exact same information can be found in four different sources, it can be considered common knowledge. Since each URL indicates a separate source, the same information disseminated on the Internet can easily be found in multiple sources, depending, however, on how we define a "source."

For example, in an essay on the importance of strikes in the early labor movement, one student wrote:

> One of the most well known of these [strikes] was the Bay View Tragedy, May 5 1886, where workers who were peacefully marching to get their 16 hour work day reduced were shot at by police, seven marchers died.

This information is not cited in the student's essay. Using a word string search on Google, I found more than four different sites had this same information but not the same phrasing that the student used. Each of the sites I viewed was an electronic version of a different newspaper account of the Bay View strike, yet each was the same story from the same wire service. So did that count as four sources or one? In the traditional sense of the word, "source" equates with a particular publication, but as the availability and duplication of electronic information increases daily, that definition and the assumptions that accompany it are not as effective as they once were. However, because of the general nature of the information and its availability on the Internet, I classified this passage and others like it as common knowledge.

At times, it was difficult to differentiate between common knowledge and a student's argument. In the same essay on unions, the student wrote:

> It is important to note though, that it is the union that has the power to strike. Employees working without a union find it not only nearly impossible to strike, but worthless. A union allows enough workers to strike that it hurts the company, however it also limits your ability to get paid more than the other workers. The unions have their good and bad points much like strikes, but a strike will almost never occur unless it is union organized.

Is this information the student gleaned from sources and class discussions or is the student making an argument? Without talking directly to the student, it is impossible to say for sure. I ultimately classified this passage as common knowledge, both because the topic of the strikes had been extensively discussed in class and the information in the passage is very vague. (The student refers to unions and strikes in general, not specific unions or events.)

Both of these examples illustrate the importance of discourse community context in determining whether or not particular information can be considered common knowledge. My initial response to the first passage was to label it patch writing because the student used the name and date of the event without citing the source. Only after investigating the possible sources of the information did I see that it could also be considered common knowledge. For the second passage, the classroom context and the evolution of that particular discourse community provided the swing vote for my decision. Had I simply read the paper as an outsider, I would have been more likely to classify that material as patch-written as well.

For students and teachers alike, deciding what is and what is not common knowledge can be both crucial and extremely frustrating. An error in judgment can result in a verdict of plagiarism from the teacher, and common knowledge is at best a slippery concept. The resources available to students offer limited help in this matter; handbook advice tends to be formulaic or nonexistent. For example, in *Doing Honest Work in College,* a text devoted to ethical academic behavior, Charles Lipson never mentions common knowledge, focusing all of his attention on various styles of citation and academic honesty, including a detailed discussion of avoiding plagiarism, both deliberate and "accidental."

In *Rules for Writers*, Diana Hacker defines common knowledge as "general information that your readers may know or could easily locate in any number of references" (403). She adds, "As a rule, when you have seen certain general information repeatedly in your reading, you don't need to cite it. However, when information has appeared in only a few sources, when it is highly specific (as with statistics), or when it is controversial, you should cite it" (403). This same advice is in both the MLA and APA sections of the handbook. However, the examples Hacker uses differ in each section. In the MLA section, she uses the facts that "Toni Morrison won the Nobel Prize in 1993 and that Emily Dickinson published only a handful of her many poems during her life" as examples of common knowledge (403). But the examples she uses in the APA section are quite different. She states, "For example, the approximate population of the United States is common knowledge among sociologists and economists, and psychologists are familiar with Freud's theory of the unconscious" (458). What's different in these two sets of examples is the specification of discourse community members, which I will discuss in more detail in a moment.

Robert Harris, author of *The Plagiarism Handbook*, defines common knowledge as "whatever an educated person would be expected to know or could locate in an ordinary encyclopedia" (19). He specifies three types: "easily observable information," "commonly reported facts," and "common sayings," each with several examples (19). He also explains that in particular instances, such as using common knowledge in a direct quote, common knowledge still needs to be cited. In a flowchart that maps the decision-making process of whether or not to cite material, Harris differentiates between material the writer thought of (a problematic distinction in itself) and information that would be considered common knowledge. Later in the book, Harris reminds his readers that "any item of background information you mention must be cited unless it is common knowledge" (23).

There are several assumptions underlying both Hacker's and Harris' approach to common knowledge:

Assumption Number 1: Students will be able to determine what their audience considers to be common knowledge. Hacker equates common knowledge with "general information . . . readers may know," while Harris uses the phrase "whatever an educated person would be expected to know." The fail-safes built into these phrases are qualifiers like *general, may, educated,* and *expected;* these vague terms require writers to make judgments about their readers' knowledge about the topic. However, without explicit experience with a discourse community, students really aren't able to make this decision. Beginning writers in particular also have difficulty with audience analysis, making it almost impossible for them to gauge what their audience does or does not know.

Assumption Number 2: The use of examples in explanations of common knowledge provides sufficient information for students to make judgments about the commonness of the information they include in their essays. The strategy of providing examples as substitutes for detailed explanations is fairly common in handbooks. The belief being enacted here is that students will be able to internalize the strategies associated with the examples and then transfer those strategies to their own writing. In Hacker's examples, one explanation mentions specific discourse communities and the other does not. The discourse communities she does mention are sociologists, economists, and psychologists, professional communities to which the majority of our students do not yet belong. However, as we can see from the examples of student work I mentioned before, knowledge about the discourse community is necessary in order to judge the commonness of the examples. Sometimes even those of us considered expert can lack the necessary knowledge base; for example, while I knew Toni Morrison had won the Nobel Prize, I didn't know in what year she won it. Does that mean I'm not an expert member of the discourse community that uses MLA for its documentation?

Assumption Number 3: Successfully integrating common knowledge into a text only involves deciding whether or not the information should be cited. In handbooks, common knowledge is defined and explained in terms of what action the writer should take—to cite the material or not. Yet studies of citation analysis show us that expert writers approach common knowledge differently, basing their decisions not on whether the information is or is not cited, but rather on how that common knowledge is rhetorically cued in the text. In her analysis of common knowledge in scientific essays, Koutsantoni details the various markers of common knowledge expert writers employ and the effect those markers have on an audience. These markers generally fall into two categories: "evaluative adjectives, such as *well-known* or *common*" and "expressions of generalized attribution, such as *it is known* [or] *it is widely accepted*" (Koutsantoni 175). These markers have multiple functions: they "stress the author's commitment to certain commonly held beliefs," they "add to the argumentative force by presenting the view as one which is not theirs alone, but one which is shared with the wider community or with relevant experts," they indicate "endorsement of sources which are highly respected in the field," and they allow the authors to "emphasize their own status as members of [the community] by showing awareness of these sources and by their relevance to their work" (Koutsantoni 176). By using these rhetorical cues, expert writers indicate which information is held in common by the community and which is new information.

Assumption Number 4: Common knowledge is an established, static set of facts. None of the reference resources I consulted portrayed common knowledge as something other than what is "known," ignoring the fact that what is "known" evolves over time. New information enters the knowledge base; old or faulty information fades out. As Hunt argues, "Information and ideas are not inert masses to be shifted and copied in much the same way two computers exchange packages of information, but rather need to be continuously reformatted, reconstituted, restructured, reshaped, and reinvented and exchanged in new forms" (2). Our cultural knowledge base increases daily; therefore, our common knowledge base increases as well. It's also true that some of what used to be common becomes uncommon: it is forgotten. Common knowledge also changes from community to community and within a community. It is not a static entity, but one that grows with the society, the group, and the individual.

Assumption Number 5: Students will be familiar enough with the field of study to be able to tell the difference between ideas that are "common" and ideas that are "controversial" (Hacker 403). When initiates enter a field of knowledge, familiarity with the dominant concepts is marginal at best. As the student continues to work and learn in a specialized field, her knowledge of the dominant ideology and information increases. The longer she remains active in the field, the more that knowledge base increases. However, undergraduate writers are at the beginning of this learning cycle and may be hard pressed to determine which ideas are common and which are not.

Assumption Number 6: The concerns of a specific discourse community are secondary to the location and prevalence of the common knowledge. Apparently where and how often we find the information overrides discourse community requirements. The majority of handbooks make no attempt to include discourse convention specifics when defining common knowledge; instead, handbooks tend to define common knowledge by where it's found, how often it's found, and whether or not the audience is likely to recognize it as common knowledge. However, as we've already seen, the context of the discourse community and the knowledge base it develops continually evolves and plays a profound role in determining what information its members hold in common and what is new information to all or some of the members.

In addition to these assumptions, the information missing from these discussions is also quite revealing. For example, there is no mention of using common knowledge to establish solidarity and credibility with readers such as Koutsantoni describes. As Ann Johns points out, members of a discourse community have shared genre knowledge, and one aspect of this is "shared knowledge of text content," which includes "the types of content and vocabulary that are brought into the text, the ways in which the content is organized, the assumptions about prior knowledge of readers and . . . appropriate use of details" (31). Certain words, ideas, and theories become repeated so often in a discourse community's communications that every other member recognizes and understands their significance. Indeed, a writer announces her membership in a particular community by employing these commonplaces appropriately. Writers who are experienced community members recognize that these commonplaces don't need to be cited because they have a more thorough understanding of the shared textual knowledge of the group; inexperienced members, on the other hand, are forced into a guessing game: to cite or not to cite?—or, following the advice of most handbooks, overcite. While this latter practice allows them to avoid plagiarism, it also announces their novice status and thus diminishes their credibility or authority with their readers. If these novice members are fortunate, they have access to more experienced members who can guide them through this decision-making process. Unfortunately, as Johns claims, "Many students receive little or no instruction" in discourse conventions and are left to discover the rules through trial and error (68). Error in this case can be an extraordinarily risky proposition for the student.

Also absent from discussions of common knowledge in handbooks and other reference texts is the effect different readers can have on a text. Handbook advice tends to portray all readers as being the same, requiring the same approach and responding in the same way. Nowhere is this less true than in the academic world, where the teacher is not only reader, but peer reviewer, judge, and sometimes executioner.

When a teacher takes it upon herself to decide whether or not information in a student's text is or is not common knowledge, she is asserting her authority over that student's text. This authority has more weight than the authority a lay reader asserts. When a lay reader makes judgments about a text, those judgments affect only her interpretation of or response to the text. A teacher, however, wields an additional authority that the average reader does not. If an average reader rejects a text, the effects on the writer are minimal. The reader might refuse to read the rest of the text, or tell a few acquaintances that she didn't like it, or she might respond to the text in writing via a letter or some other form of discourse. On the other hand, the teacher has the authority not only to reject a text she perceives as faulty, but also to prevent further dissemination of that text to other readers and impose some sort of penalty on the writer. A verdict of plagiarism or sloppy citation practices from the teacher imposes sanctions on both the writer and the text that stem from the teacher's perception of the author's strategy. If, for example, one of these sanctions is to fail the paper, then the writer's text is stopped in its tracks. Even a less severe punishment, such as requiring the student to revise the text, requires the writer to alter the text before it is read again. My argument is that this position of authority leads the teacher away from the role of reader and toward the role of judge in situations where the role of reader would be more beneficial to the student. The role of reader allows the teacher to mentally inquire into the student writer's possible motives and take into account discourse community conventions, while the role of judge requires a purely evaluative response. If teachers assume the role of reader, they can be more flexible in their responses to questions regarding common knowledge. They can suspend their judgment while reading essays, similar to what Peter Elbow encourages in the believing game, allowing different possible interpretations of common knowledge in a text rather than judging it by the standards of a discourse community with which students may have only marginal or intermittent contact.

As participants in the classroom discourse community, teachers also have the unique opportunity to introduce and prompt discussion of the conventions of discourse communities and the role common knowledge plays in community communications. Setting discussions of common knowledge in this larger context allows teachers to move beyond the formulaic handbook advice to more complex rhetorical issues such as the textual cues Koutsantoni describes and the idea of using common knowledge to establish solidarity and authorial authority with the reader.

In addition to changing the reader position they assume, teachers can also borrow inspiration from other forms of common knowledge. One of these is how common knowledge is utilized in the corporate world. Nancy

Dixon's *Common Knowledge: How Companies Thrive by Sharing What They Know* details the systems and strategies major corporations use to share common knowledge. While Dixon takes great pains to point out that her use of the term *common knowledge* refers to the "'know how' rather than the 'know what' of school learning" (11), her analysis of how companies create and disseminate information still provides us with valuable insights into new ways to view common knowledge. For example, in her discussion of how knowledge is transferred from one team to another, she describes three changes in perspective that accompany these transfers:

- The first is a shift from thinking of experts as the primary source of knowledge to thinking that everyone engaged in work tasks has knowledge someone else could use to advantage.
- The second is a shift from thinking of knowledge as residing with individuals to thinking of knowledge as embedded in a group or community.
- The third is a shift from thinking of knowledge as a stable commodity to thinking of knowledge as dynamic and ever changing. (148–49)

Each of these shifts relocates common knowledge from the individual to the community, from the static to the dynamic, to a "reciprocal model in which all contribute and all receive" (152). This corporate view of common knowledge supports the idea that common knowledge in composition can be viewed as a more complex proposition than the current characterization of it allows.

By framing conversations and instruction about common knowledge in the larger context of discourse community conventions and expectations, we can help our students move beyond the formulaic handbook approach to resolve questions on common knowledge in several ways. They will be able to approach common knowledge and citation practices from a more informed perspective, one that takes into account the effect of their audience on how and what they cite. Students will gain a more realistic picture of how information is created and transferred from one community to another, and the emphasis will shift away from the individual toward collaboration with other individuals and texts. Finally, resolving questions about the dynamics of common knowledge can promote critical thinking, discussion, and reflection about the larger issues of source citation and intertextuality. In short, we can help students develop the qualities of academic thinkers and writers we set as goals for our classes.

Works Cited

Dixon, Nancy. *Common Knowledge: How Companies Thrive by Sharing What They Know*. Boston: Harvard Business School, 2000.

Elbow, Peter. *Writing without Teachers*. New York: Oxford University Press, 1973.

Hacker, Diana. *Rules for Writers*. 5th ed. New York: Bedford/St. Martin's, 2004.

Harris, Robert. *The Plagiarism Handbook: Strategies for Preventing, Detecting, and Dealing with Plagiarism*. Los Angeles: Pyrczak, 2001.

Hunt, Russell. "Let's Hear It for Internet Plagiarism." *Teaching and Learning Bridges*, November 2004. http://www.usask.ca/tlc/bridges_journal/v2n3_nov_03/v2n3_internet_plagiarism.html, consulted December 1, 2003.

Johns, Ann M. *Text, Role, and Context: Developing Academic Literacies*. New York: Cambridge UP. 1997.

Koutsantoni, Dimitra. "Attitude, Certainty and Allusions to Common Knowledge." *Journal of English for Academic Purposes* 3 (2004): 163–82.

Lipson, Charles. *Doing Honest Work in College*. Chicago: University of Chicago Press, 2004.

Instinctual Ballast

Imitation and Creative Writing

Christina Pugh

In his *Handlist of Rhetorical Terms,* Richard A. Lanham defines mimesis as "imitation of gesture, pronunciation, or utterance; self-conscious role-playing, as when a rhapsode reenacts the poem he is reciting" (102). As defined by Lanham and discussed by thinkers from Plato to Erich Auerbach, mimesis and imitation are inseparable from the endeavor of representation itself; most creative arts are distinctly mimetic in their practice. In our contemporary landscape, however, creative *writing* is almost never taught with mimesis at the forefront of students' or teachers' minds. Instead, the pedagogical method in many workshop courses seeks to enable the student to "discover" her own voice, as if she existed in a form of literary vacuum. Students in such courses might be asked to do an occasional imitation exercise, but the serious practice of imitation is seldom pursued in any focused manner in most creative writing programs.

Even in a literary culture that continues to prize "originality," however, imitation is a viable apprenticeship for a writer. In the past few years under the auspices of the Northwestern University creative writing program, I have taught undergraduate creative writing courses that consisted *only* of reading and imitating a handful of major American poets: Robert Frost, Elizabeth Bishop, Louise Bogan, Gwendolyn Brooks, and James Merrill; and though this sort of course goes against the grain of many curricular expectations, I have been astonished at the caliber of poetic work that imitation yields from students.

Because the imitation course is an amalgam of what we might, in other circumstances, think of as discrete "literature" and "creative writing" courses, it rejects the way in which institutions cordon off complementary aspects of the mind into separate disciplines. This helps students, in turn, to begin to reject the myths and clichés of who the scholar and the poet should be: those discrete and supposedly mutually exclusive perimeters that determine how we identify ourselves as producers of literature, whether "critical" or "creative." The course thus cultivates the writer, to parse Luce Irigaray, "which is not *one*." It's built upon a radical valuation of the writing act itself—what Stevens called "the poem of the mind in the act of finding / What will suffice"—and the ways in which such an act emerges both steadily and unpredictably from a lifelong act of reading.

The task of the writer who is not *one* writer, then, is to reinscribe disciplinary boundaries that are fluid as well as rigorous. There's a way in which the straight workshop format, as practiced in some programs and institutions, can relegate the reading act to what is "not said"—almost to the realm of the unconscious. A poem might have been "influenced" by another, and we may learn as much over the course of workshop discussion; but that influence is thought to lie, almost indiscreetly, outside the artificial boundary that contains what is thought to constitute creative production. In such courses, reading is ground but not figure; the assumption, but not the task at hand. Yet this is precisely the task that writers need to consider in their own work, since text necessarily generates text. Many creative writing courses may not actively ask how to read as a writer: how should I be reading; what can I be reading; and especially: how, in this culture of images, can I line my life with words, with print? These questions are not only crucial for undergraduates, who are still very much in the stage of formation, but also should be vital to any writer for whom the re-formation of self and work remains a perennial value. By making literary texts the centerpiece of our courses rather than the background, we can teach our students not only to read as writers—"poetry is an art that reading, at its best, can imitate," Mary Kinzie explains (2)—but also to write as readers. This is a viable practice that literary critics from Helen Vendler to Judith Ryan have discussed. (Indeed, Ryan's *Rilke, Modernism, and Poetic Tradition* re-creates Rilke's writing desk.)

Italo Calvino knew quite a lot about the Reader, whom he allegorized as a character in *If on a Winter's Night a Traveler*. The male writer goes in search of this female Reader, Ludmilla by name, who keeps a crowd of picture frames in one corner of her wall:

> The frames are all different, nineteenth-century Art Nouveau floral forms, frames in silver, copper, enamel, tortoiseshell, leather, carved wood; they may reflect the notion of enhancing those fragments of real

life, but they may also be a collection of frames, and the photographs may be there only to occupy them; in fact some frames are occupied by pictures clipped from newspapers, one encloses an illegible page of an old letter, another is empty. (Calvino 144)

What is the import of that last, superfluous, melancholy frame in the Reader's house? Perhaps it constitutes a certain moment of transformation that Calvino did not fully envision—in which the reader, steeped and saturated in text, opens a portal to her own writing. The empty frame becomes incipience, or the blank page. Then the beautiful distinctions—man/woman, writer/reader—must themselves be blurred, be productively confounded, and all the genders mixed up. For the reader can only be courted by the writer *within* the self that is not one.

Saul Bellow said that the writer is a reader moved to emulation. Certainly the performing arts place a high value on emulation, or imitation, as do many pedagogical practices in the visual arts (think of aspiring painters who copy the masterpieces hanging in museums). Despite the perennial literary-critical debates regarding the role of mimesis *within* literary representation, however, few educators think of literature as a practice that a writer must learn by performing mimesis of previous writers. Nevertheless, the ballet student learns his art through a muscular, bodily mimesis of the teacher's equally muscular gesture; and here the analogy becomes more than strictly conceptual: because we need to feel poetic meter in our breath and heartbeats, we can't write iambic tetrameter without learning to walk in tetrameter first. Imitation forces us to confront the poem not as an ethereal emanation of our personal wish, but as something distinctly material: something we make through the labor of arrangement and rhetorical manipulation.

A comparison to the other arts can often bring this particular pedagogy home to skeptical students in the early days of an imitation course. That, of course, would be the time when they learn the course requirements: reading and discussing five twentieth-century poets, as well as writing both a weekly imitation poem and an analytic paper that makes an argument, via close reading, about one of the poet's poems. This is serious work—and the imitation poems are serious imitation, not parody: they are, in other words, what Nicholas Delbanco calls a "sincere imitation" (xxvi). As Delbanco elaborates, such an imitation can never be accomplished without intensive reading and study of the work to be imitated:

You cannot copy what you glance at nor remember what you speed read nor repeat what you half heard; the reason one writer chooses semicolons, or another elects an apposite comma, or a third prefers the absence of standard punctuation marks, has a great deal to do with the world view expressed, and a complex or compound sentence or parenthetical observation (such as the one we're engaged in) will represent a different way of looking at the linkages of things—the way the past impinges on the present as does the present on the future in an unbroken line of descent or argument if represented with a dash—than does a simple or short. (xxvi)

Delbanco aptly describes the way in which the imitation poems necessitate—are, in fact, constitutionally impossible *without*—intensive and sometimes self-changing reading of the poet to be imitated. I have told the students: *Put on the nerves and musculature of the poet before you begin. This is not about biography, the poet's or yours.* It's about taking your life into the poem—a different way of taking your life into your hands. For one quarter, the students learn to be sibyls: to let the poet in question speak *them.* This is not a mystical transformation; it is instead the natural outgrowth of attentive reading. Moreover, it involves much more than retaining a certain meter or line length, though it does require that, too: it also involves assimilating the ways in which a certain poet builds sentences incrementally, syntactically, across lines; the wild geography of what I call that poet's "diction universe"; what the poet would include or exclude from a particular poem. (*I want to be able to pick the poem out of a line-up,* I have told the students—and this is how the poems are evaluated and discussed in the imitation workshop.) In one particularly memorable class discussion, we debated whether or not James Merrill would have actually used the phrase "reality TV" in his work, had he lived to see it. Contrast, too, is paramount: the precise degree of microscopic sheen in Bishop's "The Bight" or "Sandpiper"—what Richard Wollheim would have described as "seeing-in"—is unthinkable in a poet like Frost. Only by dwelling within the poet's work can we access the caul of preverbal synergies that Seamus Heaney called the "instinctual ballast" of a particular poet: "What kinds of noise assuage him, what kinds of music pleasure or repel him, what messages the receiving stations of his senses are happy to pick up from the world and what ones they automatically block out" (62). For Heaney, instinctual ballast is what causes the later Yeats to clatter with consonants while Wordsworth remains the smooth and receptive oar in water, the glittering circles inscribed by the young boat-thief in book I of *The Prelude.*

Kinzie has also eloquently discussed the timbre of reading that imitation requires, as well as the primacy of the literary material at hand:

> Perceiving how shape emerges from the half-shaped background provides the reader with a lens, or vantage, similar to the writer's. But this does not require us to say much about the lives of the poets or how they went about making their works; I am more interested in how the poems themselves wrestle with their tasks and occasions. For task and occasion arise only from a clear sense of poetic mission, a mission that articulates itself most strongly when responding (among other spurs) to a poetic tradition. (14)

Such an emphasis on the material and making of the poem also gives students the freedom to cross over—to cross purportedly indelible lines that separate different races, genders, and sexual orientations: not biography, again, but the conditions or threshold of production. By its very nature, imitation challenges the received notion that writing must arise from, or be somehow ratified by, personal experience. One of the most fascinating movements in the imitation class, for me, was the pivot from the work of James Merrill to Gwendolyn Brooks, a movement that required many of the students to consider the limitations of their whiteness and to figure out how to mobilize particular aspects of African-American vernacular in a way that would have to remain "sincere," in Delbanco's terms. Brooks herself, having mastered both vernacular and more conventionally "literary" registers of speech, is a terrific model for the variegations of a writer's voice—or a writer, again, who is not *one*.

All of this certainly flies in the face of such credos as "Write what you know," "Find your own voice," "Your experience is the best subject for writing." But as someone who came to writing through and with a doctorate in literature, none of those instructions seemed right to me in the first place. With so much of my life vested in reading, in writing, how could I separate it into book and nonbook? What of my voice, or my plural voices, really belongs to me, and how would I be able to gauge the degree or percentage of that ownership? Perhaps because I did study literary theory, these ideas don't reduce me to despair; instead, they may have actually given me permission to write in the first place, despite so many creative writers' indignation over the very title of Foucault's "The Death of the Author." If I had ever found writing to be an act of the ego alone, I think my inchoate sense of modesty—or a certain love of privacy—would have prevented me from doing it. (In an essay entitled "The Uses of Doubt,"

Stacey D'Erasmo has written forcefully against the often unspoken assumption that writing must be ego-driven.) If indeed there is a way in which poetry functions as Eliot's "continual extinction of personality" (2076), can it also be a concomitant enlargement of what we consider to be the singular, limited personality as such? "Enlargement" is, of course, a world away from "inflation."

Keats's notion of "negative capability" is closely related to such enlargement. For him, the ability to be "in uncertainties, mysteries, doubts, without any irritable reaching after fact and reason" (70–71) is what Shakespeare possessed in droves, and a capacity that every poet should cultivate in herself. This is certainly a marvelous description of the writing process, but isn't it also a dead ringer for the reading act? We could say much more about the play between agency and self-dissolution in the case of the reader who is also a writer; but considered in the light of negative capability, the seeming strictness of the imitation assignments is revealed as something more than literary apprenticeship: it can constitute some of the most vertiginous artistic freedom imaginable.

An imitation course thus refines the boundaries of what we categorize as "the creative." It requires a student to do something more dangerous than to trust his own experience or to tell the story she thinks she wants to tell. Imitation unmoors the writer from her comfort zone of familiar syntax, diction, and line. If there is a philosophy subtending imitation, it is surely globally similar to that of deconstruction: both practices suggest that writing is never transparent, or innocent, or a straightforward means of self-expression.

Does anyone own his writing, then? Are imitation and plagiarism commensurate? At first blush, I'm inclined to separate them—to agree, that is, with Christopher Ricks's admonition, "Plagiarism is a dishonesty" (223). Clearly, however, plagiarism has a much more ambiguous role in the creative arts than in criticism, as poets have incorporated other poets' lines into their own work for millennia. The genre of classical poem known as the cento, which comprises one hundred borrowed lines, is an excellent example of what we might now call naturalized plagiarism. For some, Eliot's *The Waste Land*, despite its footnotes, also constitutes plagiarism writ large. The imitation course, however, does not ask students to incorporate particular lines from the master poets' work. Students are asked to put on strategies and verbal proclivities, as opposed to "lifting" pieces of text from the poet to be imitated. Indeed, such cutting and pasting would interfere with the generative writing—in another's voice—that they are being asked to do. If plagiarism has any role at all in the course, perhaps it would be the creeping and paradoxical sense of *self*-plagiarism described by William Gaddis in *Agape Agape:* "I've never seen my, seen this plagiarist because I am the other one it's exactly the opposite, I am the other" (22). I am the other: the writer who is not one.

Lastly, pedagogy seeks practical outcomes. Some might wonder how such concentrated imitation affects creative writing students and whether such a course actually allows them to remain "creative," in the popular sense of the term. In my experience, it does. Some students told me that they came to depend on the imitations: that they took great pleasure in that relinquishing of self. Many of these students also went on to write senior thesis projects in creative writing—projects that may have germinated in some of the imitation poems, but that grew in ways that exceeded the strict boundaries of the imitation course. What's more, the students also learned enormously from their own resistance to imitating particular writers. Clearly, some imitations feel easier or more "natural" than others, and these experiences help students to begin to unearth and to articulate their own "instinctual ballast," in Heaney's terms. If imitating Frost feels like the proverbial walk in the park, it's almost certain that Merrill will be more of a struggle, and this very contrast will reveal something important about the student's emerging goals and capacities as a poet.

Perhaps most importantly, the challenge of imitation spurs students (in an almost Bloomian sense) to produce poems that are fine poems in their own right, even if taken out of the strict imitation context. A couple of years ago, one of my students wrote a superb Frost imitation that was later published in a small but nationally distributed literary magazine. Thus imitation doesn't always announce itself as such to the reading public; neither, of course, does an imitative inception disqualify a work from standing as its own autonomous entity. Robert Lowell's *Imitations* volume, for example, famously troped the boundaries of imitation and "autonomous" artistic conception. More recently, Susan Stewart's *Columbarium,* winner of the National Book Critics Circle Award for poetry in 2003, has been discussed in the context of imitation.

However gratifying to the student and teacher, publication is not the ultimate goal of the imitation course. Instead, imitation allows undergraduate students to be what they are: apprentice writers. When they imitate, these students are apprenticing to the very best and are thus slowing down their own writerly gestation process in an age when the rush to publish is infecting even the undergraduate population. Writers are not made in an instant; and no matter what form our writing may eventually take, there is a very real sense in which we are the verbal concatenation of what we have read: whether our work be experimental or traditional is immaterial. Imitation recognizes and mobilizes this essential element of literary learning, and it allows students to learn viscerally from the tradition in which they strive to make their mark.

Works Cited

Calvino, Italo. *If on a Winter's Night a Traveler.* Trans. William Weaver. New York: Harcourt, 1979.

Delbanco, Nicholas. *The Sincerest Form: Writing Fiction by Imitation.* Boston: McGraw-Hill, 2004.

D'Erasmo, Stacey. "The Uses of Doubt." *Ploughshares* 28, no. 4 (2002–3): 24–35.

Eliot, T. S. "Tradition and the Individual Talent." In *The Oxford Anthology of English Literature,* ed. Frank Kermode et al., 2011–19. New York: Oxford University Press, 1973.

Gaddis, William. *Agape Agape.* New York: Viking, 2002.

Heaney, Seamus. "The Makings of a Music." In *Preoccupations: Selected Prose, 1968–1978.* New York: Farrar, Straus and Giroux, 1980. 61–78.

Keats, John. "Negative Capability." *In The Modern Tradition: Backgrounds of Modern Literature,* ed. Richard Ellmann and Charles Feidelson Jr., 70–71. New York: Oxford University Press, 1965.

Kinzie, Mary. *A Poet's Guide to Poetry.* Chicago: University of Chicago Press, 1999.

Lanham, Richard. *A Handlist of Rhetorical Terms.* 2nd ed. Berkeley and Los Angeles: University of California Press, 1991.

Ricks, Christopher. *Allusion to the Poets.* Oxford: Oxford University Press, 2002.

Ryan, Judith. *Rilke, Modernism, and Poetic Tradition.* New York: Cambridge University Press, 1999.

Stevens, Wallace. *The Collected Poems.* New York: Vintage, 1982.

The Anthology as a Literary Creation
On Innovation and Plagiarism in Textual Collections
Christopher M. Kuipers

A quick glance at almost any bookshelf, and it is obvious that anthologies are legion. Anthologies do not necessarily have "anthology" in their titles—take the tremendously popular *Chicken Soup for the Soul* series of books, for instance—but nevertheless *anthology* is the word most often used to mean a "textual collection" or "collection of excerpts." Today, the best-recognized academic anthologies are published by companies such as Norton and Longman and are aimed at college literature courses. But just as often the title *anthology* generically designates a collection of texts pertaining to almost any field. Strangely, *anthology* originally was a Greek word meaning a "literary bouquet," and referred for many centuries only to a very limited kind of textual collection, namely gatherings of short lyric poems. (The idea was that this "bouquet," like the sonnet sequences of the Renaissance, would be something you would gather and give to someone special.) This original meaning of poetic collection began to change slowly in the early decades of the twentieth century, alongside the beginnings of the "Great Books" movement, and then took a decisive turn after World War II. From that time to the present day, several thousands of works have been published bearing the title of anthology, when before there had been merely dozens. This seems to reflect the twentieth century's growing need for a basic-level term to categorize an increasingly important kind of published work—the textual collection—a need that has only accelerated into the present day, especially now with the awesome proliferation of media delivery and storage technologies. And so we have anthologies, the pragmatic concatenations of selected "original" works.

Or so it would appear to the casual book store browser who is well schooled in the meaning of "original work" and "copyrighted material."

Since the process of selection is undertaken furthest from the eventual readers of an anthology, some of the greatest and perhaps most unrecognized anthological artistry resides there. Many times anthology editors must locate the best original texts or the best translations of those texts. Under the editorship of the Romantic scholar M. H. Abrams, for instance, *The Norton Anthology of English Literature* has published versions of Romantic poems that improved upon other critical editions available at the time, with the avowed belief that students deserved the best texts possible. Other Nortons have published original translations of works—as in the scoop of Seamus Heaney's verse translation of *Beowulf* for the seventh edition of *The Norton Anthology of English Literature* ("Editors")—or have gone to great lengths to vet existing translations, as when multiple translators are used to represent the works of an individual poet.

Sometimes "selection" implies locating a work in the first place, and this in itself can be a creative endeavor. In their polemical *Pamphlet against Anthologies,* even Laura Riding and Robert Graves find time to praise those anthologists who perform "literary rescue work," the thankless unearthing of neglected authors or other worthy "fugitive pieces" that were more ephemerally published and are no longer available to the general reading public. Another kind of creative anthologizing can be found in the self-selected collections of especially influential writers. These "selected essays," "new and selected poems," and so forth are acknowledgments of the simple canonical fact that not every single production of any single author will ultimately have the same worth, yet that there is significant value in a survey of the highlights of any author's works, if only to show the evolution of theme, technique, or style. There is even more value in having a group of landmark works that are out of print or otherwise hard to come by.

While texts are still being selected, the problem of arrangement is already in the anthologist's mind. The most obvious and common kinds of anthology arrangements are alphabetical and chronological. Chance and art are often inseparable, and so even alphabetical arrangements may introduce a measure of aesthetic variation into a collection. Chronological arrangements, however, are less straightforward, and can be handled in more self-conscious ways. What date, exactly, should be used? The date of the author's birth, or the date of a work's composition, or first publication, or the revised publication? The mere establishing of all these possible dates is a labor unto itself. And once the historical dates are established, there are still ways to vary if not deviate from the arrangement, as has happened even in various anthologies from Norton, a publisher otherwise known for strict chronological ordering of selections. For instance, in the most recent edition of *The Norton Anthology of Modern Poetry,* the new category of "contemporary" has been added, and the anthology broken into two volumes to reflect this division, which nominally occurred around World War II. Interestingly, the first, "modern," volume ends with the poetry of Keith Douglas, born in 1920, and the final poem of his to be included is "Aristocrats" of 1946, a poem that seems to encapsulate a Modernist temper more characteristic of World War I. The first poet of the second, "contemporary," volume, on the other hand, is Charles Olson, born in 1910, and the first poem of Olson's in the volume is "Pacific Lament," also from 1946, but a poem that instead typifies Olson's more avant-garde "projective" verse that in turn would influence the phenomenon of Language Poetry.[1]

There are other ways to arrange selections that also introduce significant levels of creativity as editors set off both parallels and variations among the chosen texts. Recently in the many anthologies or, "readers," devoted to composition and writing courses, as well as in many introductory literary survey texts, editors have tried to differentiate their offerings by including more diverse choices not only of genres (especially with varieties of nonfiction), but also more diverse choices of authors, in order to acknowledge the wide ethnic diversity of today's world and its writers. Arranging such diverse selections is a problem that many anthologists have begun to solve with rearrangements of the texts under thematic rubrics, such as "family," "love," "death," and so on. These sections in turn include examples of poems, plays, stories, essays, and other nonfiction that illuminate the given theme. By contrast, the traditional division of such anthologies, namely the canonical triptych of fiction, poetry, and drama, seems to encourage far less editorial originality. On the other hand, even as the thematic divisions expand, many categories appear to have been imitated: given the relative openness of thematic over generic divisions, why else do various anthologies suddenly have sections devoted to such similar themes—such as "family," "love," and "death"? Strikingly, these suddenly generic headings often appear in the same order (whether such editorial imitation crosses the line to plagiarism will be considered below).

The presentation of texts within anthologies often leads back to the creativity of selection itself. It is no accident that Jahan Ramazani chose certain poems to open and close the volumes of *The Norton Anthology of Modern and Contemporary Poetry.* Just as in any creative literary work, the beginnings and ends are ripe for special effects. For instance, in the section on the English Romantic poets in the latest *Norton Anthology of World Liter-*

ature (Lawall), there are several pages of excerpts from Dorothy Words-worth's *Grasmere Journals*. By the chronologic of the anthology, she must be preceded by her brother William and must be followed by Samuel Taylor Coleridge. But this "fixed" ordering must have suggested the final words to be chosen from Dorothy—that she and William have just received a letter from Coleridge—words now appearing immediately before Coleridge's own section. More than just an anthological nicety, this clever presentation reminds readers that there was an intellectual community among these poets. In the same volume, the seemingly chance placement of Emily Dickinson next to a section featuring the Urdu poet Ghalib suggests that there really is something to the venerable concept of a "world" literature, since the spare but imagistically voluptuous poems of the recluse of Amherst resonate so closely with the tight but lavish ghazals of the classical Mughal court poet.

Where there is creative originality, there are ways of plagiarizing, and so it is in the realm of anthologies. This is remarkable indeed when coming from the position that the best anthologist is the one who adheres as closely as possible to the original text. However, the adherence to the original entails only the *transcription* of the original texts, which may not even be carried out by the editor. As Cary Nelson reminds us, transcription often happens today thanks to typesetters who work from photocopies of the original texts (320).[2] Textual transcription aside, then, wherever there is an element of editorial creativity in the anthologizing process, there can be what might be called "anthology plagiarism."

The possibility of plagiarism by anthologists was raised not long ago by David Damrosch, editor of Longman's groundbreaking anthology of British literature of 1998. When Norton published its seventh edition of its English literature anthology in 1999, under the new head editor Stephen Greenblatt, Damrosch publicly deplored the Norton's choices as plagiarism (in his words, "wholesale lifting"), since its resemblance to the Longman anthology was far closer than to previous Norton editions ("Editors"). Norton, however, responded that plagiarism in this realm seemed nonsensical. Interestingly, by the time of its second edition, Longman was imitating a selection practice earlier pioneered by the Norton: the parallel publication of novels with ancillary critical material to be assigned (and even packaged) with the anthology, thereby freeing up significant space for other selections.

As a more clear case of plagiarism by selection, there is Louis Untermeyer's inimitable editorial stunt. An early-twentieth-century poet now more remembered as a leading anthologist of the period, Untermeyer edited a series of enormously popular collections that did much to help canonize modern poetry as well as pave the way for the "critical" anthologies now ubiquitous in the classroom. Wondering whether anthologists really do copy each others' selections—"There were many instances," he recalls, "where it seemed that anthologists read only anthologies"—Untermeyer planted pseudonymous poems of his own writing in several of his own anthologies and a poetry handbook (332). With some consternation, and some glee, he found that this same poet, pseudonym and all, began appearing in other competing anthologies. One editor, whom Untermeyer does not name, went so far as to add "data available" to this mysterious author's poetry (Untermeyer 332). At least this editor may have done some checking, but none got the poetry from an "original source."

When selecting texts, if truth be told, anthologists often lean directly on other anthologists who have already made such selections. A common if unacknowledged starting point for many editors is to examine the tables of contents of similar anthologies already on the market.[3] Here is one anonymous case: when contracting to edit a literary period anthology, one of my colleagues along with some coeditors were told in no uncertain terms by their publisher that they were not allowed to have less than 80 percent of the selections contained in the current market-leading anthology for that period. Is having 20 percent "new" selections really an "original" collection? I suppose at that point it matters how often my colleague and coeditors went out of their way to procure better texts of the selections, different subselections of longer texts, and so on.

Besides plagiarism by selection, there are many cases of plagiarism by arrangement. In this unoriginal mode, the collector copies not only the original texts, but also the *ordering* of those texts used in another collection. This may be one of the oldest kinds of anthological plagiarism. The *Greek Anthology*, the medieval compendium of epigrams and other short lyric poems that became a model for all later collections of the name, was based directly on a series of earlier collections (Paton). Epigrams are typified by being brief, often no more than a couplet or two, and the *Greek Anthology* contains thousands of epigrams. Why reorganize them, especially in the laborious, copyright-free manuscript culture, and especially when the originals had cogent and even artful arrangements? Thus, although the earliest sources for the *Greek Anthology* have long been lost, scholars have observed that long "runs" of selections have been so faithfully preserved that a source anthology from centuries before can be fairly easily reconstructed (see Gutzwiller). It as if the necessary work of transcription has run amok, cutting across the divisions of selection. A more recent counterexample can be found in an anonymously edited *A Golden Treasury of English Verse* (1935), whose title page claims it is "the selection of Francis Turner Palgrave revised and enlarged." Closer examination reveals that the collection actually reproduces all of Palgrave's famous selections from 1861 and adds none; it is "enlarged" only by virtue of the engravings scattered throughout the text. The *order* of the selections, however, has been changed—effectively ruining many of Palgrave's careful arrangements—and so it is "revised" in this sense. Only by its arrangement, then, not its selections, does this collection have any claim to copyright protection.

And a thin claim it is, since even Palgrave's own original titles for otherwise untitled poems (such as Shakespeare's sonnets) have all been reproduced in this "revision." Plagiarism in anthologies might extend to the theft of footnotes and other ancillary material, but most often and unrecognized are the taking over of titles of works that originally lacked them. Of course such works must be assigned titles when they are collected so that they can be conveniently listed in tables of contents and indices. Thus deliberately untitled poems (by, e.g., Emily Dickinson and e. e. cummings) are dutifully reheaded with their own first lines, but what about untitled prose works? Take the frequently anthologized short essay by Gloria Naylor that discusses her personal experience with, and possible ways to define, the word *nigger*. It was originally published without a title as an op-ed piece, but in many anthologies it appears as "'Mommy, What Does 'Nigger' Mean?'" While it does capture Naylor's references to her childhood, this title completely destroys the surprise that Naylor had originally sprung in her essay when that shocking word makes its first appearance part way through. Other anthologists have used the more milquetoast title "The Meaning[s] of a Word." Still other editors use the more academic turn of phrase "A Question of Language," perhaps from Naylor's own introductory comments on this topic, but this gives the delaying setup without a hint that there is a punch line. It is striking that there is only one editor that I have found who actually creates an entirely unique title—"Taking Possession of a Word"—and then gives a note indicating that this title has been deliberately supplied (Meyer 1077). In other words, this anthologist was probably the first in a long time who actually bothered checking into the "original text" rather than borrowing the title of another editor, who had likely borrowed it in turn from someone else.

Similar cases of original anthologizing and anthology plagiarism might be multiplied, and they beg the question of why it is so automatic to con-

ceive of anthologies as uniformly "unoriginal," rather than as sites allowing considerable editorial innovation on the one hand and possibilities for
unacknowledged borrowing on the other. One deep-seated conceptual
frame that holds the anthology as a debased thing is the ancient organic
metaphor for textuality. Dating at least to Socrates, and famously stated in
the *Phaedrus,* this metaphor suggests that a properly executed text is an
organic whole or even a "living body." In the light of this organic
metaphor, any collection, anthology, or encyclopedia that is composed of
parts, selections, or "articles"—a word whose etymology, "limbs," is itself a
reflection of the organic metaphor—can only be a heap of disjointed members. A closely related concept is the "unit of analysis" of textual originality. That is, considerations of originality in writing tend to operate at the
rather limited scale of the *sentence* to the *paragraph.* Below this scale are the
word and short phrase, which are very hard to "steal" in any conceivable
way, and beyond lie the chapter and the entire work, the plagiarism of
which is held up as laughable in its daring. The fact that search engines like
Google also operate best at the level of the phrase or short sentence
explains why these tools are so often useful in detecting unoriginality. As if
with this unit in mind, most plagiarists do stick to shorter passages, and frequently perform sentence-level tinkering at transitional points to hide the
plagiarism. One term sometimes given to this phenomenon, namely *patch
writing,* underscores how hard the organic metaphor is to avoid in the common understanding of plagiarism: here are patches of stolen clothing,
stitched together like a fig leaf cover-up for the guilty "body" of a text.

But at certain crucial points the organic metaphor collapses. Try for
instance the following thought experiment. Imagine whatever article,
book, or other piece that you have written of which you are most proud.
Would you rather have the entire thing plagiarized word-for-word and
someone else's name put on it, or have just a fraction of it stolen and integrated seamlessly into someone else's work? Assuming that the profit to the
plagiarist is proportional to the size of the theft, we would probably prefer
the latter. However, in the pure organic mode, it makes more sense to prefer the *former.* This plagiarism of the whole work would be, as textual
organicism would have it, something like getting kidnapped, but at least
the work is out there in the same "perfected form." The latter, according to
the organic metaphor, is more like losing an arm. Given the choice in these
terms, getting kidnapped seems better than losing a limb, since kidnapping
does not necessarily involve a catastrophic bodily injury.

But this is foolish. To understand how compilations and anthologies can be original, it is essential to stop thinking of texts as fixed, unified bodies, shaped and breathed to life by semidivine authors, each with a uniquely encoded genetic identity to be defended. Obviously it *is* worse, even far worse, to have one's entire work stolen rather than just a piece of it. What fills the spaces between texts on the page is not like the open air that stands between bodies: often the text's surroundings, whether titles, notes, or even the plain white around a stanza, are not extraneous but essential to that text. The organic metaphor is thus a seriously misleading concept of what texts are. Textuality is multiple and fluid, and we never can step into the same text twice. The anthology is a salutary reminder of this. It is one place where some of the most cherished ideas about plagiarism, originality, and textual production itself simply fall apart.

Notes

1. Jahan Ramazani, a coeditor of *The Norton Anthology of Modern and Contemporary Poetry*, has indicated to me personally that this often unremarked rearrangement of the strict chronological order was indeed very much part of his editorial purpose.

2. Nelson also notes that it is thus wrongheaded to critique the relative numbers of pages allotted to individual authors, since before the appearance of the finished product the anthologist has little idea exactly how many pages this will be.

3. Take for instance the Library of America's recent anthology *American Poetry: The Twentieth Century*. According to an interview with the editors, tables of contents of various similar anthologies comprised the first step in the board's lengthy decision-making process (see http://www.loa.org/article.jsp?art=100, consulted July 9, 2007).

Works Cited

"Editors of Two Anthologies Engage in War of Words: Norton's Coup Is a Translation of 'Beowulf.'" *Chronicle of Higher Education*, November 19, 1999, A23.

A Golden Treasury of English Verse: The Selection by Francis Turner Palgrave Revised and Enlarged. New York: Hartsdale House, 1935.

Gutzwiller, Kathryn J. *Poetic Garlands: Hellenistic Epigrams in Context*. Berkeley and Los Angeles: University of California Press, 1998.

Lawall, Sarah, et al., eds. *The Norton Anthology of World Literature: 1650 to Present*. 2nd ed. 3 vols. New York: Norton, 2003.

Masters, Edgar Lee. *Spoon River Anthology: An Annotated Edition*. Ed. John E. Hallwas. Urbana: University of Illinois Press, 1992.

Meyer, Michael, ed. *Thinking and Writing about Literature: A Text and Anthology*. 2nd ed. Boston: Bedford/St. Martin's, 2001.

Nelson, Cary. "Murder in the Cathedral: Editing a Comprehensive Anthology of Modern American Poetry." *American Literary History* 14 (2002): 311–27.

Paton, W. R., trans. *The Greek Anthology.* 5 vols. 1916. Cambridge: Harvard University Press; London: Heinemann, 1960.

Ramazani, Jahan, Richard Ellmann, and Robert O'Clair, eds. *The Norton Anthology of Modern and Contemporary Poetry.* 3rd ed. 2 vols. New York: Norton, 2003.

Riding, Laura, and Robert Graves. *A Pamphlet against Anthologies.* 1928; New York: AMS, 1970.

Untermeyer, Louis. *From Another World: The Autobiography of Louis Untermeyer.* New York: Harcourt, 1939.

Economies of Plagiarism

*The i-Map and Issues of Ownership
in Information Gathering*

Kim Walden and Alan Peacock

I-map is our term for a structured process that requires students to keep track of their research activities, to record their thinking processes and activities while engaged in the gathering, evaluating, selecting, and presenting of information drawn from diverse sources. It encourages reflective practice and a self-critical examination of information-handling strategies and skills, and it results in an assessable outcome that rewards process rather than product. Among its many uses, the i-map has proved valuable in addressing those many issues of ownership and citation that cluster under the portmanteau word *plagiarism*.

Although we are specifically interested in plagiarism, in keeping with the themes of this collection, our discussion ranges widely. Before returning to the pedagogical benefits of the i-map, we will explore the challenges faced by higher education teachers. The current concerns both within educational circles and in the media about plagiarism are understood to be, in part, a manifestation of a change in our underlying relationship with information. This change is itself a consequence of economic and cultural shifts, such as the move to knowledge or information modes of wealth creation, and the widespread adoption of digital information technologies. In our discussion we use the metaphor of the "economy" because it seems to us that information is traded through gathering, refining, and presenting activities, through transactions of effort in networks of values, and that trade brings benefits through the assessment of work and the conferment of awards. We suggest that this economy has changed significantly in recent years, and it may be that its modes of operation no longer represent a shared culture across the groups who utilize and who maintain the academy.

In recent years, and in many places, the cultural economies of information handling and academic practices, as well as the ways in which they dynamically interrelate, have changed. Several factors account for those changes, including

- the deployment of information communication technologies in their myriad forms and functions
- political initiatives seeking to increase the numbers of people gaining higher-education qualifications, and broadening the access to higher education
- shifts in the way that education is funded, and changes in the modes of delivery that can be managed within the resources available (including increased student numbers and corollary reductions in time available for teaching delivery and assessment activities, distance and blended learning initiatives)
- the increasing corporatism of higher-education institutions, and the change in ethos that comes with a customer/consumer role for students

These changes, and concomitant shifts in the intellectual infrastructure of attitudes, skills, and performances through which education operates, have affected concepts of the ownership of knowledge and its expression, as well as the ways that the worth or value of knowledge is understood. We contend that recent changes have disrupted higher education's historical intellectual infrastructure; clearly some parts of the current model sit at odds with it. We note that the preexisting model of a shared intellectual community lingers on in many ways; one effect is that for adherents to the older model, plagiarism has come to represent the worst consequences of the new consumerist model of higher education. We also note that its incidence has increased (both in actual acts and in the perception of the acts), and there have been changes in the understanding of its meaning and consequences.

Although commonly described as a form of cheating, plagiarism can be understood as a behavioral activity within a community concerned with the worth of knowledge and the values of academic activities. In particular plagiarism is about attitudes to the ownership of knowledge, and taking appropriate responsibility for the expression of ideas. Plagiarism does not stand in isolation. Where it is found it exists as a pattern of transgressive behaviors, relative to other patterns that are conforming. Plagiarism is the behavioral and concrete response to traditional academic attitudes about the ownership of ideas, and about the expression of ideas, about the use and understanding of conventions of citation, reference, quotation, acknowledgment, bibliography, allusion, and intertextuality, as well as about the value of doing these things in the way the academy requires and the worth of the academy itself.

Particular ways of dealing with the ownership of ideas and the worth of expression characterize cultural activities and distinguish one from another, and are declared through sign systems of diverse kinds. Academic practice "owns" one set of attitudes and maintains a sign system through which they are demonstrated. That sign system marks the academic out among other cultural activities through the codes and modes of reference and citation that express and consolidate the academic infrastructure in both form and presence. This academic sign system performs an explicit citation function in that it marks out extracts from other texts, signaling where information and ideas have been found, through typographic differences and the ways that names and dates are used. Within these academic codes repetition creates a redundancy of utterances that, themselves, signify a form of ritual.

Using the sign system of academic citation embodies a cognitive position; a way of thinking about knowledge, and of expressing our relationship with information. As a set of marks, citation inscribes beliefs about the ownership of knowledge by others and by ourselves, about the worth of the author, the value of the academy, and the cultural systems in which those activities take place. Failure to use, or to use correctly, the codes of citation is taken as a failure in the cognitive position, and is taken to demonstrate improper attitudes about information. In turn this is understood as a form of appropriation, a taking of ownership that is not due, a form of theft, deception, or cheating, and constitutes plagiarism. At the very least, a failure to use the signs of ownership and expression is taken as an indicator of ignorance of the system, and that ignorance is seen as a failure of the individual.

In the same way that a coin or banknote has a monetary value in one country, but becomes only a souvenir or keepsake in another, so attitudes about knowledge and information circulate within cultural practices. Across the broader culture many activities embody and inscribe attitudes about ownership of knowledge that are markedly different from those of the academy. This may create eddies of resistance and flows of concordance within the experiences of groups and individuals when they engage with the academy's codes. As an example, the use of sampling in music where the pleasure of the text may in part derive from getting the reference. This is a form of implicit citation, and it can be seen to be oppositional in form and cultural meaning to the explicit citation required by the academy. Similarly, we see the complex intertextual referencing of films and computer games, those knowing, allusive in-jokes that thicken the pleasures of those texts through implicit citation. And here we note, in passing, the Modernist tradition of borrowing, best seen in the poetry of Ezra Pound and T. S. Eliot's *The Waste Land*.

This concern with ownership, expression, value, and worth supports our economic metaphor as a means of understanding plagiarism in higher education. It directs attention to networks of exchange and transaction; to cultural economies where values, behaviors, and moral judgments are inscribed in material objects such as essays, posters, and performed spoken presentations; and to an individual's expenditure of effort balanced against anticipated outcomes, rewards, and gains. In broad terms we characterize the academic as someone who balances *effort* and *values* (Szabo and Underwood; Collins, Judge, and Rickman).

Effort
- Energy required to complete task (physical and cognitive, time taken, resources needed)
- What else the energy and time could be used for (personal and social life, part-time work, other academic tasks)
- Energy available to complete
- Apprehension of task: understanding of what is required, prior experience of similar tasks, reward level from prior experience, feeling of preparedness (precursor learning, established knowledge), detailing of outcomes (format, conventions, presentation)
- Motivations of plagiarism: the effort saved by taking shortcuts (reframing task, less-than-best effort, plagiarism, other cheating)

Values
- Opportunities for plagiarism: likelihood of detection, consequences of detection, attitudes of teaching staff, moral opinions
- Relevance of task to future career aspirations ("necessary" knowledge, transferable skills)
- Worth of this task as a scholarly activity (process versus expression)
- Worth of scholarly activities generally (desire to learn, intrinsic moti-

vation, curiosity, valuing knowledge of others, valuing knowledge for itself)

- Importance of this task in relation to other activities (before or after)
- Role of higher education: functional attainment of qualification versus opportunity for betterment of self

The "intellectual infrastructure" of the academy, including its ethos and myths, sustains a particular effort:value ratio that is inscribed in the behaviors of students and teachers and in the regulations of institutions. It holds an understanding of what is normal behavior in terms of acknowledging and claiming ownership of ideas and their expression, and, by extension, an understanding of what is transgressive behavior, and what that means, in terms of the likelihood of detection, sanctions, punishments, and so on. For individuals who share the ethos, the motivations and opportunities for plagiarism are minimized, and plagiarism, when it happens, is seen as the outcome of a deliberate act that constitutes deception, cheating, gaining of unfair advantage, an evasion of the benefits of learning for oneself, and a denial of the virtuous efforts and learning of others. As the academy engages with groups that do not share that ethos, or do not understand it, or who find it contradicts value:effort balances that are embedded elsewhere and have important cultural significance for the other group(s), then incidences of plagiarism may occur inadvertently (unknowing transgressions), or may be expressions of resistance to an erosion of an alternative, preferred effort:value balance. For instance, the implicit citation strategies of popular media or the detailed knowledge web of sports fans show few signs of what academics would see as necessary and appropriate.

The intellectual infrastructure is a product of wider cultural systems than the academy alone. Broadening access means including groups that have historically had little or no access to the academy, who bring their very different cultural experiences, that is their "meme-pool" (Blackmore 41) to the intellectual community of the academy. The cognitive processes involved in maintaining, for example, a positive view of the worth of scholarly activities may require considerable additional effort for a student whose cultural milieu does not otherwise view them so positively, or holds an ambiguous view of their worth. Similarly, broadening access may mean that the need to explain and justify academic criteria to new groups leads to exposing rather than strengthening the academy's intellectual and moral standards. And that may reveal internal contradictions within the infrastructure, or open out its conflicts with other codes, modes, and values in the wider culture. The recent widespread adoption of information technologies has disrupted higher education's traditional effort:value ratio in a number of ways. We center our discussion here on two aspects in particular—shifts in the signs of ownerships of texts produced by students, and in the signs of ownership and authority in the source materials they use.

Our media habitats include myriad signs of ownership: the unique signs of a person's voice, the way a musical instrument is used, the way paint is spread on a surface, how light is manipulated, or the camera angle used. All of these are indexical signs of original ownership in the sense that they are existentially tied to the creative and expressive acts of individuals, even if they are working through mechanical or digital processes. These "autographic" (McCullough), or process, signs are as distinct and personal as, say, manuscript handwriting.

While it is banal to say that the word-processed essay has replaced the handwritten one, it is important to note that this has come with a marked shift in the signs of ownership of the material written object. Handwriting, an autographic process, inscribes personal ownership throughout the material object in the idiosyncrasies of letterforms and in minor crossings out and amendments that litter the surface. For those who will remember them, the typewritten pages of an essay, dense with white blobs of correcting fluid or the backspace overtyping of a spelling error, carry in their material form an indexical sign field of personal effort and ownership. The word-processed text, say Times Roman 12-point with double-spaced lines (even, perhaps, the format supplied as a macro), is an allographic text, one produced by the instructions sent to a machine. While such a text is a field of signs, it is not so indexical of the author as one produced by an autographic process. Personal ownership is less clearly signed in the object itself, and the evidences of cognitive ownership are equally diluted. It is possible that acts of "compilation" that appeared owned when autographically inscribed, seem less clearly owned when allographically presented. While copying out a section of a source text by hand signifies cognitive engagement of some kind, copying when done mechanically is more readily identified as plagiarism than it may have been before.

"Prior to the widespread use of the Internet," say Collins, Judge, and Rickman, "plagiarism principally entailed physically assembling hard copies of sources to plagiarise from and then transcribing and integrating them into a coherent, hopefully seamless essay format" (5). Copy and paste, an integral part of the authoring of word-processed texts, amplifies acts of compilation because it changes the economy of effort:value within the allographic relative to that which was available within the autographic. Handwriting a text, laboriously and accurately copying a section from a source text (and academic practice does require accurate quotation), may well require more effort than rephrasing the section in one's own words. *Putting it in your own words* is taken as a clear signifier of ownership, a demonstration of cognitive engagement. However, such intervention requires skills of summary, paraphrase, and précis, as well as an extensive vocabulary of terms, phrases, and words. Bernstein's work on elaborated and restricted codes suggests that those may well be sociolinguistic performances and cognitive skills indigenous in some social groups, but not all. A student with little sociolinguistic experience of, and expertise in, rephrasing to a uniform authorial voice will relate to rewording a section of a source in a way very different from a student who finds rewording it straightforward and who also very likely shares the effort:value position of the academy.

The resources of the Internet, and other information available in electronic form, are often experienced, and their ownership thought of, as a "commons." That is to say, they are experienced like a public park, say, rather than a cinema. Websites are like a park because access is free and requires no simple payment and because what happens there is unstructured—in a park you can picnic, play games, lounge, chatter, do what you will. In a cinema a particular event takes place; it is organized, structured, and provided for you at a given time. A park is made up of air, sky, grass, the natural world (and increasingly signed as "natural" as styles of municipal gardening shift from formal beds and clocks to simulated wildernesses), while the cinema experience, the darkness, volume of sound, brightness of light, construction of narrative, is markedly artificial. The pleasures of a park are largely a product of one's own actions; the pleasures of the cinema are provided for you. Set against the park, the cinema is more readily identifiable as a consumable product. Set against the cinema, the park is difficult to understand as a consumable object.

The sign systems of activities and pleasures, ownership and payment, for a park or a cinema distinctly communicate different concepts of product and ownership. The film-viewing experience is clearly identifiable and so can be clearly owned and purchased through payment. The less distinct ownership of the park, and of the experiences there, models the apparently freely accessible digital resources available online, and the user experience of being there. If we think of payment for the Web, it is as a payment to a phone company or to a broadband provider for the line not the content, rather like paying the bus fare to the park. And when we get there, as in the park, the pleasures come from what we do, through our own effort, from our own ergodic activities (Aarseth 1). A key concept in the current discussion of hypertext and hypermedia, *ergodic* is derived from the two roots of *ergos*, "work," and *hodos*, "path." It describes the path through a hypertext that is formed by the reader's work, his mainly intellectual effort in following links, making choices between them, understanding how this-that-is-here-now relates to that-which-has-been-before, and which constructs the particular instance of a hypertext. In terms of our discussion of effort:value balance, this is a useful concept, as it reminds us that when using hypertexts, and the Web especially, the effort involved seems to emphasize the personal effort of the reader, and the uniqueness of her experience, which, of course, she feels she owns.

The park experience itself is not readily identifiable; it is intangible, indistinct, and particularly individual. Ownership of the place, and the experiences had there are unclear. The signs of ownership in a cinema are at once identifiable and tangible and can be shared with many others. Access is ritualized (often architecturally, certainly in the exchange of money for ticket), and there is a clear and distinct organization, structure, provision—an identifiable product that is owned somewhere. In the clarity of its signs of ownership and its implicit acts of provision the cinema models the "book and library" and the canon as a source of information, while the park models online information gathering.

While the historical intellectual infrastructure of the academy references the "cinema" model of ownership in its implicit understanding of effort:value, the increasing use of Internet and digital resources exposes students to the "park" model of the ownership of the material they work with. Access is free, the place is unstructured, and what comes from being there is the outcome of your personal activities and effort. When compared to the "book and library," the sign systems implicit in the experience of the Web make ownership less distinct, harder to be clear about; it may create the illusion that the stuff is unowned, and that what is found is somehow the product of the user's efforts and so owned by him. This confusion of ownership is compounded by the incunabula nature of the Web itself where conventions of declaring identity and ownership are not established, where the stable sign system of ownership needed for citation is not necessarily present, and where the concept of ownership collides with ideas about authority, reliability, or standing of a source. Confusions of ownership such as this mark a shift in the intellectual infrastructure and in the play of effort and values. We suggest that often that shift requires of the student a greater effort, and of a different kind, than required in a "book and library" structure. That additional effort may not be readily accommodated in assessment tasks that reward content and product rather than practice and process; in turn, it creates conditions in effort:value ratios such that plagiarism may appear to be to the individual's advantage.

Within the broader economy, effort required to take ownership of information is balanced against effort required to locate the information. This equation has shifted from acts of finding books, often named within a canon and distributed on shelves, to acts of searching for information sources—and this has implications for ownership in significant and subtle ways. Library books, as tangible objects, are clearly owned, often inscribed with library index numbers and institution stamps; they have authority embodied in their presence. The process by which they have come into being and into place gives, of itself, the imprimatur of an authoritative and reliable source. And the same extends to individually owned copies of the library book; the signs inscribed by the library on its book are carried as ghostly echoes on the ones students own and carry around. Online information is not only less clearly owned and ownable, but it also has less clear authority partly because we have, as yet, no sign system for that authority. Finding a book brings the authority of the source, while searching for information online means having to gauge, evaluate, and establish the value of the source itself, a significant shift in the play of effort within acts of studentship.

This is made more complex by the fact that information can change and become outdated. Books change relatively slowly and stay out-of-date longer. Internet resources potentially change very rapidly but maintain currency. In terms of how memes are understood, these are the relative balances of fecundity, felicity, and longevity. From the library of books to the Internet, knowledge has become transient and contingent, as it can be superseded tomorrow by a newer version, and so the older version is no longer valid. Given that it needs less effort to find the new version than to recall the older one, because memorizing and recalling take more effort, and, besides, what was memorized is no longer valid, it makes sense economically not to own, as such, but to know how to find when needed. However, the academy asks for quotation and reference partly to show that a student has taken ownership of ideas. But if powerful parallel sign systems indicate those ideas are contingent and transient, then the purpose of quotation and reference is reframed and may seem questionable. The historical ethos of the academy values a play of fecundity, felicity, and longevity that is antithetical to online information sources, and possibly to the aspirations of many students and their perception of the skills needed for employment. In a time of rapidly changing knowledge, and a shifting currency of what it is valuable to know, how do students understand the relevance of their studies, how can they gauge their "need for knowledge in the future," or judge the "future usefulness of knowledge gained through sincere work" (Szabo and Underwood 182)?

In educational systems whose response to rapid change is (quite rightly) to emphasize transferable skills, the balances of the intellectual infrastructure shift significantly. Transferable skills are inherently about knowing *how to* rather than knowing *about,* about processes rather than content, because content is contingent but processes can be used in many places. However, it may be quite difficult for students to identify the relevance of transferable skills in learning and assessment processes that emphasize the assessment of product and content *(about)* rather than practice and process *(how to),* if they do not understand the context of their learning of transferable skills and are not able to see what knowing *how to* means. These thoughts, and others, led us to develop ways we could enhance students' information-handling skills, to enable them to recognize and value transferable skills, and to be rewarded for process as well as product. That developed into the i-map.

The i-Map

The i-map is a way of recording the research stages of a project, focusing on the information-handling process. It produces an artifact that can be assessed against stated criteria, and so can be used to reward the information-handling skills involved in many academic activities. An i-map logs such things as finding sources, reading and evaluating them, taking ownership of ideas, formulating a response or argument, citing sources when appropriate, and building a bibliography, in a visual account of the process.

An i-map may include the following:

- Annotated book-lists, articles, website URLs, databases, electronic journals, media sources (newspapers, newsgroups, blogs, discussion boards)

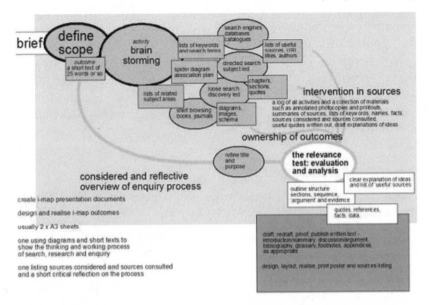

Doing an I-Map: A Typical Process of Enquiry Leading to a Written
Text or Poster

- Diagrams: brainstorms, spiders, flow diagrams, pie charts showing
  connections and relationships between elements
- Graphic elements: symbols, drawings, boxes, circles, arrows, colors,
  highlights that organize elements into relationships
- Words: keywords, search term strings, definitions, quotations, bon
  mots
- Images: book covers, film stills, screen grabs, case studies, and any
  illustrations that are useful to an understanding of the subject

It uses space, layout, typography, lines and arrows to build sequence, links,
and interrelationships within the visual representation. The act of creating
an i-map requires reflective thinking about the process, and inscribes that
reflection in the visual representation. The i-map is a pedagogic strategy
that enables teachers to identify transferable process skills, and to reward
them by shifting the emphasis away from a single-end-point, content-led
submission. It enables the assessment of information-handling skills based
on evidence rather than inferred from the qualities of a written text. The
i-map rebalances the play of effort and values in the economies of aca-

demic activities, lessening the motivation to plagiarize, as well as reducing the opportunities for plagiarism, while providing a place to develop information-handling skills and to discuss the myriad issues around the ownership of knowledge, the uses of information, and the values of the academy. More information about the i-maps and examples of i-maps created by some of our students are online at http://www.art-design.herts.ac.uk/a/mihs/index.htm.

Works Cited

Aarseth, Espen J., *Cybertexts*. Baltimore: Johns Hopkins University Press, 1997.

Bernstein, Basil, "Elaborated and Restricted Codes: Their Social Origins and Some Consequences." *American Anthropologist,* n. s. 66 no. 3, pt. 2 (December 1964): 55–69. The Ethnography of Communication. Online at http://www.jstor.org/view/ 00027294/ap020359/02a00040/0

Blackmore, Susan, *The Meme Machine*. Oxford: Oxford University Press, 1999.

Collins, Alan, Guy Judge, and Neil Rickman. "Thinking Economically about Plagiarism." *Proceedings of the 39th Annual Meeting of the Canadian Economics Association/Association canadienne d'economique,* McMaster University, Hamilton, May 2005. http://economics.ca/2005/papers/0308.pdf, consulted July 4, 2007.

Graham, Roz, and Mike Hart. "Plagiarism Is a Complex Issue, but—Universities Must Articulate a Moral Vision and Live up to It!" http://mike-hart.com/cv/papers/plag_com2.doc, consulted July 9, 2007.

McCullough, Malcolm. *Abstracting Craft: The Practiced Digital Hand*. Cambridge: MIT Press, 1998.

Szabo, Attilla, and Jean Underwood. "Cybercheats: Is Information and Communication Technology Fuelling Academic Dishonesty?" *Active Learning in Higher Education* 5, no. 2 (2004): 180–99. http://alh.sagepub.com/cgi/content/abstract/5/2/180, consulted July 9, 2007.

"Fair Use," Copyright Law, and the Composition Teacher

Martine Courant Rife

In our roles as writing teachers, we have been asked to adopt postmodern practices, including releasing old-fashioned notions of single authorship and an obsolete pedagogy that forbids plagiarism under a "detect and punish" regime (DeVoss and Porter 198; DeVoss and Rosati). Instead, we are to teach "digital ethics" and fair use. What exactly is "fair use"? This is a doctrine writing teachers need to understand because, while public figures such as Lawrence Lessig, Jessica Litman, and Siva Vaidhyanathan argue that the law needs to be changed, we have classes to teach. Writing teachers increasingly teach writing on networked computers, and therefore our need to understand the basic doctrine of fair use is as great as our need to understand the rules against plagiarism. This essay first reviews current U.S. copyright law, and then briefly traces the concept of fair use from its inception as "fair abridgment" in eighteenth-century England to its current interpretation in U.S. case law.

Overview of Current U.S. Copyright Law

U.S. copyright law has become a confusing mix of statutes and rulings that can encompass invention, imitation, compilation, and appropriation. A variety of stakeholders have fought to establish control over intellectual property (IP) for commercial purposes; in the process, the noncommercial, educational uses have come under increasing pressure. These influential interactions include the habits of writers, agents, and publishers, and such varied secondary uses as film and recording companies (Vaidhyanathan; Porter; DeVoss and Porter; Hart-Davidson; Bartow). The tension between stakeholders who wish to share and stakeholders who wish to contain and control information is viewed as a "battle," "war," and "fight" (Litman; Yu; DeVoss and Porter 185). The writing student and teacher have become actors, willingly or not, in determining how copyright operates (Porter). Indeed, writing teachers are key players in these "battles" because students often have an unclear notion of what constitutes appropriate use and citation; too often their only knowledge of copyright comes from the current publicity over downloading music.

U.S. copyright law is a statutory law; therefore one must always begin by reading the statute. A full copy of copyright statute, Title 17, U.S. Code, is readily available on the Web (United States Copyright Office). Underlying the U.S. Code, the Constitution grants Congress the power "to promote the progress of science and useful arts, by securing for limited times to authors and inventors the exclusive right to their respective writings and discoveries" (Art. 1, Sec. 8). Under Title 17, copyright holders receive a limited monopoly with respect to certain uses of their work. Section 102 of the the Copyright Law of 1976 (effective 1978) states that all original, fixed works are protected, including literary, musical, and dramatic works, dance, pictures and sculptures, movies and other audiovisual works, sound recordings, and architectural works. As of 1978, works that are original and fixed do not need to be registered in order to receive copyright protection. Instead, a limited monopoly is automatically granted to the copyright owner. Because copyright protection is automatic, all works are copyrighted unless an owner opts out of the system by taking affirmative steps, such as marking his work with language that gives up any of the copyrights. To completely opt out of our current copyright regime, an author donates her work to the public domain. To partially opt out, an author might license for money or donate one or more of her "copyrights" to others. For example, a Creative Commons Attribution-ShareAlike license (Creative Commons) allows others to use the designated work noncommercially, as long as they give the copyright owner credit and allow others to use their work. The ShareAlike license divvies up the copyrights held by the owner, and makes the use of those rights conditional on certain requirements.

"Fair Use" from Its Inception to Current Interpretation in U.S. Case Law

Copyrights can be divided among different stakeholders because a copyright is a bundle of rights. While copyright law defines the kind of work protected, it also defines the strands in this bundle of protections. Section 106 gives copyright holders exclusive rights to reproduce, prepare derivations, distribute, publicly display, and perform the copyrighted work. It is this bundle of rights that copyright holders may parse out to others, or donate completely to the public domain. To say or write, "I own the copyright in that piece" is vague. When I hear this, I wonder, which right of copyright? Instead, to be clear, one might say or write, "I own all rights conferred to me by copyright law," or, "I reserve all rights," or, "I have licensed the right to copy, perform, distribute, and display my work, but I've retained the right to create derivative works." For example, the Creative Commons ShareAlike license creates a hybrid license that conditionally gives away strands in the bundle of rights: to make derivative works, perform, publicly display, and make and distribute copies, as long as the users of those rights credit the copyright holder, and use the material for noncommercial purposes. However, a license to use is not fair use. It is a contractual arrangement set up by copyright holders. "Copyright" could become worthless under a clever publisher's agreement. It is not unheard of for publishers to offer authors contracts that give publishers all rights under the copyright statute, but leave the author with the "copyright"—an empty shell with no rights attached.

Fair use is a doctrine that preserves certain types of uses not protected by copyright. Therefore, to use a work under fair use is never to infringe on the owner's copyright. Section 107 defines fair use as codified by the courts and contains the prose we as educators so often rely on as we venture into the digital writing realm with our students:

§ 107. Limitations on exclusive rights: fair use
Notwithstanding the provisions of sections 106 and 106A, the fair use of a copyrighted work, including such use by reproduction in copies or phonorecords [*sic*] or by any other means specified by that section, for purposes such as criticism, comment, news reporting, teaching (including multiple copies for classroom use), scholarship, or research, is not an infringement of copyright. In determining whether the use made of a work in any particular case is a fair use the factors to be considered shall include—
(1) the purpose and character of the use, including whether such use is of a commercial nature or is for nonprofit educational purposes;
(2) the nature of the copyrighted work;
(3) the amount and substantiality of the portion used in relation to the copyrighted work as a whole; and

(4) the effect of the use upon the potential market for or value of the copyrighted work. (U.S. Code, Title 17, Sec. 107)

Section 107 defines four elements to be used by the courts when making a fair-use determination. It also clearly states that fair use is a "limitation"; plus, the statute says the listed uses are "not an infringement." Section 107 provides the exception to the copyright owner's right to use. However, court interpretation has complicated this clarity. Legal scholars tell us fair use is nothing more than a skimpy sliver, or a concept now being compacted into ineffectuality (Lessig; Bartow).

The term *fair use* first arose in the American judicial system in the case of *Lawrence v. Dana* (1869). However, the concept, known as *fair abridgment*, appeared in the early English cases of *Gyles v. Wilcox* (1740), *Dodsely v. Kinnersley* (1761), *Cary v. Kearsely* (1802), and *Roworth v. Wilkes* (1807) (Duhl). While the term *fair use* did not appear in American courts until 1869, the English concept was appropriated in the 1841 case of *Folsom v. Marsh*. In the *Folsom* case, the defendant had written a biography of George Washington. The plaintiff claimed the defendant used excerpts of letters from the plaintiff's earlier published and copyrighted biography. While the defendant had copied 353 pages of the plaintiff's multivolume work, the copied material amounted to less than 6 percent of the total. However, the court held for the plaintiff, finding that the defendant had copied the most important material in the plaintiff's earlier volumes. In the opinion, Justice Story set out the framework that was codified over 130 years later in Section 107 of the 1976 Copyright Act. Judge Story included concerns about how much of the original work was taken, and stated that the issue was one of whether "piracy" occurred; he factored in comparative use as well as "the nature, extent, and value of the materials thus used; the objects of each work," considered whether there were "common sources of information" and asked if the alleged infringer had used the "same common diligence in the selection and arrangement of the materials" as the author of the original work *(Folsom)*. Judge Story emphasized that writers should be able to use others' work for "purposes of fair and reasonable criticism," but noted that the court must "look to the nature and objects of the selections made, the quantity and value of the materials used, and the degree in which the use may prejudice the sale, or diminish the profits, or supersede the objects, of the original work." Judge Story's discussion in the *Folsom* case sets forth the elements that were later folded into the four-factors fair-use test of Section 107.

Judge Story's 1841 opinion is accepted as part of our current fair-use analysis (Bartow; Duhl). However, judges struggle with case-by-case fact-specific analyses, applying the doctrine inconsistently, and they thereby increase public confusion (Duhl). This uncertainty permeates composition and rhetoric pedagogy and policy, culminating in what DeVoss and Porter describe as a potential floundering effect reflected in inconsistent teaching and professional practices (197). By studying the history of fair use along with current court interpretations, we can further our knowledge of this important doctrine and help our students contextualize both their use of the Web and their Web-composing practices. Fair use has only been considered four times by the Supreme Court since the enactment of the Copyright Act of 1976. Those four cases and their holdings are *Sony Corp of America v. Universal Studios, Inc.* (1984), *Harper & Row, Publishers, Inc. v. Nation Enterprises* (1985), *Stewart v. Abend* (1990), and *Campbell v. Acuff-Rose Music, Inc.* (1994).

In *Sony* the Court held that sale of VCRs did not equal contributory infringement of the plaintiff's copyrights. The Court concluded that since most VCR use was private, legal taping for later viewing, and that the plaintiffs had failed to establish harm to the potential markets for Universal Studios, that VCRs fell under fair use. In *Harper & Row*, former president Gerald Ford's memoirs were being prepared for publication by Nation Enterprises. Harper & Row published a magazine article containing excerpts. Using a fact-specific analysis, the Court held that the publication by Harper & Row, prior to the memoir release by Nation Enterprises, harmed the potential market. The Court held the use was not fair use. In *Stewart* the Court focused on copyright protection of the owner's exclusive right to create derivative works. Cornell Woolrich is the author of the story "It Had to be Murder." *Rear Window* is based largely on Woolrich's story. When MCA rereleased the film, suit was brought. The Court held that the film was not a "new work" falling under the protection of fair use. Other factors taken into account by the Court were the commercial nature of the work, the fact that the original work was creative rather than factual, and the fact that the rerelease harmed the copyright holder's ability to find new markets. In the final Supreme Court opinion, *Campbell*, 2 Live Crew created a parody of the Roy Orbison song "Pretty Woman." Balancing the four factors set forth in the fair-use doctrine, the Court held that the defendant's use was fair. The Court noted that the public-interest benefits of transformed songs were important, but remanded the case to the lower court for consideration on the issue of harm to the copyright holder's market.

To these four Supreme Court cases, I am going to add a fifth: *MGM v. Grokster* (2005). Even though *Grokster* did not directly consider fair use, it did directly interpret and narrow the holding in *Sony*. Disturbingly, the majority opinion failed to mention fair use as a factor in its considerations, while Justices Ginsberg and Breyer (in their respective concurrences) only mention the concept in passing (Porter and Rife). In *Grokster* the Court discussed the *Sony* case as it considered whether P2P (person-to-person) software distributors StreamCast and Grokster were vicariously liable for the copyright infringing uses of individual users of their software. The Court vacated the judgment of the lower court and found Grokster and Stream-Cast could be liable for damages and subject to injunction. The Court narrowed the protection of *Sony* (and thus the protection of fair use), stating that the Ninth Circuit holding in favor of Grokster was imbued with a misreading of *Sony*. Thus a determination of infringement in P2P contexts (dual-use distribution technologies) depends on a two-part test pursuant to *Grokster*. First one looks to the *Sony* safe harbor to see if there is substantial noninfringing use. If the use passes this standard, one then looks to whether the distributor showed intent to induce others to infringe.

In *Grokster,* the Court said that the supposed central question in *Sony,* whether or not substantial noninfringing uses exist for a certain product, is *not* the sole determining question on the issue of legal liability. The question instead is *What is the intent of the distributor?* If it is to cause others to infringe, then the distributor is liable regardless of whether or not substantial noninfringing uses are possible. In his concurrence Justice Breyer stated that the Court had gone from an environment of certainty (are there substantial noninfringing uses?) to an environment of uncertainty (what is the intent?). It is important to note that Justice Souter, who wrote the main opinion, never mentioned fair use. We could read *Grokster* as saying that what was once fair use, the private copying via taping of copyrighted materials (TV programs, music) is no longer defined as fair use. On the other hand, we might read *Grokster* as placing a lot of stock in "intent." We might draw the conclusion that as long as we as educators do not *intend* to break the law we are safe from liability (Porter and Rife). In *Grokster,* the Court rhetorically read a number of organizational communications in order to make its determination on whether or not intent to induce infringement was present. I conclude from the *Grokster* case that it is not enough simply to hold our good-faith intent in mind; we must also document and reflect on how we teach others to use technology that includes replicating work by others.

According to Duhl, the first four cases show the Supreme Court's reluctance to define clear boundaries for the fair-use doctrine. As a result, both copyright holders and users/remixers like us and our students are held in a legal limbo. And why should the Court make any concrete, universal determinations when no pressure is applied? The industry stakeholders would rather the educational institutions live in fear, adopting limiting and restrictive IP policies; these interests would rather we did not know exactly how to operate, and that we work under concerns of infringement liability. The uncertainty of the fair-use doctrine in educational settings is amplified by the lack of a Supreme Court opinion. On the other hand, because of quickly changing information streams and technological innovation, the uncertain, open-ended language of the fair-use doctrine may serve us well (Rife). To gain a better grasp of the language that is there, to push on the boundaries of legal interpretations of that language, to exploit the slipperiness of the U.S. fair-use doctrine for purposes of education, is to give ourselves and our students the critical agency we and they need in order to compose robust texts, including multimedia texts, in the digital age. Our understanding of the fair-use doctrine can be improved significantly by looking not only at the Supreme Court opinions, but also at the lower-court judicial opinions, some of which have dealt directly with determinations of fair use in an educational-copying context. In the 1914 case of *Macmillan v. King*, the court held that it was not fair use for a tutor to create an outline, incorporating quotes and following the organizational structure of a Harvard University professor's economic textbook. In a later 1962 case, the court held that when a teacher distributed a musical arrangement adapted from a copyrighted musical composition, it was not fair use *(Wihtol)*. In *Encyclopedia Britannica Educational Corp. v. Crooks* (1982) the court held that the practice of a nonprofit educational services cooperative, in taping educational, state-funded television programs for collection and nonprofit, scholastic viewing later, was not a fair use. The next year the court held it was not a fair use for a home economics teacher to make "fifteen copies of an eleven page excerpt of a thirty-five page cake decorating booklet for her students" (Bartow 11).

Pursuant to a line of cases commonly referred to as the copy-shop cases *(Basic Books, Harper & Row v. Tyco, Addison-Wesley, Princeton University Press v. Michigan Document Service, Inc. [MDS])*, settlements have been made such that course packs cannot be copied unless accompanied by written permission of the copyright holder, or a statement from faculty members certifying the copies were in compliance with guidelines. Universities have thus agreed to adopt guidelines, and if faculty do not follow the guidelines, they face personal liability. The *Princeton v. MDS* is worth special remark since it includes three major presses, Princeton University Press, Macmillan, and St. Martin's Press suing a photocopy shop, Michigan Document Services (MDS). The court found MDS's copying to be a willful infringement. Damages against MDS were $30,000 statutory damages, $326,318.52 attorney's fees, and injunctive relief. In *MDS* the publishers targeted Mr. Smith (like MGM targeting Grokster), a fair-use crusader and owner of MDS, and brought him down. The *MDS* case reminds us always to do a complete rhetorical evaluation of case law and consider all stakeholder interests when making a fair-use determination. We are stakeholders on both sides of the issue, the copyright holders and those who need to use others' works in order to do writing and research. Ann Bartow asserts that under current court rulings, the reproduction of copyrighted materials for educational purposes is a "commercial" use; since any commercial use creates a presumptive harm to the copyright holder's market, and market harm is the single most important factor in current judgments, reproducing copyrighted material for educational use no longer falls under fair use.

Bartow reminds us that the Internet has so blended public and private, commercial and noncommercial, that every use is deemed "commercial." How these photocopying cases translate to other kinds of copying or remixing that go on in the classroom and beyond, remains uncertain. We can suspect that big media and publishers, once their attention is had, will unify for strength. Bartow argues that the courts could easily find faculty members as liable, if not more liable, than the copy shops. She speculates that the reasons that faculty members are usually not sued might be fear of bad press, or because under Section 504 of the Copyright Act, multiple-copying educators are only liable for actual damages, which are usually nominal. In order to maintain such limited liability, educators must be acting under a good-faith belief that they are not infringing. How can any of us be acting under "good faith" if we do not understand basic copyright law and fair use? And how can we expect our students to act in "good faith" if we do not teach them what the issues are? Additionally, if our institutions have restrictive guidelines that we disobey, you can bet that the courts will not listen to our pleas when we explain. Judges love to use "official guidelines" as heuristics for evaluation. Our institutional guidelines will be used, and the courts will tell us that, if we do not approve of the guidelines, we should change them rather than engage in blatant civil disobedience.

While Bartow recommends active assertion of our copyrights, even subversion of overly restrictive rules, Lessig tells us that our overreliance on fair use restricts our ability to freely exchange information without fear of legal liability (139–45). Lessig rightly points out that since under our current law, every use is a *regulated* use (because of automatic copyright protection on all fixed works), our *only* justification for unauthorized use is "fair use." Because the fair-use doctrine was not created to bear this burden, he argues (145), the law should be changed.

Yes, the law needs to be changed, but it seems unlikely at the present moment especially since automatic copyright protection is needed for the United States to be in compliance with international IP treaties. In the meantime, as educators we must operate under some understanding of the doctrine as it stands. Of course we should be concerned with fair-use policy and the trend of recent U.S. courts that repeatedly emphasizes the "property rights of the author as the paramount purpose of copyright law" (Vaidhyanathan 80). At the end of the twentieth century and the beginning of the twenty-first, U.S. courts have repeatedly emphasized the protection of property rights of the publishers and media conglomerates as the paramount purpose of copyright law. For example, the recent post-*Grokster* Seventh Circuit fair-use case, *BMG Music, et al. v. Cecilia Gonzalez* (December 2005), held that private downloading of music from the Internet was not a fair use even though the individual already owned some of the CDs featuring the downloaded songs because doing so impinged on the copyright holder's ability to enter new markets. Courts are increasingly focusing on the market impact of any use. Pursuant to *Gonzalez,* even though money or profit is not sought by the user of copyrighted works, the user can still be held to infringe on others' markets. U.S. copyright law has almost been rewritten by the courts and Congress so as to eliminate any consideration whatsoever based on public good.

Writing scholars and teachers are in a unique position to engage in civic participation, advocacy, and teaching, so as to emphasize the public good in sharing information as fully as possible, while still giving credit. It might be that we as educators need to convene and craft our own fair-use guidelines that will allow us to be able to teach in digital environments. After all, our students are not normally selling their classroom assignments for money, and yet under *Gonzalez,* their cutting and pasting of images and texts off the Web could be interpreted as impeding the copyright holders' ability to enter the "new" market of new media composing in the educational setting.

Conclusion

I encourage digital literacies if students can situate their fair use of material within the current copyright regime. Students should be introduced to basic IP concepts and categories such as trademark, service mark, copyright, and plagiarism, and should know where to find needed definitions effectively and efficiently. Students should be able to make at least cursory evaluations regarding where information comes from, who owns it, and what rights are offered. Working with students to uncover the intricacies of IP law and fair use, focusing on key legal cases, helps students understand the economic, legal, and social issues surrounding the use of information. By discussing legal damages assessed in various infringement cases, by talking about lawsuits such as *Folsom, Sony, Campbell, Napster, Grokster, Google Print,* and *Kelly v. Arriba Soft,*[1] students can understand the potential implications of using others' work. By looking at culturally significant perspectives embodied in law and governmental agencies, such as the United States Patent and Trademarks Office's database of Native American insignia, students can make autonomous decisions about their own comfort level and definition of ethical and legal use. There are no fixed lines or rules here. Students need to know what their options are in order to act responsibly and within their own political, social, and personal beliefs. Studying the history of fair use helps them understand the impact of recent court decisions. As educators, the discourse of fair use should be just as much ours as is the discourse of "writing."

Note

1. *Google Print* and *Kelly* are both search engine fair-use cases. *Kelly* held that the use of thumbnail images as search tools was a fair use (Band). The American Association of Publishers lawsuit against Google Print is still being decided at this writing; however on January 25, 2006, Electronic Frontier Foundation carried a story reporting that the Nevada District court ruled that the Google cache is a fair use. This holding could influence the larger *Google Print* case (see "Google Cache").

Works Cited

A&M Records, Inc. v. Napster, Inc. (9th Cir. 2001). 239 F.3d 1004).
Addison-Wesley Publishing Co., Inc. et al. v. New York University, et al., 1983 Copyright L. Dec. ¶ 25,544 (S.D.N.Y. 1983).
Band, Jonathan. "The Google Print Library Project: A Copyright Analysis." 2005. http://www.policyband.com/doc/googleprint.pdf, consulted February 2, 2006.

Bartow, Ann. "Educational Fair Use in Copyright: Reclaiming the Right to Photocopy Freely." *University of Pittsburgh Law Review* 60 (1998): 149–230. http://ssrn .com/abstract=506983, consulted April 10, 2005.

Basic Books, Inc. v. Kinko's Graphic Corp. 758 F. Supp. 1522 (S.D.N.Y. 1991).

BMG Music, et al. v. Cecilia Gonzalez. 430 F.3d 888 (7th Cir. 2005) (No. 05–1314).

Breyer, Stephen, and Sandra O'Connor. Concurring Opinion, *MGM v. Grokster,* 545 U.S. 1 (2005). http://www.eff.org/IP/P2P/MGM_v_Grokster/04–480.pdf, consulted July 9, 2007.

Campbell v. Acuff-Rose Music, Inc. 510 U.S. 569, 583–85 (1994).

Cary v. Kearsely. 4 Esp. 168, 170 Eng. Rep. 679 (1802).

Creative Commons. June 7, 2006. http://www.creativecommons.org, consulted July 5, 2007.

DeVoss, Dànielle Nicole, and James E. Porter. "Why Napster Matters to Writing: File-sharing as a New Ethic of Digital Delivery." *Computers and Composition* 23 (2005): 178–210.

DeVoss, Danielle, and Annette C. Rosati. "'It Wasn't Me Was It?' Plagiarism and the Web." *Computers and Composition* 19 (2002): 191–203.

Dodsely v. Kinnersley. 27 Eng. Rep. 270 (Ch. 1761).

Duhl, Gregory E. "Old Lyrics, Knock-off Videos, and Copycat Comic Books: The Fourth Fair Use Factor in U.S. Copyright Law." *Syracuse Law Review* 54 (2004): 665–738.

Electronic Frontier Foundation. http://www.eff.org, consulted June 6, 2006.

Encyclopedia Britannica Educational Corp. v. Crooks. 542 F. Supp. 1156 (W.D.N.Y. 1982).

Folsom v. Marsh. 9 F. Cas. 342, 6 Hunt Mer. Mag. 175 (C.C.D. Mass. 1841). http://www.faculty.piercelaw.edu/redfield/library/Pdf/case-folsom.marsh.pdf, consulted April 17, 2005.

Ginsberg, Ruth Bader, William Rehnquist, and Anthony Kennedy. Concurring Opinion, *MGM v. Grokster,* 545 U.S. 1 (2005). http://www.eff.org/IP/P2P/MGM_v_ Grokster/04–480.pdf, consulted July 9, 2007.

"Google Cache Ruled Fair Use." http://www.eff.org/deeplinks/archives/004344.php, consulted July 9, 2007.

Gyles v. Wilcox. 26 Eng. Rep. 489 (Ch. 1740).

Hart-Davidson, Bill. "On Writing, Technical Communication, and Information Technology: The Core Competencies of Technical Communication." *Technical Communication* 48, no. 2 (2001): 145–55.

Harper & Row, Publishers, Inc. v. Nation Enters. 471 U.S. 539 (1985).

Harper & Row v. Tyco Copy Services, 1981 U.S. Dist. LEXIS 13113, Copy.L. Rep. (CCH) P25230 (D. Conn. Jan. 19, 1981).

Kelly v. Arriba Soft. 336 F.3d 811 (9th Cir. 2003).

Lawrence v. Dana. 15 F. Cas. 26, 40 (C.C.D. Mass. 1869) (No. 8136).

Lessig, Lawrence. *Free Culture: How Big Media Uses Technology and the Law to Lock Down Culture and Control Creativity.* New York: Penguin, 2004.

Litman, Jessica. *Digital Copyright.* Amherst, New York: Prometheus Books, 2001.

Marcus v. Rowley. 695 F.2d 1171 (9th Cir. 1983).

Macmillan Co. v. King, 223 F. 862 (D. Mass. 1914).

MGM v. Grokster. 545 U.S. 1 (2005). http://www.eff.org/IP/P2P/MGM_v_Grokster/ 04–480.pdf, consulted July 9, 2007.

Porter, James. "The Chilling of Digital Information: Technical Communicators as Public Advocates." In *Technical Communication and the World Wide Web in the New Millennium,* ed. Michael Day and Carol Lipson, 243–59. Mahway, NJ: Erlbaum, 2005.

Porter, James, and Martine Courant Rife. "MGM v. Grokster: Implications for Educators and Writing Teachers." WIDEpaper no. 1, June 2005. http://www.wide.msu .edu/widepapers/grokster, consulted June 28, 2005.

Princeton University Press v. Michigan Document Services., Inc. 1996 FED App. 0357P (6th Cir.) http://fairuse.stanford.edu/primary_materials/cases/michigan_document_ services/110896cofadec.html, consulted July 25, 2007.

Rife, Martine Courant. "Global Literacies for Judges: Canadian/US Judicial Opinion Approaches to Globalization in Copyright Contexts." May 5, 2006. http://papers .ssrn.com/sol3/papers.cfm?abstract_id=900743, consulted June 5, 2006.

Roworth v. Wilkes. 170 Eng. Rep. 889 (1807).

Sony Corp of America v. Universal Studios, Inc. 464 U.S. 417 (1984).

Stewart v. Abend. 495 U.S. 207 (1990).

United States Copyright Office. http://www.copyright.gov, consulted June 5, 2006.

United States Patent and Trademark Office. "Frequently Asked Questions about the Database of Native American Tribal Insignia." 2003. http://www.uspto.gov/web/ offices/tac/tribalfaq.htm, consulted April 2, 2005.

United States Patent and Trademark Office. "Trademark, Copyright or Patent?" 2004. http://www.uspto.gov/web/offices/tac/doc/basic/trade_defin.htm, consulted April 17, 2005.

Vaidhyanathan, Siva. *Copyrights and Copywrongs: The Rise of Intellectual Property and How It Threatens Creativity.* New York: New York University Press, 2001.

Wihtol v. Crow. 309 F.2d 777 (8th Cir.). 1962.

Yu, Peter K. "The Escalating Copyright Wars." *Hostra Law Review* 32 (2004): 907–51. http://ssrn.com/anstract=436693, consulted September 20, 2004.

Plagiarism

History and the Disciplining of Plagiarism

Michael Grossberg

I begin this essay with a story. It comes from a meeting of the Board of Editors of the *American Historical Review (AHR)* during my years as editor of the journal. The board, which consists of twelve prominent historians from around the country, sets policy for the journal. Like other editors of peer-reviewed journals, I wanted to speed up the publication process and thought I could do so by sending article manuscripts to reviewers electronically. When I proposed doing that, I expected resistance but not the kind I got. I thought I would have to deal with technophobia; instead I met the fear of plagiarism. Board members worried that if readers received manuscripts electronically, they would not be able to resist the temptation to lift information and ideas from them; conversely, they thought that established customary practices inhibited readers from plagiarizing print manuscripts. My proposal gave them an occasion to express their anxieties about the disciplining of plagiarism. As a result I had to scuttle the plan.

The *AHR* editorial board response suggests that plagiarism is understood by many academics to be a growing problem aided and abetted by technological change, declining ethical standards, and dwindling faith in disciplinary controls. As the story suggests, these worries have combined to make uncertainty a dominant disciplinary response to plagiarism. And so as my contribution to this volume, I want to use experiences in the trenches of struggles over plagiarism as a history journal editor to discuss three prime sources of that uncertainty. I will focus on professional, not student, writing because I think it most directly raises the disciplining challenges surfacing in current debates about plagiarism (Grossberg).

The Definition

Changing definitions are surely one source of uncertainty about the disciplining of plagiarism. Plagiarism has never been and is not now a stable term—it has and will continue to change. But there have been some consistent elements in our understanding and use of the concept. Historians, for example, have had a quite well developed definition of plagiarism with two critical components: organizational and experiential.

The most influential organizational definition of plagiarism has been promulgated by the major society of professional historians in the United States, the American Historical Association (AHA). Created in 1884, the AHA adopted a formal definition of plagiarism in 1987. As is often the case, a bitterly contested case identified a problem that compelled the search for a solution. In this instance, a tenure battle at Texas Tech University exposed the lack of clear standards for judging plagiarism among professional historians. Historian Jayme Sokolow stood accused of appropriating the work of another historian, Stephen Nissenbaum, in a book manuscript about early-nineteenth-century sexual and health reformers. Though the university denied Sokolow's bid for tenure, the difficulties that Nissenbaum and others faced in pursuing charges of plagiarism led the AHA to craft an official definition (Mallon 144–93; Weiner 195–200)

The resulting definition contains five central tenets. First, and most basically, it defined plagiarism as appropriating "the exact wording of another author without attribution." Second, it broadened the ethical misdeed to include the appropriation without proper attribution of another person's concepts, theories, rhetorical strategies, and interpretations. Third, the AHA definition declared plagiarism to be the failure to acknowledge the work of another, regardless of intent or of monetary or other form of gain. Fourth, the definition also recognized that the appropriation of another's words or ideas without proper attribution constituted an ethical and professional but not a legal infraction unless it slid into copyright infringement. Finally, the AHA declared enforcement to be a collective responsibility:

> All historians share responsibility for maintenance of the highest standards of intellectual integrity. When appraising manuscripts for publication, reviewing books, or evaluating peers for placement, promotion, and tenure, scholars must evaluate the honesty and reliability with which the historian uses primary and secondary source materials. Schol-

arship flourishes in an atmosphere of openness and candor, which should include the scrutiny and discussion of academic deception. (American Historical Association)

The AHA definition has become the most authoritative formal statement on plagiarism in my discipline.

I think the AHA definition of plagiarism is very compelling and useful. However, its meaning comes not simply from the wording in the statement itself but also from a complementary set of shared experiential definitions of plagiarism. Despite disclaimers like those in the AHA definition, the language and labels of criminal violation permeate all discussions of plagiarism and define it in most people's minds. It is considered theft, the act of stealing another's words or ideas and therefore one of the most serious of all academic crimes. It thus incurs a proportionate condemnation, activating what, in another context, sociolegal scholar Mona Lynch calls the "discourse of disgust" (530). By that she means words that aim to shame, ostracize, and condemn violators with labels like *thief* and *fraud*. Such shaming epithets pervade cases of plagiarism. Equally critical to an experiential definition of plagiarism is an understanding of it as professional victimization. Anger and a sense of powerlessness boil up when we see our ideas and research appropriated by someone else and presented as his own without acknowledging his source. I have tried to capture this feeling by suggesting that like the characters in Ray Bradbury's *Fahrenheit 451*, our books and articles constitute our intellectual personas in very fundamental ways. They are elemental parts of our self-definition as scholars and thus we feel their misappropriation as a personal violation (Grossberg, "Plagiarism," 1334).

As a journal editor, I also realized something of the Dreyfus-like experience that faces those charged with plagiarism. Like the French Jew falsely accused of treason by a virulently anti-Semitic military, those who think that they have been unfairly indicted with stealing someone else's words or ideas suffer an acute sense of anguish and unfairness that is also a critical part of the experiential definition of plagiarism. As I have learned in messages from those in the plagiarism dock, they fear dishonor and a blighted career and seek a means of vindication and redemption. These fears are well founded, as widely published author and federal judge Richard Posner makes clear: "The label 'plagiarist' can ruin a writer, destroy a scholarly career, blast a politician's chances for election, and cause the expulsion of a student from a college or university." Thus the ways we experience plagiarism create a complicated sense of victimization and vulnerability that are also critical to definitions of plagiarism.

Historian's definitions of plagiarism express beliefs and practices common to the humanities. They reveal the power of and dependence on the written word in our disciplines and thus our commensurate fear about its misappropriation. Yet, to return to my opening story, the existence of clear organizational and experiential definitions did not quell the concerns of *AHR* board members. It did not, in part, because my colleagues understood quite clearly that neither component of the definition has been static or stable. And the sense that we are in a period of changing definitions is one of the key sources of uncertainty today about plagiarism. For instance, though the basic elements of the AHA definition have remained in place for almost two decades, it has been revised a number of times as controversial cases exposed it limitations. Changes were made in 1990, 1993, 1995, and 2002. Further revisions seem inevitable, and that knowledge breeds uncertainty.

The Moment

We are obviously in a time of heightened concern about plagiarism. Indeed, this volume and the conference that spawned it are examples of our current apprehension about the misappropriation of words and ideas. As a historian, my response to the emergence of such widespread anxiety about a particular problem is to ask questions about periodization: What is distinctive about this moment of time that makes us so concerned about plagiarism?

One answer, perhaps tautologically, is simply to say that right now plagiarism is a very visible problem ("Professor Copycat"). There has been a series of outing of historian plagiarists, most notably Doris Kearns Goodwin and the late Stephen Ambrose. Panels on the subject have been staged at meetings of several historical associations. Three books by historians on plagiarism and related scandals have been published over the last couple of years; their titles are evocative: Ron Robin, *Scandals and Scoundrels: Seven Cases That Shook the Academy;* Peter Charles Hoffer, *Past Imperfect: Facts, Fictions, Fraud; American History from Bancroft and Parkman to Ambrose, Bellesiles, Ellis, and Goodwin;* and Jon Weiner, *Historians in Trouble: Plagiarism, Fraud, and Politics in the Ivory Tower.* The editor of the *History News Network,* an online newsletter, reported that he had received so many tips about purported plagiarism that he only investigates well-known scholars. Another historian created a website, "Famous Plagiarists," that included a special section on history and a rogues' gallery of famous historian plagiarists. Finally, when Public Broadcasting Service's *Newshour* host Jim Lehrer decided to write a murder mystery about plagiarism, of course he peopled it with historians, in this case biographers of the nation's founders (Robin; Hoffer, *Past Imperfect;* Weiner; "Famous Plagiarists"; Lehrer).

Another reason for our present concern with plagiarism is a feeling that it may be on the increase. For example, Daniel Callahan has written about growth of what he terms a cheating culture, presenting a rise in plagiarism as a prime illustration (see his book *The Cheating Culture* and the associated website). Others, though, argue that the significant change has been in our ability to detect plagiarism. The debate reminds me of disputes in my own realm of scholarship, family history and policy, about whether or not child abuse has increased, decreased, or stayed the same over time. In both cases, it is likely impossible to find a definitive answer. And thus I think the more compelling question to ask is why are we so concerned with plagiarism right now?

As my *AHR* editorial board story suggests, technology has played a critical role in making plagiarism so important to us today. Computers and the Internet have vastly increased the amount of information we can obtain and created new skills in cutting and pasting that heighten our sense of vulnerability to plagiarism. Blogs, personal websites, library repositories, pre-print services, and search engines like Google have altered scholarship in ways that may well challenge a shared meaning of plagiarism, especially by encouraging the idea of information as common property available for use by all of us (Robin 55–56). At the same time, technology has created powerful new devices for tracking down plagiarism. Students have been the initial target of these software tools; Turnitin.com, for example, is now mandatory in many secondary schools. But technological policing is being applied to professionals as well. Indeed the creator of another program, Copyguard, contends that it would have caught the disputed passages in the books by Goodwin and Ambrose (Ralli). In fact a Google search did catch historian Brian Le Beau, then dean of arts and sciences at the University of Missouri, Kansas City, after he posted a speech on a dean's listserve. A reader looking for a particular phrase discovered that Le Beau had appropriated the work of African-American scholar Cornel West without proper attribution (Bartlett, "Missouri Dean"; Carnevale). So one of the reasons for the distinctiveness of this moment is that technology has increased our sense of both vulnerability and accountability.

Another source of our present concern about plagiarism is the impact of the law on all discussions of the misappropriation of words and ideas. Though plagiarism is not a legal violation, libel certainly is a legal matter (Stearns). Fear of libel suits and other forms of litigation hovers over the entire subject of plagiarism because the calamitous consequences of calling someone a plagiarist can send disputants to lawyers and perhaps court-rooms. The University of Dayton, to cite one example, successfully defended its decision to fire a faculty member for plagiarism; but winning the lawsuit cost the school almost two hundred thousand dollars in legal fees and administrative time (Glenn). Incidents like this intimidate schol-ars, universities, professional organizations, and publishers. As a result, every discussion about the issue turns to questions about the legal conse-quences of filing or defending charges of plagiarism.

I have tried to capture the ordering power of law by drawing on a metaphor crafted by the famous nineteenth-century French chronicler of American mores, Alexis de Tocqueville: the shadow of the law. He used it to describe the power of the formal agencies of law to influence the ideas and actions of people even if they never enter a law office or courtroom. The law creates a sense of expectations, entitlement, and penalties that govern us as we bargain in its shadow. Specific accusations of plagiarism pull accused, accuser, and others like editors, publishers, and universities into this shaded space. In terms of plagiarism, it is right now a frightening place where fears of litigation stifle needed disciplinary debate and action and thus condition our response not only to the act of misappropriation itself but also to technological changes that increase our ability to identify plagiarism (Grossberg, *Judgment*, 2–3, 34–35, 238–39; Grossberg, "Plagia-rism," 1338).

Uncertainty about the nature and meaning of authorship is yet another reason for the distinctiveness of this moment. Studies in the history of the book and scholarship in literary criticism have compelled us to reexamine our foundational belief in the author as an original thinker. This has also led us to reconsider whether an author has or should have a property claim to words, ideas, and evidence clashes, and also whether such claims clash with an equally vital commitment to the free flow of information. Plagia-rism emerged in early modern Europe from the confluence of technologi-cal, intellectual, and legal change that promoted exclusive and exclusion-ary authorial rights. In our time, postmodern claims about the cultural contingency of all social constructions have fostered uncertainty about the link between textual construction and ownership that challenge that understanding of plagiarism. Writing theorist Susan H. McLeod warns us, "We ignore the recent, local cultural history of copyright and plagiarism at our peril. The notion of stealing ideas or words is not only modern, it is also profoundly Western. Students from Middle Eastern, Asian, and African cultures are baffled by the notion that one can 'own' ideas" (Swearingen 21). Students from this country may be baffled as well. The culture of media sharing promoted by the Internet may well be teaching students an idea of information as an "intellectual commons" open to all uses that is at odds with the beliefs of most of the faculty and most definitions of plagiarism, including the one I cited from the AHA (Creative Commons).

These uncertainties about the property claims of authors are reinforced in a discipline like mine by an understanding of scholarship not simply as the product of individual insight but as accumulating and cumulative knowledge that is shared within and between generations; what historian William Cronon calls "a continuum of intellectual indebtedness" (Hoffer, "Reflections"). Thus *New Yorker* writer Malcolm Gladwell derides what he calls plagiarism fundamentalists, who, he says, "encourage us to pretend that these chains of influence and evolution do not exist and that a writer's words have a virgin birth and should have an eternal life" (48). Complaints like his suggest that property rights claims to scholarship based on assertions of authorial originality ignore the interdependence of scholars and undermine scholarly communication in history and all disciplines. Such contentions complicate our understanding of plagiarism. They make us worry that a restrictive definition of plagiarism and activist plagiarism policing will stifle needed disciplinary debates.

I think the market is the final major source of our plagiarism anxieties. Again my discipline is a revealing example in a couple of ways. First, persistent worries about declining monograph sales have increased pressure for academics and university presses to abandon the narrow monograph for broader analyses that appeal to larger groups of readers. The effort to write for a more inclusive audience is a very useful development in many ways, but the resulting rise in synthetic writing also heightens the need to rely on the work of others. And a greater use of secondary sources raises questions about plagiarism and the legitimate limits of paraphrasing. Just how much tinkering turns someone else's words and ideas into your own is a particularly gray area in any effort to define and police plagiarism, as both Goodwin and Ambrose discovered. It challenges all of those who write synthetic work (Hoffer, *Past Imperfect,* 180–201). Second, and I think more consequential, has been the impact of an expanding market for popular history evident in the large audiences for Ken Burns's documentaries and the huge readership of David McCullough's best-selling books. Successes like theirs have led to the rise of a cadre of historical popularizers, historians who write about the past as a popular, public, and often very profitable enterprise with sales not only to readers but to book-of-the-month clubs, cable channel producers, and Hollywood moviemakers. Most popularizers are not formal academics; they are, however, the prize catches in plagiarism hunts because of their notoriety (Robin 7, 31–32).

Historical popularizing is not a new endeavor, though it may well be garnering greater influence and rewards than in the past. What is new is an attempt to carve out a special ethical place for popularizers in the discipline. Judge Posner argued for such a policy during a panel discussion at the 2003 annual meeting of the American Historical Association. He contended that since the job of a historian writing for a popular audience is the dissemination of ideas by telling a good yarn rather than developing a discipline through original research, plagiarism by popularizers is simply not as significant an ethical violation as it is when done by an academic historian. Posner contended that plagiarism by popularizers simply did less serious damage to the discipline than the misappropriation of words and ideas by academic historians. Thus, he concluded, the penalties should be less as well (Postel). Posner's assertion is reinforced by policies at journals like the one I edited. The *AHR*'s definition of reviewable books excluded many of those published by popularizers because it gave pride of place to works of original scholarship. Consequently, none of Ambrose's recent books have been reviewed in the *AHR*. Such a policy exempts his books and many others from the disciplining that comes in scholarly book reviews ("Book Reviewing"). Posner's proposal and the *AHR* policy suggest the existence of differential standards for plagiarism in history writing that is another source of the uncertainty of this moment.

What to Do?

Crafting appropriate responses to our heightened concern about plagiarism has become a major challenge for all of those involved in academic writing. It requires individuals and organizations willing to tackle the problem and able to construct procedures that can effectively resolve the varied contemporary problems raised by plagiarism. Limited success in both endeavors is a final source of the uncertainty at this moment.

Until recently, the AHA had a settled procedure for resolving plagiarism accusations. It was one of the few professional organizations willing to police itself in this manner. In 1974 the AHA established a Professional Division and charged it with monitoring ethical issues in the discipline. The committee was staffed by representatives elected by the association's members. In 1987 the AHA published its first "Statement on Standards of Professional Conduct"; it defined various forms of professional misconduct—including plagiarism—and charged the Professional Division with enforcing the new guidelines. The division had an adjudication procedure to police historians' ethical misdeeds: aggrieved individuals could file charges against another historian and the division would then notify the accused of the charge, investigate the accusation, and inform the parties of its finding. Notification of a finding of misconduct was the primary sanction. The entire process was confidential, though the AHA asserted a discretionary power to publicize a judgment if the situation warranted. The process operated in Tocqueville's shadow of the law, consistently dominated by concerns about lawsuits.

Questions about its effectiveness and legitimacy plagued the AHA disciplining process from the start. The most searching and publicized complaints emerged out of an investigation of plagiarism charges against historian Stephen B. Oates filed in 1990. Oates had written widely read biographies of Abraham Lincoln and Martin Luther King. He denied the accusation and won the support of many of his fellow historians. He also refused to participate in the investigation. The process dragged on for over two years and in the end members of the Professional Division found that Oates had been careless in his use of other scholars' work, but they did not issue a specific finding of plagiarism. Oates challenged the legitimacy of the AHA procedure, which he likened to the Star Chamber, and threatened to sue the organization. He argued that since he was not a member of the AHA it had no jurisdiction over him; and he rejected the association's definition of plagiarism as overly broad. The battle continued into the new century and exposed many of the investigatory and enforcement problems of the system (Mallon 189–93; Hoffer, *Past Imperfect,* 135–39; Robin 36–45).

Critics argued that the rule of confidentiality underscored the timidity and ineffectiveness of the AHA's efforts to police professional misconduct. Because it refused to publicize findings of misconduct, no one but the parties involved knew if a historian had been accused or found guilty of plagiarizing. Ohio State historian Judy Tzu-Chun Wu learned that lesson in 2002 when she charged Wichita State historian Benson Tong with plagiarism. She later reported that the Professional Division agreed with her that

Tong has appropriated words and ideas from her dissertation and published them as his own in a book. Nevertheless, since only she and Tong knew the result, she resorted to self-policing for redress. Wu informed his department and publisher of the finding. Though Tong lost his bid for tenure, he found another job and his book remains in print. Following its procedures, the AHA refused to say whether it had even handled the case (Bartlett and Smallwood).

Incidents like the Oates and Wu cases generated uncertainties about the AHA process. Critics repeatedly argued that the procedure offered individuals a very limited remedy and, because of the commitment to confidentiality, the decisions rarely had a significant impact on the larger discipline or served to educate historians about plagiarism or other forms of misconduct. On the other hand, they acknowledged, the AHA remained one of the few professional associations that even attempted to police the ethics of its members. And its procedure did offer aggrieved individuals a place to seek redress. Nevertheless, the concerns mounted and undermined the system. The AHA abandoned it in the fall of 2003. AHA staff members and elected officials concluded that the process had "proven to be ineffective for responding to misconduct in the historical profession." In its place they proposed that the association should take the lead in educating the public and historians about "plagiarism, falsification of evidence, and other violations of scholarly integrity" ("AHA Announces").

The demise of AHA's adjudication of professional misconduct charges illustrates the difficulties of devising effective ways to police plagiarism and thus is itself another source of the uncertainties of this moment. Now historians, like most academics, have no formally recognized mechanism for resolving charges of plagiarism. Three alternatives have been suggested; each is problematic in its own fashion (Glenn).

As in most disciplines, history journals are now the front line of plagiarism struggles. Few are prepared to assume this responsibility; most have no established guidelines or procedures for dealing with claims by authors that a book or an article contains misappropriated words or ideas. I made that discovery at the *AHR*. The customary practice had been to refer accusers to the AHA and thus rely on its process to police plagiarism. When that system collapsed, the journal staff decided to revise the *AHR* book review guidelines and accept the responsibility for publishing charges of plagiarism. The new guidelines relied on the AHA definition of plagiarism and used the publication of parallel passages from the disputed texts as the prime method of exposure (Grossberg, "Plagiarism," 1338–39). A few other history journals also created new policies; most of these have adopted an approach much like the adjudicatory system formerly used by the AHA (*Journal of the Gilded Age;* Society for French Historical Studies). Even in these cases, however, the role of journals has raised as many questions as it has resolved: How can journals justify the power to investigate charges of plagiarism? What responsibility do journals have to notify the publishers of plagiarized books or other journals when plagiarism charges are filed? Should journals share their findings with each other? With history departments and organizations and with publishers? What is the liability of a journal, publisher, and individual editor in plagiarism cases? These and many other questions suggest the uncertainties of making journals the primary plagiarism police (Kahl).

The other prime candidate to handle accusations of plagiarism is the university. In this case, an aggrieved individual could lodge a charge of plagiarism against a faculty member with the accused academic's home institution. The appeal of university responsibility for policing plagiarism is that these institutions have established procedures for dealing with faculty misconduct, the power to compel participation and information gathering, the resources to support such investigations, and the ability to apply effective sanctions. Some universities have assumed this responsibility. For instance, in 2003 the United States Naval Academy investigated charges of plagiarism leveled against historian Brian VanDeMark. A committee substantiated accusations that his book on the development of the atomic bomb, *Pandora's Keeper: Nine Men and the Atomic Bomb,* contained plagiarized material. The Naval Academy stripped him of tenure, demoted him from associate to assistant professor, and cut his salary (Bartlett, "Naval Academy"; Steinberg; HNN Staff). Yet there are not many examples of similar actions by other universities. And thus turning to the university to resolve the problem of plagiarism also raises uncertainties. As former University of Nebraska vice chancellor Richard C. Edwards declared: "I find that all of the possible candidates for policing plagiarism (among faculty)— the 'own' university of someone accused of plagiarism, the professional journals, or the professional societies—are deeply flawed and likely to be very timid, with a different politics playing out in each. The own university is likely to have many personal connections and other pressures that may work to limit the appetite for calling it plagiarism."

Finally, another solution has emerged in the last few years. Historian Ron Robin has championed the policing of professional misconduct by the new interpretive communities being constructed through the mediums like the

Internet and reviewing mechanisms like those on Amazon.com. He argues that since the professional association, scholarly journal, and university have been unable to enforce ethical standards, we must rely on such communities and on public exposure as the most effective way to control plagiarism:

> To be sure, public scandals may occur more frequently, but they do not necessarily represent either disciplinary turmoil or the wholesale jetti-soning of standards. In a somewhat counterintuitive manner, the mod-ern-day version of vox populi is decidedly averse to revisionism and intolerant of deviancy . . . the participation of amateur scholars, gradu-ate students, and laypersons in Internet forums and other modes of dis-cussion suggest widespread rejection of those who seek to experiment with the canon, retool scholarly guidelines, or transgress conventional rules or regulation. The public scandal is, then, border control by other means. (Robin 232)

However, it is not clear if public monitoring can discipline professional misconduct, including plagiarism, any more effectively than the alterna-tives I have mentioned. For example, historian Peter Hoffer surveyed reviews of popular history books on Amazon.com and found that accusa-tions of misconduct against authors like Ambrose and Goodwin made little difference to ordinary readers. Their books continued to sell quite well despite the charges. He concluded that for many people reading is enter-tainment, not a critical intellectual act that should be policed for violations like plagiarism (Hoffer, *Past Imperfect*, 2005–7). Even so, communal moni-toring is developing and warrants our attention.

I want to conclude by returning to the opposition of the *AHR* Board of Editors to digital manuscript reviews for fear of plagiarism. We cannot fol-low that example and respond to our fears about plagiarism with distrust and resistance to change. Instead I think we have to seize this moment of intense concern to craft new understandings of plagiarism and new ways to discipline the misappropriation of other people's words and ideas. And that can only be done by raising these issues at every opportunity and in every relevant forum from journal pages and graduate seminars to conference panels and Internet discussion forums.

Works Cited

"AHA Announces Changes in Efforts Relating to Professional Misconduct." Press release, May 3, 2003. http://www.historians.org/press/PR_Adjudication.htm, consulted July 4, 2007.

American Historical Association. "Statement on Standards of Professional Conduct." Adopted January 6, 2005. http://www.historians.org/pubs/Free/Professional Standards.cfm#Plagiarism, consulted July 4, 2007.

Bartlett, Thomas."Missouri Dean Appears to Have Plagiarized a Speech by Cornel West." *Chronicle of Higher Education,* June 24, 2005. http://chronicle.com/ weekly/v51/i42/42a01301.htm, consulted July 4, 2007.

Bartlett, Thomas."Naval Academy Demotes Professor Accused of Plagiarism in a Book on the A-Bomb." *Chronicle of Higher Education,* November 7, 2003. http://chronicle.com/weekly/v50/i11/11a01201.htm, consulted July 4, 2007.

Bartlett, Thomas, and Scott Smallwood. "Four Academic Plagiarists You've Never Heard Of: How Many More Are Out There?" *Chronicle of Higher Education,* December 17, 2004. http://chronicle.com/free/v51/i17/17a00802.htm, consulted July 4, 2007.

"Book Reviewing in the *AHR.*" http://www.historycooperative.org/ahr/guidebkrv .html, consulted July 4, 2007.

Callahan, Daniel. *The Cheating Culture: Why More Americans Are Doing Wrong to Get Ahead.* Orlando: Harcourt, 2004.

Callahan, Daniel. *The Cheating Culture.* www.cheatingculture.com, consulted July 4, 2007.

Carnevale, Dan."Plagiarizing Dean Is Put on Leave." *Chronicle of Higher Education,* July 1, 2005. http://chronicle.com/weekly/v51/i43/43a01004.htm, consulted July 4, 2007.

Creative Commons. http://creativecommons.org, consulted July 4, 2007.

Edwards, Richard. Letter to author. March 22, 2004.

Famous Plagiarists. "Historians and Their Cut-n-Paste Scholarship." http://www .famousplagiarists.com/history.htm, consulted July 4, 2007.

Gladwell, Malcolm."Something Borrowed: Should a Charge of Plagiarism Ruin Your Life?" *New Yorker,* November 22, 2004, 40–48.

Glenn, David. "Judge or Judge Not?" *Chronicle of Higher Education,* December 17, 2004. http://chronicle.com/free/v51/i17/17a01601.htm, consulted July 4, 2007.

Grossberg, Michael. *A Judgment for Solomon: The d'Hauteville Case and Legal Experience in Antebellum America.* New York: Cambridge University Press, 1995.

Grossberg, Michael. "Plagiarism and Professional Ethics—a Journal Editor's View." *Journal of American History* 90 (2004): 1333–40.

HNN Staff. "Brian VanDeMark: Accused of Plagiarism." May 31, 2003. http://hnn .us/articles/1477.html, consulted July 4, 2007.

Hoffer, Peter Charles. *Past Imperfect: Facts, Fictions, Fraud; American History from Bancroft and Parkman to Ambrose, Bellesiles, Ellis, and Goodwin.* New York: Public Affairs, 2004.

Hoffer, Peter Charles. "Reflections on Plagiarism—Part 1: 'A Guide for the Perplexed.'" *Perspectives* (American Historical Association), February 2004. http://www.historians.org/perspectives/issues/2004/0402/0402vie1.cfm, consulted July 4, 2007.

Journal of the Gilded Age and Progressive Era. "SHGAPE/JGAPE Plagiarism Policy." December 11, 2004 . http://www.jgape.org/plagiarism.php, consulted July 4, 2007.

Kahl, Caryln E. "Plagiarism Policies and Historical Journals." *Editing History* (Conference of Historical Journals) 21, no. 2 (2005): 1–3.

Lehrer, Jim. *The Franklin Affair*. New York: Random House, 2005.

Lynch, Mona. "Pedophiles and Cyber-Predators as Contaminating Forces: The Language of Disgust, Pollution, and Boundary Invasions in Federal Debates on Sex Offender Legislation." *Law and Social Inquiry* 27 (2002): 529–66.

Mallon, Thomas. *Stolen Words*. New York: Ticknor and Fields, 1989.

Posner, Richard. "On Plagiarism: In the Wake of Recent Scandals Some Distinctions Are in Order." *Atlantic Monthly,* April 2002. http://www.theatlantic.com/issues/2002/04/posner.htm, consulted July 4, 2007.

Postel, Danny. "In Wake of Controversies, Historians Debate Causes and Prevalence of Plagiarism." *Chronicle of Higher Education,* January 6, 2003. http://chronicle.com/daily/2003/01/2003010603n.htm, consulted July 4, 2007.

"Professor Copycat." *Chronicle of Higher Education,* December 17, 2004. http://chronicle.com/weekly/v51/i17/17a00801.htm, consulted July 4, 2007.

Ralli, Tania. "Software Strives to Spot Plagiarism before Publication." *New York Times,* September 5, 2005. http://www.nytimes.com/2005/09/05/technology/05plagiarism.html?ex=1283572800&en=35522b480d567b03&ei=5088&partner=rss nyt&emc=rss, consulted July 4, 2007.

Robin, Ron. *Scandals and Scoundrels: Seven Cases That Shook the Academy*. Berkeley and Los Angeles: University of California Press, 2004.

Society for French Historical Studies. "H-France Bylaws, Guidelines, and Policies." Revised April 1, 2005. http://www.h-france.net/policies.html#policies, consulted July 4, 2007.

Steinberg, Jacques. "New Book Includes Passages from Others." *New York Times,* May 31, 2003, B9.

Stearns, Laurie. "Copy Wrong: Plagiarism, Process, Property, and the Law." In *Perspectives on Plagiarism and Intellectual Property in a Postmodern World,* ed. Lise Buranen and Alice N. Roy, 5–18. Albany: State University of New York Press, 1999.

Swearingen, C. Jan. "Originality, Authenticity, Imitation, and Plagiarism: Augustine's Chinese Cousins." In *Perspectives on Plagiarism and Intellectual Property in a Postmodern World,* ed. Lise Buranen and Alice N. Roy, 19–30. Albany: State University of New York Press, 1999.

Weiner, Jon. *Historians in Trouble: Plagiarism, Fraud, and Politics in the Ivory Tower.* New York: New Press, 2005.

Plagiarism and Copyright Infringement

The Costs of Confusion

Laura J. Murray

In August 2005, a translator sent a question to "The Ethicist" at the *New York Times*—aka Randy Cohen. She had discovered that a Hungarian encyclopedia article that she had been hired to translate for an American reference work, and that pretended to be new research, had in fact been "copied in large part from a lexicon published in 1929." She supposed there were copyright issues, and asked whether she should report the discovery to her American employer. The Ethicist advised that she should. "Intellectual integrity can be maintained only if members of your community report transgressions," he said. "Without this self-policing, the field cannot sustain its own values." What interests me here is the failure on the part of both translator and journalist to distinguish clearly between copyright infringement and plagiarism. The translator is mistaken in framing her question around copyright. An article from 1929 might still fall under copyright, depending on when its author died—but getting permission to publish is hardly likely to cause much problem. The real issues for the translator's editors are these: who is to be paid for the work, and does the work being delivered represent up-to-date research? Cohen's focus on problems of academic practice in his reply is therefore quite appropriate. In the next paragraph, he does note that "the copyright question is a legal one (with a potential pitfall for your boss), and hence beyond my purview." But although he makes a distinction between two realms of transgression, Cohen misses an opportunity to clarify the nature of the distinction. He doesn't even name the problem "plagiarism."

Insofar as there are two realms of transgression referred to in Cohen's discussion, one (unnamed) is governed by ethical principles and community values, and the other (copyright) by legal rules. In this implicit claim,

Cohen shares a widespread hunch about the difference between plagiarism and copyright infringement: that plagiarism is a matter of ethics, and copyright is a matter of law. But despite the popularity of this formulation, it is not in fact the nature of the distinction. As a falsification of research methodology, plagiarism is arguably more dangerous as a threat to the stability of knowledge verification systems than as an ethical transgression (see Rose). Furthermore, plagiarism includes unintentional acts, even if these tend not to be punished so severely, so on these grounds as well, ethics cannot be said to be at its core. On the legal side, it is true that in principle the law may be distinguished from ethical judgments. However, public discussions and legal rulings concerning copyright are heavily freighted with ethical ballast—just like those concerning other crimes. Thus ethics infuse both plagiarism and copyright discourses, and cannot be used as a fundamental criterion for distinguishing between them.

Another common idea about the distinction between the two transgressions, also evoked by Cohen's brief musings, is that plagiarism is a matter of etiquette or community norms, and copyright is a matter of law. This distinction has some merit. Whereas copyright is a crime against the individual (the source), plagiarism is widely understood as a crime against the group (the audience), and in its threat to social relations it is rather like a flaunting of etiquette. Seen as a breach of sincerity (or of the collectively defended illusion of sincerity), plagiarism is felt to insult and embarrass others, and is censured rather performatively as a ritual of social control.

However, the etiquette distinction neglects the fact that not only the identity of the "victim" but the nature of each transgressive act is quite different. Plagiarism and copyright infringement do not describe the same array of actions. The crucial and almost always unrecognized distinction between the two infractions is that plagiarism is use or reuse of words or ideas without *acknowledgment,* whereas copyright infringement is use or reuse of words or ideas without *permission.* Plagiarism and copyright infringement are transgressions against two distinct but overlapping economies of knowledge: citation systems and market systems.

Citation systems are multiple and often informal. They include "reputation" economies in the arts and marketing; blogging, "playlist," and hypertext practices; and protocols for tracing circulation of stories and other oral genres. In these economies, being identified as a source bestows cultural capital, and perhaps, eventually, increased income, but does not result in direct payment. Stopping to ask permission would run completely counter to the principles of these economies: the goal of all participants is free, cited circulation. Of course citation economies do not operate "purely" or in isolation: they intersect in various ways with market economies of knowledge, regulated through intellectual property law. But their dynamism is based on a certain independence and distinctness.

Academic citation is one of the most formalized citation systems. While its logic may be self-evident to its practitioners, this article argues that academics ought to devote more effort to understanding and displaying its vitality, capacity, and governance mechanisms, and demonstrating its points of distinction from the copyright system. It is in their interest as researchers to do so, because various windows in copyright law that allow academic research to proceed—provisions such as limited term, fair use (or fair dealing in Canada and other countries), the first-sale doctrine, and so on—are closed or closing rapidly. In the United States, the 1998 lengthening of copyright term and other restrictions of the 2001 Digital Millennium Copyright Act have impeded the operation of citation economies. Canada has not yet ratified the 1996 World Intellectual Property Organization "Internet treaties," but it is poised to follow in U.S. footsteps. A solid grasp of the principles behind citation may help to protect established research practices. But it is also in academics' interest as citizens and teachers to clarify the distinction. As I will argue, defenses of academic citation may draw attention to the dynamism and importance of other citational economies, and this in turn may help students to understand the logic and advantages of academic citation. Strategies for preventing plagiarism could be framed in more positive terms.

Copyright law is only one of the threats to academic citation practice. Challenged by universities' desire to generate income from intellectual property licensing, this system also appears to be under threat from students' easy access to plagiarizable sources on the Internet. These situations may invite a certain nostalgia for days of yore, but at the same time, studies of science research and publishing have critiqued the academic citation system's ideological underpinnings and practical mechanics (McSherry; Galison and Biagoli), and composition and literature scholars have taken issue with its promotion of inaccurate or unproductive models of authorship (e.g., Howard; Lunsford). I fully acknowledge the power of these critiques. In fact I am inspired by Corynne McSherry's paraphrase of the contention of Jacques Derrida and Bill Readings that "academics must take responsibility for enacting a community of thought that, because it does not pretend to be either disinterested or secluded from society, will no longer work to legitimate particular inquiries, polices, and property claims"

(19). In this spirit, I think it urgently necessary to emphasize distinctions between citation and copyright systems, both despite and because of their intersections and internal contradictions. Thus while I am taken by Lisa Maruca's claim that "the increased vigilance over source use that results because of and as part of the plagiarism panic may be actually increasing the domain of copyright" (10), I would focus on developing models for educating students about citation that do *not* play into corporate copyright. And whereas Debora Halbert sees the citation system and the copyright system as equally obsessed with individual genius and property (111), I would suggest that citation acts as a powerful reminder of the collaborative and collective nature of knowledge.

As I have pointed out, the essential distinction between citation and copyright is that proper citation practice turns on acknowledgment, whereas proper copyright practice turns on permission. It is a tenet of academic freedom that one does not ask permission before critiquing the work of another. As awkward as it may be to say it in our present intense environment of antipiracy rhetoric, unauthorized copying is what we are all about in the university—with the larger goal of creating new ideas and arguments from the fabric of those already existing. It is understood in academic circles that once a work has been published, its pieces are available for free use. Free, that is, in the sense of free speech, not free beer, in the terms of the open-source software people: one has to pay to buy a book or a subscription, but one does not have to ask permission to read or to quote.[1] In copyright law, this is called "fair use," or in Canada "fair dealing"—that is, the provision that allows us to quote without permission. It is seen as something of an exception in copyright law. But in citation cultures, this freedom is not an exception: it is the foundation. The copyright system and citation systems are based on entirely different foundations. They are both concerned with policing inappropriate reproduction, but their definition of inappropriate is very different.[2] As Laurie Stearns puts it, "Attribution of authorship is the highly personal connection between author and work, but the interest that copyright protects is the impersonal connection between owner and property" (12).

Academics are especially well positioned to understand these distinctions because citation is the currency of our research. By explaining to students and university administrators that unauthorized, *cited* use of others' work is essential to our mode of knowledge production, university writing teachers can contribute to a larger citizens' movement to design and clarify nonproperty economies of knowledge, a movement that includes open-source software, the Creative Commons license, defense of the public domain, and all manner of documentation and education initiatives.[3] And this in turn may make it easier to discourage students from plagiarizing. Consider these words of Rosemary Coombe:

> Too much of what we now protect under the guise of authorship is not creativity or innovation, but merely investment. Too much of the world's creativity is unrecognized, and when it is recognized, our global intellectual property regimes provide rights without recognizing the responsibilities that many peoples in the world hold—responsibilities to others, to their ancestors, to future generations, and to the plants, animals, and spirits that occupy and animate the worlds they inhabit. Can authorship be revitalized to encompass this wider field of human obligation and energy? Can the exercise of intellectual property rights . . . be limited and shaped to address a larger range of social objectives? (1173)

In her allusion to the struggles of indigenous peoples, Coombe is evoking a realm of struggle and discussion far removed from the university classroom. But the gist of her words would not be startling to most university students, who along with their generation as a whole and many other citizens as well feel that copyright law in its current and emerging form is morally bankrupt and economically unjust. Consumers are urged to "respect" the rights of others, when those others—especially large corporations—do not seem to practice respect, or even recognize the existence of interests other than their own.

In this context, teachers and students can explore the idea that respect and submission are not identical—surely a proposition attractive to adolescents and young adults. In copyright, at least as corporate lobbyists see it, there is only one way to show respect: asking permission. But in a citation system, one shows respect when one finds another's work useful and acknowledges its author—even if one goes on to criticize, adapt, augment, or even dismiss it. I explain to students that for individual participants, the academic citation system has a relatively low bureaucracy and cost overhead. It is much more easily compatible with freedom of expression than copyright. It is a way of building prestige and networking; it doesn't cost anything; and it can help in democratizing communication and making authority more transparent. Placing academic citation in the context of other citation economies in which students participate can also be productive. Internet links are one endless chain of footnotes, only handier. Blogs invite their readers to trace back through their sources like any good academic historian. Some students will already know about Creative Commons, a circulation system based on citation (all of its licenses require attribution); students might be assigned to choose an appropriate Creative Commons license for a piece of work, and explain their choice. Citation economies may be hip, but they are ancient. Janet Giltrow discusses citation compellingly in terms of the norms of conversation (33–36). In ordinary conversation, it is often wise to cite the source of a joke or anecdote or notable fact. Why? Because it is normal to cite: it is part of the social fabric and habitual modes of speech. Because sometimes it bolsters social status to declare a prestigious source. Or because it helps your listener to evaluate your information: if you don't say where you got it, they may ask. Through discussing conversational and online practices, students may understand better the logic of academic citation.

What happens if we don't make the distinction? I have space here to present one cautionary case study. Simon Fraser University in Vancouver, Canada, posts two documents online dictating copyright rules to graduate students submitting theses. SFU tells such students that they must obtain permission for use of images or more than five hundred words or 2 percent of the work of others (Simpson, "Copyright Workshop," 2). When "earmarking graphics for later use, [students should] immediately send for copyright permission" (1); it advises asking them to imagine themselves arguing before a judge in a lawsuit as they decide the scope of their permission-seeking efforts (3). In these and other sections, the SFU documents present erroneous interpretations of Canadian copyright law, which in fact offers a number of "users' rights," including fair dealing, a provision recently substantially bolstered by the Supreme Court in the *CCH Canadian Ltd. v. Law Society of Upper Canada* case.[4] But for the purposes of the present discussion, it is most important to note the massive change to established academic practice represented in these SFU rules. In ignoring fair dealing and other users' rights, SFU is allowing its students far less room to maneuver than Canadian law permits, burdening them with the difficult, time-consuming, sometimes expensive or impossible, and often unnecessary task of negotiating permission.[5]

There are two connections here to citation and plagiarism. First, the most obvious: SFU is handing over to the copyright system various regulatory functions that could be handled, and normally are handled, by the citation system. Students are advised that asking permission to quote the work of others will produce "enhancement of your reputation," and assist in "opening up relationships with originators," "establishing personal acceptance in the community of scholars," and "extending your career/job network" (5). In bold print, we read the following: "It cannot be over-emphasized that 'used by permission of . . .' appearing in captions and foot-notes of a thesis or project report greatly enhances the reputation of both the author of the current work and originators of borrowed work" (5). Here, the authorizing and networking functions of citation have been transferred to the copyright system, at the cost of academic freedom for the student, who now must grovel for permission where she previously only had to footnote with grace.

The second connection to citation is more insidious. Simon Fraser's guidelines represent not only an importation of copyright thinking, but an unwitting export of some expectations from citation practice. In the aca-demic citation system, it is expected that all sources, no matter how old, will be cited—ideas, facts, expressions, arguments—with the tiny exception of "common knowledge." The copyright system, given its "fair use" or "fair dealing" provisions, limited copyright term, focus on "expressions" and not facts or ideas, and other user-rights mechanisms, simply does not require permission for all the acts that require citation in the citation sys-tem. Designed to "promote the progress of science and the useful arts," as the U.S. Constitution puts it, copyright needs windows of unauthorized use as much as it needs permission requirements. As I noted earlier, many forces have been closing or trying to close these windows, or telling people that they are closed—or that they never existed. One reason that academics may not see the windows, it seems to me, is that they don't have counter-parts in the citation system. If "total citation" is expected, "total permis-sion" may be expected too. SFU's interpretation of the law makes more sense than it should to students and professors because of the confusion between citation and copyright principles.

Simon Fraser's policies, though thankfully not typical according to my surveys so far, represent a useful warning. Often at the request of confused faculty and students, university and college administrators are developing more and more finely grained interpretations of copyright law. And yet these policies have a double purpose: they aim to protect the institution from litigation, and may only secondarily defend academic freedom and modes of knowledge production. My contention here is that copyright's intrusion into everyday academic life is facilitated by the absence of a robust understanding of the academic citation system. It is crucial for aca-demics and students to understand that permission is not part of the citation system—otherwise they will not see what they are giving away in this increasingly copyrighteous world. Of course, we all operate in the market as well, as purchasers and writers of books and other media, and here copyright regulates our exchanges. I am not questioning the right of copyright owners to control republication of substantial parts of their work. But even in the world of copyright, we have a right to repeat people's words in order to hold them accountable, bring them into dialogue, or use them as a springboard.

In all countries around the world, citizens' rights to use materials they purchase or to make their own contributions to culture are eroded by creeping digital rights management and its extra carapace of copyright law. With analog technologies, citizens could lend, borrow, collage, and give away cultural materials—books, pages, clippings, records. Although digital technologies have the potential to increase these recirculation abilities, in fact we are seeing them reduced. Standing up for user rights such as fair use or fair dealing, then, has repercussions outside the world of writers and teachers, to the world of private use, where citizens' abilities to incorporate small pieces of cultural materials into their relationships and lives is being commodified and controlled to a whole new extent. It is crucial that the principle of some degree of free use of materials under copyright be articulated as a public good—not just, as corporate copyright lobbyists insist, the accident of primitive technologies now improved upon. In defining the citation system, we are helping to animate user rights often presented as "loopholes" to be "plugged." Just as apparently useless wetlands may be key to maintaining a healthy environment, copyright "loopholes" are microclimates that foster creativity, innovation, and democracy. Happily, as teachers and researchers and writers, academics know this well; it is merely a matter of getting the message out, and happily once again, we have in our students an audience at hand.

Notes

1. For the classic explanation, see "Free Software Definition."

2. Other differences between the systems exist. In general, the citation system covers more ground than the copyright system. There is no fixed term for "citation protection": you have to cite a source no matter how many centuries old, whereas you only have to ask for permission through seventy years after the death of the author (in the United States), or fifty years after (in Canada). You have to cite ideas and facts, but you don't need copyright clearance for them. The only exception in academic citation is "common knowledge," a much tinier window than fair use or

fair dealing. One is supposed to cite short sequences of words that one could use without permission as "fair use" or "fair dealing." And a purchased essay is plagiarism, but not copyright infringement because it is contractually assigned to the student customer.

3. For example, see the Free Software Foundation (http://www.fsf.org), the Electronic Frontier Foundation (www.eff.org), the Internet Archive (http://www.archive .org/index.php), www.chillingeffects.org, and www.creativecommons.org. In Canada, http://www.digital-copyright.ca and http://forumonpublicdomain.ca, www.cippic.ca, and www.michaelgeist.ca embody and document efforts toward public interest copyright advocacy.

4. No Canadian statute or case law sets specific quantity limits on fair dealing; instead, *CCH* offers a multipart test featuring assessments of the purpose, character, and amount of the dealing, the nature of the work, available alternatives, and the effect of the dealing on the work (at par. 53). *CCH* pronounces that "the fair dealing exception, like other exceptions in the Copyright Act, is a user's right. In order to maintain the proper balance between the rights of a copyright owner and users' interests, it must not be interpreted restrictively" (at par. 48). Especially pertinent to the SFU rules, *CCH* suggests that judges look to "custom or practice in a particular trade or industry" (at par. 55) in adjudicating fair dealing, and it raises the possibility that fair dealing with an entire image may be possible (at par. 56). It is nothing short of astonishing that few universities in Canada have harkened to this landmark case (see Geist).

5. I certainly do not doubt the sincerity of Penny Simpson, the SFU thesis librarian and the author of the two documents, who seeks to save students from becoming "involuntary cannon fodder" (e-mail, February 20, 2006). However, her belief that the "rights perspective" is a "rather defiant, rather adolescent approach" (e-mail, February 15, 2006) compared to the maturity offered by her restrictive interpretation of the law is troubling, to say the least. Students, it should surely be acknowledged, own their own copyright, and the decisions in this realm should ultimately rest with them.

Works Cited

Buranen, Lise, and Alice M. Roy, eds. *Perspectives on Plagiarism and Intellectual Property in a Postmodern World*. Albany: State University of New York Press, 1999.

CCH Canadian Ltd. v. Law Society of Upper Canada. SCC 13 CanLII. Supreme Court of Canada. 2004. www.canlii.org/ca/cas/scc/2004/2004scc13.html, consulted July 9, 2007.

Cohen, Randy. "Translating Copycat." *New York Times,* August 14, 2005, late ed., sec. 6, p. 18.

Coombe, Rosemary J. "Fear, Hope, and Longing for the Future of Authorship and a Revitalized Public Domain in Global Regimes of Intellectual Property." *DePaul Law Review* 52 (Summer 2003): 1171–91.

"The Free Software Definition." http://www.gnu.org/philosophy/free-sw.html, consulted July 5, 2007.

Galison, Peter, and Mario Biagoli, eds. *Scientific Authorship: Credit and Intellectual Property in Science*. New York: Routledge, 2003.

Geist, Michael. "Education Summit Shouldn't Be Only about Money." *Toronto Star,* August 29, 2005. http://www.michaelgeist.ca/index.php?option=content& task=view&id=940, consulted December 28, 2006.

Giltrow, Janet. *Academic Writing*. 3rd ed. Peterborough: Broadview, 2002.

Halbert, Debora. "Poaching and Plagiarizing: Property, Plagiarism, and Feminist Futures." In *Perspectives on Plagiarism and Intellectual Property in a Postmodern World,* ed. Lise Buranen and Alice M. Roy, 111–20. Albany: State University of New York Press, 1999.

Howard, Rebecca Moore. "The New Abolitionism Comes to Plagiarism." In *Perspectives on Plagiarism and Intellectual Property in a Postmodern World,* ed. Lise Buranen and Alice M. Roy, 87–98. Albany: State University of New York Press, 1999.

Lunsford, Andrea. "Foreword: Who Owns Language?" In *Perspectives on Plagiarism and Intellectual Property in a Postmodern World,* ed. Lise Buranen and Alice M. Roy, ix–xii. Albany: State University of New York Press, 1999.

Maruca, Lisa. "The Plagiarism Panic: Digital Policing in the New Intellectual Property Regime." Presented at the AHRB Copyright Research Network, Conference on New Directions in Copyright, June 30, 2004. http://www.copyright.bbk.ac.uk/ contents/publications/conferences/2004/lmaruca.pdf, consulted August 11, 2005.

McSherry, Corynne. *Who Owns Academic Work? Battling for Control of Intellectual Property*. Cambridge: Harvard University Press, 2001.

Rose, Shirley K. "The Role of Scholarly Citations in Disciplinary Economics." In *Perspectives on Plagiarism and Intellectual Property in a Postmodern World,* ed. Lise Buranen and Alice M. Roy, 241–49. Albany: State University of New York Press, 1999.

Simpson, Penny. "Working within Copyright Requirements: How Do You Decide?" Guidelines for thesis students, Simon Fraser University, 2003. http://www.lib.sfu .ca/researchhelp/writing/thesesregulations/WorkingWithinCopyright.pdf, consulted December 28, 2005.

Simpson, Penny. "Copyright Workshop." *Simon Fraser University Library,* 2004. http://www.lib.sfu.ca/researchhelp/writing/thesesregulations/WorkshopCopy right.pdf, consulted December 28, 2005.

Stearns, Laurie. "Copy Wrong: Plagiarism, Process, Property, and the Law." In *Perspectives on Plagiarism and Intellectual Property in a Postmodern World,* ed. Lise Buranen and Alice M. Roy, 5–18. Albany: State University of New York Press, 1999.

Plagiarism, a Turnitin Trial, and an Experience of Cultural Disorientation

Lisa Emerson

In October 2003, all faculty at Massey University, a research university in New Zealand, were invited to join a university-wide trial of Turnitin.com, a plagiarism detection system being considered for widespread use to combat a perceived "plagiarism epidemic." The university framed the Turnitin trial as an investigation into issues of academic integrity and a step in strengthening academic misconduct procedures, with no reference to plagiarism as an issue of academic writing. This is not, perhaps, surprising since rhetoric and composition is an emerging discipline in New Zealand and is not yet fully established as part of the curriculum. As the only full-time faculty member employed at this time to teach academic writing at the university, I joined the trial, hoping to bring a different perspective on the issue.

The purpose of this essay is to consider the value of Turnitin primarily from the context of reflecting, as a writing teacher, on what the trial taught me about writing, about my role as a writing teacher, about students and learning, and on the gaps that exist in our understanding of and relationship with one another in the student-teacher relationship. To deepen my reflection, I have used a form of reflective practice established by Donald Schön and developed by the British school of action research (see, for example, Whitehead and McNiff). This reflective paradigm, as described by Richard Winter, Alyson Buck, and Paula Sobiechowska, "requires more than observation. It requires us to engage in a process of introspection leading to self-clarification" (186). This essay summarizes the process of observation and self-clarification I engaged in as part of the university trial.

The Project

The university trial involved ten faculty members across a range of disciplines. My part of the trial took place in a thirteen-week communication in science course that is compulsory for all freshman science students. The course is taught through a combination of lectures and tutorials and is fully internally assessed. Demographically, the class is unusually homogeneous for a New Zealand context, with an even gender split and very few ESL students (predominantly Asian, but with some Maori speakers); 90 percent of the class are recent school leavers.

I wanted to start with an understanding of my students' knowledge of what constituted plagiarism. My perception, based on teaching experience, was that students entered university unprepared to use academic sources in their writing. However, attitudes of others within the university challenged my perception. I was unprepared for the level of anger expressed by some colleagues joining the Turnitin trial. Many of these faculty, particularly those working in fields with large numbers of ESL students, animatedly discussed the "plagiarism epidemic" (although there are no studies on rates of plagiarism in New Zealand universities) and expressed pleasure, almost jubilation, that these graceless students would be found and punished. Such a perspective appeared to be supported, though reinterpreted, by an article written by a student in the student newspaper entitled "George Bush Cheats so Why Can't I?" In this piece, Jess Cameron suggests that the code of behavior established by political and business leaders in recent years means that "an unstable foundation of morals regarding cheating and plagiarism for 'Gen X' is set" (16). Claiming that plagiarism is a result of cynicism, and laughing at claims of "unintentional plagiarism," she challenges so-called liberal attitudes and calls for a harder line on plagiarism, which she describes as devaluing her own educational achievement.

So were my perceptions wrong? To investigate whether students understood what plagiarism is, I conducted a survey based on Julio Soto and Elizabeth McGee's study, modified to meet a New Zealand context. Student responses were analyzed using the Statistical Analysis System. The results showed a discrepancy between students' initial confidence and subsequent ability to answer the specific questions. A majority of students (69 percent) rated their understanding of plagiarism as either good or very good. Their answers to the more specific questions, however, showed that their confidence was misplaced (table 1). Although most students could correctly answer simple questions about plagiarism (92 percent correctly identified that including copied text without a citation is plagiarism), they had difficulty with the more complex questions and showed particular confusion over paraphrasing and the distinctions between correct formatting for paraphrasing and quoting. Only 12 percent of students correctly identified that copied material needs to be formatted correctly as well as referenced with a citation. Of those students who felt their understanding of plagiarism was good, only 11 percent answered this question correctly, and only 19 percent of those who said their understanding of plagiarism was very good.

This first-year class, then, was insufficiently prepared to use secondary sources with confidence. They initially overestimated their skills and showed that, while they understood the broad terms, they had insufficient knowledge of the distinctions between paraphrasing and quoting, and of how to acknowledge sources. This confirmed my perception that New Zealand students do not understand the complexities of using secondary sources and what constitutes plagiarism and that education on these matters is imperative.

Turnitin.com is an international website that checks all submitted papers against its ever-growing body of previously submitted papers, as

Table 1

Percentage of Correct Reponses to Survey Questions, by Students' Perception of Their Own Understanding of Plagiarism and as a Class Total

	Perception of Understanding[a]				Overall Class ($n = 132$)
	Very Good	Good	Fair	Poor	
Including copied text from a paper or digital source without a citation in an assignment is plagiarism	100	98	85	50	92
Including copied text from a paper or digital source with a proper citation in an assignment is plagiarism	19	11	12	0	12
Including copied text from a paper or digital source within quotation marks with a proper citation in an assignment is not plagiarism	89	80	71	38	77
Including a quote without a citation in an assignment is plagiarism	100	88	76	50	85
Proper paraphrasing involves summarizing, synthesizing, and citing read information in my own words	58	61	38	37	53

[a]Percentage of students within each perception ranking was 20, 49, 25, and 6 percent respectively.

well as commercial databases of journals and periodicals. Once a paper is submitted, it belongs to Turnitin, as the company is popularly known. I used Turnitin on a single assignment, a report on an aspect of science and ethics. The report is designed to be "plagiarism-proof" in that it asks students to link the scientific issue to some specific course material on ethics, and also asks them to address the New Zealand context (which discourages students from uncritically modifying material from international websites). Turnitin was contextualized within a detailed educational package. In 2004, students attended a lecture on using secondary sources and American Psychological Association (APA) referencing conventions. They then worked in groups on integrating sources within their own text and using referencing conventions. Activities included interactive exercises designed to illustrate the differences between paraphrasing and quoting. The following week, a peer review exercise on the assignment included questions and discussion on each student's use of sources. Students also had access to paper-based resources on integrating sources and APA referencing. In 2005, we added another support mechanism: brief individual conferences with an adjunct teaching assistant for each student. Questions asked during the conference included, "Do you think you may have used any unacknowledged quotations in your work?" and "Do you understand the conventions of APA referencing—is there anything you would like to discuss about this?" Adjuncts wrote summaries of students' responses, and each student wrote a reply to their comments, explaining how they would change their assignment if needed.

Assignments for both cohorts were processed through Turnitin and the individual reports sorted into four categories: no plagiarism, minor plagiarism (defined as less than six sentences of consecutive or nonconsecutive copied material with no form of in-text citation, or quotations treated as paraphrases, i.e., quoted with an in-text citation), moderate plagiarism (six to eight sentences of consecutive or nonconsecutive copied material with no form of in-text citation), and major plagiarism (nine sentences or more of consecutive or nonconsecutive copied material with no form of in-text citation). Results are detailed in table 2.

Because we did not measure plagiarism rates prior to 2004, we cannot state whether student plagiarism rates decreased due to the use of Turnitin or the educational package—or, indeed, whether rates had changed at all. While other faculty within the trial reported that they believed there were decreased rates of plagiarism as a result of the Turnitin trial, there are no quantitative data to confirm this. However, in my own case, the results suggest that the individual conferences had a substantial impact on the rate of plagiarism detected, effectively halving it across all categories.

Two more specific findings also emerged from these results following an analysis of the conference review sheets in the second part of the project. Students who experience problems with the less severe forms of plagiarism may be exhibiting errors in the academic writing *process,* rather than misunderstanding how to use conventions. Every student in the 2005 cohort identified as having plagiarism problems had attended an individual conference prior to submission of the assignment. However, all but one had attended with an incomplete assignment draft and had been identified as not having completed in-line citations. Adjuncts discussed the issue with these students, who promised to insert in-line citations. These facts suggest an error not of understanding but of technique. Second, the conference appeared to have a substantial impact on the outcomes for ESL students. Four of the students classified as having major plagiarism problems in 2004 were ESL students, but none of the students in 2005 showing plagiarism problems of any kind were ESL students. Instead, ESL students were more likely to overuse quotations. It is interesting that the introduction of the conference, rather than the introduction of an educational strategy and detection device, proved to be the decisive factor in almost eliminating plagiarism in our (admitted small) sample of ESL students. We were unable to establish, through analysis of the assignments and conference sheets, why the conference was successful in addressing plagiarism among ESL students. Further research is needed.

Reflections of a Writing Teacher

After so many years of working with academic writing, I find it disconcerting that I still misunderstand how students process information and how

TABLE 2

Occurrence of Students (*n*, %) within Three Levels of
Plagiarism for Two Cohorts in 2004 (*n* = 142) and
2005 (*n* = 171) for the Same Assignment

Plagiarism Level	2004	2005
Major	5 (3.5)	1 (0.6)
Moderate	9 (6.3)	5 (2.9)
Minor	9 (6.3)	5 (2.9)
Total	23 (16.1)	11 (6.4)

they write. The study clearly showed that the students who used a "patch writing" technique (Howard) were engaged in a writing process that could lead to accidental plagiarism. Although the workshop included interactive exercises, these did not satisfactorily model the writing process or ensure that students integrated and acknowledged sources as part of their thinking and drafting process. This was a fundamental error in the pedagogy we employed. The lecture itself, by presenting the conventions of citation outside of process, may have misled some students. We also presented sources as something separate from the students' own thinking. And we failed to address adequately the complexities of voice in academic writing, of how to locate one's own voice within the context of academic sources; yes, we touched on this—but such a fundamental, complex, and shifting issue requires more than a thirty-minute exercise. Clearly, some revision of pedagogy is required—and, somehow, more teaching time.

A second key aspect of my reflection has been the impact of the conference on plagiarism. Building a relationship with a reliable mentor may dramatically affect a student's experience of her or his position within the academic community. Jonathan Hall suggests that plagiarism may be partly a result of the depersonalization of tertiary education:

> The modern university is big, bustling and impersonal. Students often feel like teachers don't know their names or care about their problems. . . . The plagiarism crisis is not something that dropped out of the sky without our complicity or our participation. . . . If, as the traditional consensus has it, the plagiarist has become cynical, it may be partly because he or she believes we are cynical too. (13)

Individual contact with an adjunct who is available to discuss the student's assignment and personal confusions may be a key difference between the classes of 2004 and 2005. And perhaps it is not surprising that this has an impact on ESL students, who are doubly disenfranchised by language and culture. As a teacher I find this outcome heartening—it suggests a simple and easily implemented solution that we can explain clearly to colleagues and that can easily become part of a broader strategy on plagiarism.

But what of Turnitin.com? Researchers in the field and individual faculty who have used Turnitin tend to have very clear views one way or another: either it is "the best thing we have ever had to combat plagiarism" (personal communication) or it is a reprehensible tool that undermines students' rights, supports the commodification of education, and creates a spirit of distrust and fear (McKeever; Marsh). After my involvement in the trial, I initially held an ambivalent view. In both 2004 and 2005 we found a student who had copied the work of another student from a different tutorial group. Since their work was marked by different tutors, under ordinary circumstances they would not have been caught. As teachers we like to think we can spot plagiarism without additional tools, but this trial convinced me otherwise.

The deterrent effect of plagiarism detection systems remains anecdotal until empirical studies support this claim. Nevertheless, I do think there is evidence that Turnitin can be used as an educational tool. This point is well articulated by another faculty member involved with the trial:

> I use Turnitin as an alerting system, but I don't rely on its judgement because I feel the nature of copying, and particularly the level of intent, need case-by-case discerning. During this particular trial, Turnitin helped me to identify one group whose work contained two chunks of material copied from a website without attribution. I don't think I would have picked it up without Turnitin, as it was integrated quite seamlessly. However, my feeling upon reading the context in which the material had been used (to provide background and company profile to a case study) was that it was not deliberate plagiarism but rather a misunderstanding about the best way to provide such background and profile.
>
> I showed the students the Turnitin report, discussed correct referencing requirements with them, and had them explain to me why what they had done could be problematic. I never accused them of plagiarism. . . . However I made very clear to them that if they did this kind of thing again, they could risk being accused of plagiarism, and the penalties were severe. I then had them resubmit the work, and this time it was not only correctly attributed, but they had seen how to put the background they needed into their own words and make it work for their argument. . . . I was really pleased with this outcome. I had the feeling that the students would not copy again, *(a)* because they knew it could be easily detected (and I think there was a clear deterrent effect on the whole class simply because of the visibility of plagiarism issues due to our in-class discussions of Turnitin and the trial) and *(b)* because they had worked through the issue of making source materials work for them instead of work against them.
>
> They were happy, and I was happy, and having an independent report like Turnitin helped clarify what was needed and enabled us to have an objective discussion without the students feeling that I, per-

sonally, was judging them or accusing them of anything. I think having Turnitin to refer to made the students much less defensive towards me than I have previously experienced when having to deal with plagiarism problems I have detected myself. (Personal communication, October 6, 2004)

This is an example of Turnitin used with subtlety and skill, and would, on its own, incline me toward encouraging the use of Turnitin.com. If Turnitin could be used by teachers committed to teaching academic writing skills, who could (and would) sensitively read the reports, and who understood the distinction between fraud and incorrect or inadequate use of sources, and if this tool was used in conjunction with an effective educational package that addressed process and voice and personal conferences with tutors, then we might make a strong case for Turnitin.

However, there are a lot of subordinate clauses here. We cannot assume that Turnitin will only be used by such instructors—given the level of anger and anxiety around plagiarism, there is plenty of evidence to suggest that it is more likely to be used by those concerned solely with detection and punishment. In such hands, Turnitin becomes a blunt instrument to accuse those struggling to grasp a complex intellectual skill of moral failure—with huge repercussions for those students.

Just as important, in considering Turnitin, are issues of trust and respect. Plagiarism has been characterized as a breakdown in the student-teacher relationship—a student, in plagiarizing, snaps the relationship of trust and respect between herself and her instructor (though the causes of this breach may, of course, be complex). One perspective on Turnitin is that its use constitutes a breaking of that trust relationship *by the instructor.* If we treat all students as potential cheats, how can they approach us with confidence? A focus on detection and punishment combined with a tool that suggests an instructor's fundamental lack of confidence cannot be conducive to effective learning. Can the detection capabilities of a system such as Turnitin compensate for such a breach in the educative relationship?

So what shifted my ambivalence? Cynthia Hoogland develops Donald Schön's idea that stories are fundamental to the reflective process. She suggests that "stories conjoin emotions and intellect. . . . they are what head-talk becomes when it is joined to the body, or what ideas are fused to lived experience" (216). So let me end with a conceit, a narrative of something I experienced at the Sweetland Writing Center's 2005 Originality, Imitation, and Plagiarism conference:

The trip to the Michigan conference was my first extended visit to the United States. I arrived in Ann Arbor in a cab from Detroit, tired after the long-haul trip, and suddenly aware of an anxious thought: people tip in the United States. I had never tipped in my life—what should I do? The only person I could ask was the cab driver. He said 20 percent was compulsory. Wasn't that rather a lot, I asked. No, ma'am, he said, quite normal. So, I paid the 20 percent and asked the clerk in the hotel lobby whether 20 percent was a compulsory tip. She was not impressed.

Later that day, I headed out for a meal. Before I left, I asked the hotel clerk to explain the rules of tipping. "It's simple," she said. "You just tip 15 percent for good service in a place where you're *served*." "Like a restaurant?" I said. *Yes.* "What about McDonald's?" *No.* OK, I thought, slightly more complex than it appears.

As it turned out, over the next few days, tipping became a matter of outlandish proportions for me. Sitting in a Starbucks café I would think, "Is this the equivalent of a restaurant or McDonald's?" Then there was the matter of what "good service" meant. Did it mean "normal, to-be-expected kind of service," or did it mean "exceptionally helpful and charming kind of service"? Did you tip 15 percent for normal and 20 or more for exceptional? Or 10 percent for normal and 15 percent for exceptional? And what about *shops?*

The hotel clerk became a vital source of information, greeting me at the end of each day with the wry, amused smile of the native and, "Now, how was the situation today, Professor?"

Some days, finishing a meal at the end of a long day, I would feel so confused that I would shrug my shoulders and walk out without tipping. Other times I just tipped the coins in my wallet (how many?—didn't care) into the jar in a form of mindless overcompensation. Some days, maybe, I got it right.

It is probably not necessary for me to spell out the elements of this extended metaphor, but I will mention just a few. First, the rules in both instances appear to be simple but are surprisingly complex, and implementation of the principles requires extensive cultural experience and the exercise of judgment arising from that experience. Second, to those who work within the cultural context, the rules appear to be clear and the complexities of usage almost invisible. Only the novices flounder and therefore see the issue as significant.

But there is a poignant difference between the two situations. When I failed to come to terms with the complexities of the situation, when I walked away without tipping, there were no repercussions. Despite this,

I found the situation confusing and confidence-sapping (I'm used to under-standing the basic social rules of modern living—how come I couldn't do this simple thing?). Had I known that moral censure, personal and family shame, and failure to achieve lifelong dreams might ensue from a single error in grasping these culturally determined practices, then the stress would have been considerably higher. I wanted to be able to tip—it wasn't that I didn't care or didn't try. But I sometimes failed out of frustration at my inability to grasp the complexities. If we had added to the situation a device that would unerringly detect every error I made, I would probably have taken the safe route (McDonald's every day?) or tipped excessively at every possible moment. Anything else would have been too difficult.

Originality, Imitation, and Plagiarism: A Cross-Disciplinary Conference on Writing was a valuable professional experience for me. But nothing at the conference taught me so much about students' experiences of learning to use secondary sources in their writing as did the practical experience of learning to tip. I realize that the idea expressed by this conceit is neither original nor revolutionary; I know that a cornerstone of our pedagogy is the idea that learning academic writing is a form of enculturation (Howard; Price). Although I knew this concept intellectually, I had never *felt* it; I'd never experienced the dilemma from the inside. Through this episode I experienced the plagiarizing student's cultural disorientation.

A significant person in the story is the hotel clerk. At times she was mystified by my confusion but always willing to unravel for me what was second nature to her. Had she been harried and cynical ("Foreigners can never understand the most basic issues"), and judged with the power and inclination to punish my errors, then I would never have learned the basics of this cultural practice. In reversing the role I customarily play, I saw again the attributes of an effective teacher—patience, lightheartedness, interest, a willingness to explore new ideas or revisit old ones, a constant courteous-ness and respect—and a willingness to laugh at mistakes.

Conclusions

Massey University has made the decision to continue and extend the use of Turnitin.com, and a role has emerged for me in talking to faculty about rel-evant research and providing a context of educative support. Recently, three tertiary institutions in our city have come together to research a multistrategy approach to teaching information literacy and secondary source usage, and to develop learning tools that may be used widely across tertiary institutions. If we cannot prevent our institutions from using detection systems, then we must become involved in how they use them, and work to provide an educational context to mitigate their effects.

Plagiarism is a complex, multifaceted term that encompasses quite differently motivated behavior. This study has produced some clear results regarding the effect of conferences on plagiarism rates of all students and ESL students in particular. Although Turnitin has potential as an educational tool, we cannot, given the present climate of antagonism regarding plagiarism, have confidence in its being used in this way unless we become involved in how the institution approaches its use. A potentially punitive and insensitive detection tool is unlikely to encourage learning, and the power of detection does not compensate for the breaking of the pedagogical relationship between student and teacher. If Turnitin is here to stay, then as writing teachers we have a task ahead of us.

Acknowledgments

Thank you to Malcolm Rees, Bruce MacKay, and the participants in the Turnitin trial, particularly Elspeth Tilley and John Walker.

Works Cited

Cameron, Jess. "George Bush Cheats so Why Can't I?" *Chaff* 70, no. 18 (2004): 16.

Carroll, Jude. *A Handbook for Deterring Plagiarism in Higher Education.* Oxford: Oxford Centre for Staff and Learning Development, 2002.

Hall, Jonathan. "Plagiarism across the Curriculum: How Academic Communities Can Meet the Challenge of the Undocumented Writer." *Across the Disciplines: Academic Perspectives on Language, Learning, and Academic Writing*, 2005. http://wac.colostate.edu/atd/articles/hall2005.cfm, consulted August 30, 2005.

Hoogland, Cynthia. *Cuba Journal: Language and Writing.* Windsor, ON: Black Moss Press, 2003.

Howard, Rebecca Moore. *Standing in the Shadow of Giants: Plagiarists, Authors, Collaborators.* Stamford, CT: Ablex, 1999.

Johnson, Andrew and Rosemary Clerehan. "A Rheme of One's Own: How 'Original' Do We Expect Students to Be?" *Journal of University Teaching and Learning Practice* 2, no. 3a (2005): 37–47.

Larkham, P. J., and S. Manns. "Plagiarism and Its Treatment in Higher Education." *Journal of Further and Higher Education* 26, no. 4 (2002): 341–49.

Macdonald, Ranald, and Jude Carroll. "Plagiarism—a Complex Issue Requiring a Holistic Institutional Approach." *Assessment and Evaluation in Higher Education* 31, no. 2 (2006): 233–45.

Marsh, Bill. "Turnitin.com and the Scriptural Enterprise of Plagiarism Detection." *Computers and Composition* 21, no. 4 (2004): 427–38.

McKeever, Lucy. "Online Plagiarism Detection Services—Saviour or Scourge?" *Assessment and Evaluation in Higher Education* 31, no. 2 (2006): 155–66.

Price, Margaret. "Beyond 'Gotcha!': Situating Plagiarism in Policy and Pedagogy." *College Composition and Communication* 54, no. 1 (2002): 88–114.

Schön, Donald. *The Reflective Practitioner: How Professionals Think in Action.* London: Arena, 1991.

Soto, Julio G., and Elizabeth McGee. "Plagiarism Avoidance." *Journal of College Science Teaching* 33, no. 7 (2004): 42–48.

Whitehead, Jack, and Jean McNiff. *Action Research: Living Theory.* London: Sage, 2005.

Winter, Richard, Alyson Buck, and Paula Sobiechowska. *Professional Experience and the Investigative Imagination: The Art of Reflective Writing.* London: Routledge, 1999.

Academic Plagiarism and the Limits of Theft

Stefan Senders

When students plagiarize, are they "stealing"? Or are they merely demonstrating their lack of engagement with "the academic community"? This essay traces one case of plagiarism from its inception in student writing to its resolution in administrative discipline. The student was brought before the Committee on Standards, a quasi-juridical board charged with determining the "guilt" or "innocence" of the student, and with suggesting appropriate discipline. Throughout the process, all parties—the student, professor, deans, and faculty-based disciplinary committee—held different views of what had occurred and what was at stake. Was plagiarism to be viewed primarily as a theft, as a breach of community norms, as a betrayal of the ethical foundation of the teacher-student relationship, or perhaps as a disciplinary misunderstanding?

Educators, it seems, make sense of student plagiarism in two ways.[1] Some argue that students don't know *how* to cite sources or make "proper" use of texts; others assume students know full well what is expected of them, and that when they plagiarize, they cheat. The first approach sees plagiarism as a symptom of ignorance, a condition curable with education. The second approach sees plagiarism as simple fraud, an act sharing semantic space with cribbing, lying, and the stealing of test questions. Rebecca Moore Howard ("Plagiarism"), expanding the pedagogical position, has argued that *plagiarism* is a scare word, and that we should instead view it as one of a wide range of borderline textual practices that function as signs of social transition; students plagiarize, from this perspective, because they have not mastered the norms of scholarly writing and therefore do not see themselves as full participants in that community of writers. Despite such admonitions, however, most teachers assume that students do understand academic norms, but they simply choose not to recognize or act on them.

am sympathetic to the argument that "plagiarism" is a product of socioliterary transition; I agree that if students felt more engaged, more participatory, in their scholarship and writing, they would be far less likely to plagiarize. But strangely, that argument doesn't make sense to my students, who say, almost in unison, that plagiarism is "taking the words of others," that it is "a kind of stealing," and that it is "bad." Admittedly, when I have actually found students doing what I would consider "plagiarizing," they frequently claim ignorance. Aware in the abstract, ignorant in the breech; makes sense to me.

I say that with some cynicism, of course. Plagiarism, my students say, is "bad," but more importantly it "isn't worth it," or it is "for cowards." They tell me that plagiarism is "stealing," yet they also tell me that they routinely, and illegally, download music. I question their claims about the "moral" wrongness of plagiarism, and I have concluded that my students are giving me what they think I want to hear—a legalistic doctrine that defines plagiarism as "stealing."

My students *do know* that plagiarism is regarded as transgressive by the academic community; they also *know* a great deal about the details of academic norms—that paraphrase and websites need citation, that quotes must be exact, that even ideas must be referenced; they *know* that the dominant model for plagiarism is not cooperation or transitional textuality, but *theft*. But for all they do know, many of them *don't believe*. I think there is good reason for this. As Stuart Green argues, plagiarism fits well into the legal model of theft, so long as it is recognized that the "property" that is stolen is not the plagiarized language itself, but the *credit* due the author. That is, plagiarists don't "steal" words, but they do steal the rewards that attach to the public recognition of authorship, which are credit, prestige, and authority.

Among students, the societal norm that "stealing is wrong" does not appear particularly robust.[2] Students routinely download files and music illegally, and they don't have much compunction about it. One student interviewed in a recent survey said, "There are so many people doing this that the risks are so low. . . . It's like shoplifting without the risk or retribution" (Wong). Clearly the issue here is not the applicability of a moral norm prohibiting theft, but an economic norm in favor of the calculation of profit and loss. But even for the students who think stealing *is* wrong, and I mean *really wrong*, plagiarism doesn't look like *normal* theft. From the perspective of the thief, stealing is a way to get things. You want bread, you steal bread; you want jewelry, you steal jewelry; you want music, you steal music. But when students plagiarize, they "steal" *things,* usually words, that they frequently don't want or care about, or even hold onto for long. From a legal perspective, there's not much difference between stealing something and keeping it, and stealing something and giving it away, but subjectively, the two practices apparently look quite distinct.

Students and "authors" do not participate in the same economy. If it isn't *words and ideas,* but is in fact *credit* that is being stolen, do students understand this? They do, of course, understand the idea of credit, but in most cases they consider that credit to be of a very different sort than that accumulated by a professional author. To put it another way, rarely, if ever, is an author deprived of credit when my students reproduce her work. Students do get something out of it: time, excitement, and the possibility of a better grade, but when students "steal" from professional authors, they receive only a form of *token-credit,* a token only valuable within the walls and rules of the house. Students think plagiarism is a bad thing because it can be dangerous to them—they might be caught. It's like a computer virus—the thing that worries them when they download illegal software. It is, moreover, a calculation, a playing of the odds, a game, and the theme song of the game is this: Practice "safe writing," don't catch anything, don't get caught.

At my college, the faculty handbook positions plagiarism squarely in the discourse of the law. Listen to the resonance of courtroom drama (emphasis added):

> All **cases** of **suspected** plagiarism or cheating, whether deliberate or seemingly inadvertent, **must be so reported**, in order to invoke the **hearing** procedure a student **accused** of plagiarism may request a Committee on Standards hearing. . . . If the student is **exonerated** . . . If **sus-**
> p   e   n   d   e   d
> . . . [N]ormally, **guilt or innocence** of plagiarism or cheating is determined by the Committee on Standards and the dean primarily on the basis of the **factual evidence** submitted by the instructor. . . . **A student's ignorance of what constitutes these offenses or of the rules concerning them is not considered to bear on this question.** If a student is **judged guilty,** circumstances surrounding his or her action may be taken into consideration in determining appropriate **penalties.** (Hobart and William Smith Colleges)

The language is of cases, suspects, reports, hearings, accusation, innocence, guilt, exoneration, evidence, judgment, and penalty. The process, it appears, is invoked automatically. Even the mechanics of the appeal is crafted to have the look and feel of the law.

In three cases I have participated in, my account was taken first, and the student was asked if she had anything to say in response. The faculty members of the Committee on Standards then addressed questions to the student: Do you know what plagiarism is? Do you think what you did is plagiarism? Were you aware at the time that what you were doing was considered plagiarism? Where did the material that was not yours come from? Did you do what you did deliberately? Once the committee had heard the "evidence," it asked us both to leave the room while they deliberated in secret before inviting us back to hear the "verdict." What is striking about the process is the degree to which it is framed and elaborated as a judicial one. What is even more striking, however, is that while there is quasi-legal language, there *is no law*. There is no set code that governs the rules of evidence, the limits of plagiarism, the limits of accusation, or the reasonable extent of punishment. There is no direct or open appeal to precedent, and if members of the committee have any knowledge of past cases, it is purely accidental.

National estimates suggest that between 20 and 40 percent of college students cheat or plagiarize.[3] Yet at my school, in 2004, only three cases came before the deans. Out of a student population of just under two thousand, that's a little more than one-tenth of 1 percent. It's possible that our school is special, and that the students don't cheat here, but it seems unlikely; according to the deans, most cases of plagiarism are "handled" by professors individually. I have learned, based on anecdotal evidence, that in my school plagiarism is quite widespread, but that it is rarely acknowledged, and even more rarely "prosecuted."

In practice, then, our claims that "plagiarism is theft," and the corollary that their prosecution is somehow "legal," are undermined by the weakness of our legal theater. We are not convincing because, at least at a communal level, *we don't believe that student plagiarism is theft.*[4] Our claims are inauthentic and false, and so, to the sharp eyes of our students, who have surely had plenty of practice in spotting just such inauthenticity in other authorities, we look foolish, not to mention hypocritical.

We can assume that if our students suspect us of hypocrisy, their suspicions are confirmed when we press them to work cooperatively on papers, to workshop and peer-edit, and to discuss their forming work freely in class and in our offices. We tell them to do it themselves, and to do it with others. It's an unhappy mix.

I have argued that the claim that plagiarism is theft, or stealing, may make sense among professionals, but it fails to do so among students or in the academic-pedagogical context generally. It fails because (1) norms concerning the morality of theft are changing, particularly among our student population; (2) subjectively, from the student's point of view, plagiarism does not meet the definition of theft, in that the plagiarist *does not get what she steals;* (3) to the extent that credit is stolen, the meaning of "credit" is not the same for professionals and students (thus students do not see themselves as "stealing" something that they could in fact steal) (4) our use of a quasi-legal theater to sustain an antiplagiarism norm has been ill-conceived, and it has therefore not been successful; and finally, (5) in our teaching we have not adequately articulated the relationship between ostensibly "original" work and "collaborative" work, and we have thus failed to displace the assumptive norm that originality is "better" than collaborative work. In such a context, it's no wonder that plagiarism might not seem like a big deal to students.

But plagiarism is a big deal to me, and it is to many teachers I know. It is important to me not because it is "criminal," but because it undermines the intimacy that helps make teaching possible and rewarding. Plagiarism displaces that intimacy with a new form of relationship, one characterized by instrumentality, deception, and infidelity. Arguably, we have set the stage for such a disruption, but we nonetheless depend on pedagogical intimacy to make teaching work. From this perspective, plagiarism is not an *act;* it is a relationship, a social form that, while always transgressive and often disruptive, can on occasion offer teachers and students unanticipated opportunities.

My students, by and large, are well prepared and willing. But last year, after receiving a wave of papers from my first-year writing seminar, I noticed that the work I was receiving was surely plagiarized. We had been reading George Orwell's *1984,* and the students had produced copious freewriting about the novel, engaged in peer-critique, and had chosen essay topics in consultation with me. The process was as much about topic choice and development as it was about the finer points of the essay.[5]

It wasn't hard to tell which papers had been written and which had been clipped, and I developed a functional, if somewhat cynical, approach to the preliminary triage. If a sentence had even a breath of grace, I checked to see if Google knew anything about it. My first inquiry brought up one student's paper as the first hit; he had simply cut and pasted it as a whole—almost whole; the omissions from the original were almost as telling as the plagiarism itself. The student removed from the essay the only passage that suggested even the slightest intellectual challenge. Once I had received, and identified, the first piece of plagiarism, I began filing through the papers on my desk, looking for sentences that seemed out of place. I was angry. I Googled a few and came up with hits. I began to get the picture: the papers had been assembled, half-written, pasted-down—they were plagiarized.

I was struck by my students' skepticism about their own writing and "voice." They seemed so sure that they had nothing to say, and no voice to say it in, that I wouldn't notice that the papers weren't theirs. Their skepticism certainly clarified my task: to help them realize that they might have something to say and a way to say it. The disjuncture between the students' misperception of their own "voices," specifically that they do not have them, and the perception of readers of their work, who perceive those voices clearly, suggests a kind of rhetorical self-negation, almost a blindness with respect to authorial self. Student plagiarism, from this perspective, might best be seen as a dysfunctional manifestation of a psycho-rhetorical disorder, a kind of displacement, a failure of identification in which the literary self is absent or unavailable.

I have many times been told that before accusing someone of plagiarism, I should be sure of my claim. The first paper was too blatant a misrepresentation to have been rooted in ignorance, but I suspected that I'd find more plagiarism, as it seemed plausible that *some* of it might have been somehow innocent, or at least ignorant. When I next met my class I had the students write a brief essay in answer to the question, "What is plagiarism?" I wanted a signed statement from each of them. There was no confusion; with only a couple of exceptions, the students agreed that plagiarism is "using someone else's words without attribution. Stealing someone else's words or ideas." A few called it a "coward's way out," and worried "it was something that could get you into big trouble" because "you could have plagiarized without your knowing what you've done."[6]

I then told my class about the papers, and I let them know I was angry. I suggested that if any of them was worried about whether or not they'd plagiarized, that they should come see me. That day, as my office hours approached, students began lining up outside my door. In the end, twelve out of my thirty-four students came to meet with me. There was, it seemed, a lot to worry about. Most of the students were worried for no reason. A few had failed to cite properly, but it was clear to me that most of their failures were clumsy, not deceptive. One student, though, walked in my door, sat down, looked at the floor and said: "I did it. You were talking about me, right?" And it was true. We talked for a while. Why had he done it? He told me that he was stressed-out. He had been having trouble with his girl-friend. Some of his family members were sick. His team had been taking a lot of his time, and his courses had all somehow gotten backed up. He apologized and wondered what would happen. I told him to go, directly, to the deans.

The next student entered my office, smiled, and said that she thought I might have found some of her writing troubling. I agreed that I had (hers had been one of the papers I had first picked up), and I gave her my copy of her paper, on which I had marked a couple of passages I knew she had not written. She looked at the paper, sighed, and agreed that the passages were not hers, and that it hadn't been the right thing to do. But, she said, she hadn't exactly been clear about how to cite, and she didn't really think that what she had done was as bad as it appeared. She just hadn't known what to do. It was simple ignorance. I resisted the impulse to punish. "Fine," I told her, "I will work with you. Why don't you take your paper back and cite each bit that isn't yours, and indicate which bits are yours. I've shown you how to cite (and don't worry, I'm not worrying about the little things) so you can go do it. We'll work in good faith."

I soon received an e-mail with a new version of her paper attached. She had cited every passage I'd marked. It seemed like a good resolution, until I saw a suspiciously graceful phrase. Sure enough, she had cited the marked passages, but no others; the paper appeared to be a complex pastiche of pastes, patch writing, paraphrase, and unmarked quotations, and she was hoping to get out with the least trouble she could manage. I sent her an e-mail containing a single question mark and the Web address from "Spark-notes" from which some of the remaining material had come.

We agreed that she would identify all the material that she had written herself, and cite what she had taken from other sources. She would have to go before the Committee on Standards, which would decide on the conse-quences of her case. I recommended that she speak to the dean immedi-ately. As it turned out, she had been brought before the Committee on Standards once before on a similar charge—she had been caught cheating on a science test. (She hadn't really cheated, she said.) Because my case was not her first offense, the penalties were likely to be more severe than usual, and might include expulsion; she was terrified and began to e-mail me mul-tiple times a day. She was sure that if she were to be expelled her parents "would kill her," and that she "couldn't accept it."[7]

I suggested that she write a letter of appeal to the committee, in hopes of reducing her punishment. She latched onto the idea, and when I suggested that she start the process using the very production techniques we had discussed in class, she agreed enthusiastically. Which is to say, she became a writer, and I a writing teacher. She wrote:

> I have begun loop writing on the points that we picked out of my freewriting. . . . I am thinking that I should continue loop writing this weekend and then have a rough draft of my appeal to forward you this weekend or show you Monday. Do you think we should meet another time or I should get this put together now that I have my strong points?
>
> I having been working away at my appeal and doing lots of loop writing and I have a question about the order of my points in my appeal.

But it wasn't all good. There was also fear.

> Professor H. spoke with a reliable source and was told, just like I was told, that I must write my appeal based on the four criteria from the handbook. As we both know, I really do not have anything to go on from there.
>
> . . . I intend to turn in the appeal tomorrow, but am obviously very concerned. I have spoken with a couple of other professors for advice and to request letters of reference, and one thing they suggested was that I ask you directly to drop the charges. I feel awkward asking you this via email, . . . but, again, I do not think my violations warrant removal from school. I realize this would require a drastic step on your part, but I would be willing to make it up to you however you see fit, on my honor (which I can assure you remains intact). I realize you are trying to bring attention to this issue and think we could team-up to do so. I am at your mercy and would be greatly indebted to you if you would drop the charges.
>
> . . . Please, can you give me another chance to prove to you and myself that I can change and get through what I have done.

The student stopped coming to class, but became intensely engaged in writing. She drafted proposals for antiplagiarism education programs, developed a Sapir-Whorf hypothesis for her own plagiarism, arguing that in mathematics scholars "plug in" formulas and variables without attribution, and because she saw herself as a math major, not a humanities major, she should reasonably be expected to follow the norms of mathematics. She wrote letters to other professors seeking advice and assistance, and she even asked me to write a letter on her behalf, which I did—with significant reservations and caveats (I would have been more supportive if she hadn't written to the dean to say that she "had not been dishonest").

Eventually her case came up, and she and I were called to stand before the committee to explain the case. She came to the hearing, like any smart defendant, well dressed—in a respectable dark blue pantsuit—and she read a long prepared statement to the committee in which she argued that "something has to be done about the problem of plagiarism at this school," and that she was the one who could help. The gesture was, in part, one of contrition, but one that at the same time confirmed a fundamental disruption of her ability to perceive her own ethos. Her statement was heard, and apparently ignored; because she had been found guilty of cheating once before, she was expelled—temporarily. The student and her mother, who had inquired about the potential for a lawsuit, eventually and reluctantly accepted her punishment. The student is now back on campus, doing fairly well, and the case appears resolved.

My student, then, despite all the pain and anguish that accompanied her "trial," became, even if only for a few weeks, a writer, and she saw and worked with me in my role as a writing teacher. From a pedagogical perspective, the incident was a success; the student, once so disengaged from learning, had seen with near-blinding clarity the reasons for writing drafts, for conferencing, for editing, and for thinking hard about writing. There were other unexpected effects. Quiet students began to find their voices, and marginal writers became suddenly attentive to writing and to detail. In some cases it looked like simple fear; they were afraid that they would do something wrong and get nailed for it. But in others, it seemed that the intensity of our relationship had suddenly increased. Students and teacher were made more distant, but also brought closer together; the apparently "criminal" act became a pedagogical encounter. Plagiarism, to quote Howard ("Sexuality")—with a slight shift in emphasis—did "cultural work."

A number of my colleagues have suggested that plagiarism is the product of poor teaching, that it comes from lackluster classroom theater and vague assignments. While it is true that we can do a great deal to preempt transgression, it strikes me as odd that we should be expected to shoulder the burden alone. The best advice, clearly, is to teach with as much vigor and engagement as possible. Yet we also have to wonder why the vocabulary we share with our students is often so limited; why my students were so easily ready to feel and express remorse, but not to engage in intellectual inquiry, or to engage with the "academic community."

The *act* of plagiarism brings into play new *actors*. The "academic community," usually nothing more than a vague shadow to the student, suddenly appears to both faculty and student newly materialized. The college's handbook, the signal of bureaucratic authority, takes on new power as all parties turn to it for rule. And in its black-and-white text, where statements are phrased in the imperative mood (the student *will* receive a grade of F in the course), the players find thin guidance, as imperative text gives way to contingent reality. Each individual player will take on many roles. The teacher will become investigator, police, judge, and finally (perhaps) executioner. The student, once seen as a person of *potential,* will appear to the college and professor as a somewhat more fixed quality—a violator, a cheater perhaps, or in more friendly times, an ignoramus. The student's immediate context, usually invisible to all concerned, will take on heightened significance, and may emerge into light. The student will turn reprobate, criminal, fool, child, lawyer, and perhaps belligerent.

As the stage becomes crowded, the relationships among all the players will gain heightened significance, and they too will shift shape. Between student and teacher will emerge, perhaps, a newly charged Oedipal dynamic, as the urge to "kill the father" seems more and more apt. Perhaps the student will feel the need to confess, and if he does, then to whom shall he confess? So perhaps the professor, if she is warm, will become confessor and potential redeemer, or if she is cool will stand as accuser and interrogator, rejecting all confession as irrelevant. The professor, too, will have new social needs: what is her obligation to the "academic community," and how is that community represented in the immediate circumstances of her collegiate surroundings? Who are the deans, and what role will they play in shaping her response? What does she owe them?

In her bad dreams all her students will hand in identical essays, each cut-and-pasted from the same foolish website, and in the morning or in class, she will look at them with suspicion. And perhaps she will feel angry, and even though she might attempt to hide that anger, judging it misplaced, she can hardly do so successfully, and the classroom will take on a new atmosphere, one potentially poisonous, but just as conceivably nurturing. Or, just as likely, she has learned that each case deserves to be heard and understood on its own merits, and she will wonder just how little do her students really know, and just how do they regard the school in which they study. Of course, she will feel some measure of affront, probably laced with humor, that her students thought *she wouldn't notice!* And then she would realize how little they understand about the subtlety of voice and rhythm, and how much work she has to do. She might go home to a companion, who will share her anger and outrage and humor, and she will find from the disruption of her classroom intimacy a new intimacy elsewhere.

Of course, it is just as likely that another professor will see the same paper differently, perhaps not *notice* anything wrong, or at very least *not enough* to make a stink about. After all, these things take time and energy, and they might not be worth it. And so this professor will distance herself from her classes, sensing, rightly, that something is off somehow, but that it isn't worth getting into. Thus the professor will begin to experience *removal,* or *dismissal,* and will feel, probably, a sense of increased interaction with her own self and work. She might feel more powerful than she did earlier, as she was able to detect the plagiarism and to determine the outcome of that detection without any interference from outside authorities.

From a legalistic perspective, plagiarism has a slippery quality, shifting as it does from theft to defamation to fraud to passing off (Green). From a social analytic perspective, however, it's much easier to assess. First, plagiarism is not simply an *act,* it is a categorical designation for a range of *relationships,* all of which center on a subjective sense of transgression. Only by analyzing the way the relationship of plagiarism takes shape can we say whether it is best fit by paradigms of "theft," "fraud," "infidelity," or even excessive intimacy. Moreover, by viewing plagiarism as a relationship, we become more aware of its productivity, of the ways it shapes and refigures other identities and relationships. Plagiarism from this perspective comes to serve not merely as prohibition, but as an illumination of our pedagogical and administrative practices. When we cling to the juridical metaphor to define plagiarism, moreover, we become its slaves, and we might wish, finally, to be stolen away, liberated, plagiarized.

Notes

1. I owe special thanks to my students, and to Antonia Saxon, George Cooper, Allison Truitt, and Ann Russ for their discussion, comments, questions, and suggestions. I also owe what I hope are obvious intellectual debts to Rebecca Moore Howard and Stuart Green.

2. Many authors have made historical arguments to the effect that the moral prohibition against stealing has weakened in recent years. I have seen no evidence that either supports or refutes the claim. It is clear, however, that the prohibition is not as powerful as many people, particularly authorities and property owners, would like it to be.

3. McCabe and Trevino suggest that rates are even higher. Here I use conservative numbers, such as those used by the University of Illinois. Similar statistics are widely available on the Web.

4. We tend to recognize it as a transgression, but only very rarely do we imagine that a particular case of plagiarism involves theft from the author. It is often true that teachers experience plagiarism as a personal affront, or a breach of implicit contract, but in such cases the offense is not against an author, rather it is against the teacher.

5. Topics ranged from a discussion of hypnotism to an analysis of the Abu Ghraib prison scandal. Some students wanted to write about Orwell's dystopia and its "relation" to current U.S. politics. I discouraged them, suggesting that they would find it difficult to carve out much writing space from the dense critique available on the Web. Three chose to write on the topic against my advice, and of those students, two plagiarized. I later learned that there are extensive Web resources for students writing about any "classic" work. The available material ranges from complete essays to public advice boards. In the Orwell thread on "Sparknotes," for example, students posted queries and comments such as these:

> hey guys.
> i need help with the following: i have to do a diary entry (winston's point of view). i still don't know what i should do it about. any suggestions? it's writer's block for me right now. i must write a minimum of 500 words max of 1,000. i must respect the language, style and setting.
> any suggestions please email me @ . . .
> thanx!

> Essay on Newspeak
> posted by *sonofdabitch* on 6/5 4:23 PM
> The topic of my essay is an explanation of Newspeak. I'll have to write more than 1000 words. The problem is that I can't find a lot of material on the topic besides the appendix. Can anybody give me some advice ?

> connecting to todays world
> posted by *petercom10* on 9/11 3:08 PM
> if you want to connect newspeak to something similar in our current society, euphamisms are similar to newspeak in that it changes what you are saying by making your speech seem milder and politacally correct

6. Their responses, for all their uniformity, were suggestive. To see plagiarism as the "coward's way out" suggests a linkage to a guiding notion of masculinity—plagiarism is for pussies (for more on this line of inquiry, see Howard, "Sexuality"). The idea that plagiarism is something that could somehow sneak up on you suggests that students see it as part of a tactical tool-kit of teachers, who are in opposition to the student.

7. At one point she went so far as to draft a letter to the dean in which she said that she "could not accept expulsion." I had to point out to her that she was in no position to accept or reject anything. The incident indicated (again) a profound

ethos disruption, the rhetorical equivalent of a personality disorder.

Works Cited

Green, Stuart P. "Plagiarism, Norms, and the Limits of Theft Law: Some Observations on the Use of Criminal Sanctions in Enforcing Intellectual Property Rights." *Hastings Law Journal* 54 (2002): 167–242.

Hobart and William Smith Colleges. *Faculty Handbook.* https://campus.hws.edu/aca /provost/ handbook/faculty_handbook_part_3.pdf, consulted May 15, 2007.

Howard, Rebecca Moore."Plagiarism: What Should a Teacher Do?" Paper presented at the Conference on College Composition and Communication, Denver, March 2001.

Howard, Rebecca Moore. "Sexuality, Textuality: The Cultural Work of Plagiarism." *College English* 62 (March 2000): 473–91.

McCabe, Donald, and Linda Trevino. "What We Know about Cheating in College." *Change* 28, no. 1 (1996): 28–33.

"SafeAssignment: Easily Deter Plagiarism in Your Class Using SafeAssignment for Blackboard." University of Illinois at Chicago. http://www.uic.edu/depts/accc/ itl/ safeassignment.html, consulted June 2, 2006.

Wong, Brad. "Illegal Downloads Don't Pose Ethical Problem for College Students." *Seattle Post Intelligencer,* June 30, 2005. http://seattlepi.nwsource.com/printer2/ index.asp?ploc=t&refer=http://seattlepi.nwsource.com/business/ 230702_down- loads30.html, consulted May 15, 2007.

Insider Writing

Plagiarism-Proof Assignments

Lynn Z. Bloom

Whose words these are, I think I know . . .

It was the best of assignments . . . . Newcomers to St. Louis in 1974, we had chosen to live in Clayton because of its excellent public schools. So my heart leapt up when I beheld the instructions for our son's very first sixth grade English assignment, "Write a poem in the manner of Robert Frost." This Laird did, refusing—as usual—to let us even see his work until he brought it home with the teacher's comments. I do not remember the poem, alas, but I do remember how all changed, changed utterly when at the bottom of the quatrains appeared, in impeccable copperplate, the teacher's only observation: "This is a very good poem—if YOU wrote it." Maintaining my customary decorum—I had yet (nor have I still) to punch any rogue and peasant slave in the nose—I suppressed my outrage and asked Laird, "May I complain to your teacher?" "Over my dead body," quoth the innocent (not his exact words), so I forbore.

This cynical skepticism reveals how even good assignments can go bad if a teacher doesn't trust her convictions, or her students. Today she'd have gone straight to the Internet, where a Google search would reveal some 32,800 hits for the combination of "Robert Frost" and "Whose woods these are" in English alone. What a waste of time, and what a displacement of intellectual energy! Laird's teacher was, in fact, on the right track and should have had confidence in the integrity of her assignment, recognizing that it was, if not plagiarism-proof, then plagiarism-resistant. For hers was a classic "insider writing" assignment.

As teachers, we need to exploit the broad spectrum of possibilities for insider writing assignments—those that inspire originality *because* they are plagiarism-proof. To do so, we need to examine how we ourselves understand our own discipline as insiders. Whatever we take for granted as disciplinary assumptions and knowledge, norms and values; how and why we do our work; and what we consider big issues, ongoing problems, can become the basis for writing assignments that will invite students to look inside, to understand, to remember.

Why the Current Concern with Plagiarism-Proof Writing Assignments?

It is far easier, more intellectually interesting, and more ethically satisfying to prevent plagiarism than to track it down. It's far more productive and a lot more fun for teachers and students alike to work in the atmosphere of trust that insider assignments engender, with their implications of collegial creativity, rather than with the suspicion adhering to more conventional assignments. Innovative assignments resistant to plagiarism are particularly important in an era when student culture implicitly condones copying software and downloading MP3 files, is dependent on Internet search engines, and believes that even copyrighted information is there for the taking. These *insider writing* assignments are original in conception; they encourage student writers to be original, thoughtful, and engaged; they can be revised and refined anew for every student in every class. They assume and operate on the assumption that students will actively participate as insiders in investigating the topic at hand, and in creating some of the issues and materials to be studied, and not simply approach topics from the outside as passive consumers of ancillary sources.

Insider Writing versus Outsider Writing
Outsider Writing

Robert Scholes claims that in writing conventional critical papers students are put in the position of trying to second guess the teacher's interpretation of unassailable iconic texts. They too often feel forced to read and write as aliens, bowing in reverence before the sacred texts of the literary canon, "'the best that has been thought and said,'" offered up by teachers serving as "priests and priestesses in the service of a secular scripture" (12–13ff.). The same obsequiousness prevails when students, novices to the subject at hand, rely heavily on experts on any topic, in any field. Students, writing of necessity as outsiders, see themselves as pressured to consult the experts, to patch together others' ideas and words (see Howard) in the hope of coming closer to understanding the subject than they would if they depended on their own ideas. Yet as outsiders suppressing their own judgments, student writers serving as ventriloquists of published scholars are not positioned to own the primary material or to trust their opinions of it. With so little of themselves in their writing, they have little incentive to care very much about their work.

Insider Writing

In contrast, when students write from *inside* the problem, issue, or literary or historical work at hand, they operate as engaged participants rather than as alien outsiders whose understanding comes through what others— sometimes centuries of others—have had to say on the subject. As I explain below, through the examples of my own literature course and those in other disciplines, teachers in all fields can construct assignments that compel their students to understand the perspectives, values, beliefs, norms, and customs as insiders. By creating dialogues, dramatizations, primary documents, or position papers in the process, students are directed to produce meaning, rather than to reproduce received opinion.

With such assignments, student authors perforce have to accept and assume some authority for knowing and understanding the problem or issue at hand. Admittedly, this authority is limited by the students' actual experience with or understanding of the situation they're writing about, as it would be in most undergraduate papers. Yet these assignments have considerable integrity, and consequently, so do the students. Teachers whose courses are described below (see also Adler-Kassner, Crooks, and Watters; Downing, Hurlbert, and Mathieu; Flower; Grobman) claim that because as a rule the students are heavily invested in the lively dialogues or events in which they're participating, they work harder, learn more (they generally have to buttress their insider understanding with outside sources), and write far more convincingly than with the usual routine academic exercises. Because these writing assignments are highly specific to both the courses and to the individual student's participation in them, they're more varied, more interesting, and nearly impossible to plagiarize. As the context changes every semester, so do the assignments; students have to construct their specifically nuanced topic from the ground up, every time.

How Insider Writing Works: Model Courses

Coming of Age in American Autobiography, a course I've taught over the years to honors freshmen and a variety of upper-division undergraduates, took on new vitality when I changed the writing assignments from conventional papers of literary criticism to imaginative scenarios in which the students created or reconceived the autobiographers and significant moments in these lives. My students examine autobiographies, including those of Benjamin Franklin, Frederick Douglass (the 1845 version), Harriet Jacobs, Henry David Thoreau, Annie Dillard, Richard Wright, and Maxine Hong Kingston, in their human, historical, and literary contexts in order to understand as readers, critics, and writers the significant issues and problems of the autobiographer's art.

The students analyze the ways autobiographers shape their self-presentations in a variety of roles: as members of a particular gender, ethnicity, or social class; as individuals in family, occupational, and other group contexts; and as people fulfilling particular destinies or roles in a specific historical context. To accomplish these aims the students "become" the characters they are writing about through employing a variety of literary forms, including monologues, dialogues, dramas, philosophical presentations, letters of job application or professional vitas, and imaginary journal entries.

Among the many possibilities for writing is an assignment that asks pairs of students to "write a dialogue between Franklin and Douglass in which they discuss, debate, and ultimately define the meaning(s) of one of the following concepts as it pertains to either coming of age as an individual or as a nation (or both): independence, self-reliance, defiance of authority, citizenship, maturity, contributions to/engagement in the larger society." Another asks student duos to

> Design a twenty-first-century house for Thoreau (will it be static or mobile, rigid or free form?), in an appropriate setting (will it remain at Walden Pond? Or will you relocate it? Why?). One of you (as Annie Dillard) acts as the decorator, while the other is the environmental engineer and landscaper. Remembering Frank Lloyd Wright's dictum, "Form follows function," this dwelling and its environment should reflect and symbolize the predominant values of both Thoreau and Dillard. These characteristics are reflected in the appended list, "Writing in the Manner of Thoreau and Other Nature Writers" [see appendix]. You may include illustrations—a drawing, floor plan, sketches, photos, whatever, ad-lib.

Because the papers have to be historically accurate, characters from different times must have a plausible way of communicating with one another, one that respects the era and the ethos of each; the students may choose a contemporary or future time if they wish. One memorable presentation was that of an engineering student, who delightedly filled all the whiteboards in the classroom with diagrams of an environmentally friendly geodesic dome, from various angles, employing mathematical formulas to illustrate its ecological properties. Other briefer writings involved keeping a Thoreauvian journal; telling a joke Dillard's family would appreciate; making a list imitating Richard Wright's lists of sensory encounters with objects and phenomena; and constructing a cautionary tale analogous to "No Name Woman," which opens Kingston's *Woman Warrior.*

I consider these assignments *historical rendering* because they are embedded in factual information. My students, however, call them *creative writing,* in part because they're highly unusual in freedom, form, and voice for academic writing, and they are unique in the students' experience. Students deadened by conventional expectations revive as they reanimate their subject in a process that compels independent thought and allows them to tap wells of creativity they didn't know they had. While working with partners, they learn from one another—not so much factual information, which both have to find from external sources—but perspective, pacing, the sound and sense of sentences, dialogue, organization. Many seem surprised that such enjoyable assignments require them to work harder than they expected to, even though they are sharing the work, and at how extensively they need to revise (often, by supplying additional evidence or information) once the class has heard their intermediate version.

Of course, to fully experience autobiography as a literary form, it is essential for the students to write an autobiographical essay, thereby to understand the genre as insiders once again, in this case as real-time, real-world autobiographers. This is, perhaps, the ultimate "insider" writing, the quintessence of a paper impossible to plagiarize. Students still have to figure out ways to make accounts of first true love, recognition of life's unfairness or random chance, experience with war or exile or divorce or death meaningful in new ways to the jaded reader. Thus, about midway through the semester, when the students felt comfortable with each other and with me, I ask them to "tell a true story of your experience with an event, person or group; recognition or development of a belief or value system; or other phenomenon that was pivotal in your coming of age and/or understanding of the world." In the interests of full disclosure, I share with them my autobiographical "Living to Tell the Tale: The Complicated Ethics of Creative Nonfiction." Here I use the story of discovering my twinhood, whose existence and neonatal death my parents had concealed from me (including denial, altering my birth certificate, swearing talkative relatives to secrecy) as the vehicle for exploring such fundamental issues as "Who owns the story?" "Who has the right to tell/suppress/interpret it?—for what readers?" and more. The implied message is clear: if I can do this, making myself vulnerable to readers and at the same time transforming life into art, so can they.

Although these assignments specify three to five pages, most of the students write double or triple that number, not counting revisions. They expect to be able to dash off a personal reminiscence; then artistic and philosophical and ethical issues intervene, and they revise again and again. And again. In an era when many students take writing-intensive courses simply to fill a requirement, this is surely an index of student investment. And yes, of course, I too invest a lot of time responding to these multiple drafts, but the results are worth our collective effort, say the student evaluations, enthusiastic affirmations of this writing that, as one student said, "makes me better than I am."

My students' class presentations stimulate lively, invested, and involved discussion. The students come alive when they read these papers, individually or in pairs, to their primary audience, the class; their discussions are energetic, enthusiastic, and engaged. When I asked the students to evaluate each assignment individually, to a person they loved "trying new modes of writing and getting into the heads of the authors we were reading." They write, "I was pleasantly surprised with the assignments. I liked them a great deal more than the simple, mechanical, and stereotypical critical papers I was used to." The autobiography, voted "the best paper of the year," provided further validation of insider writing: "It gave everyone a hands-on experience with the genre. While I found writing about myself exceedingly difficult, this assignment gave me a great appreciation of the subject matter of this course."

Other Sample: Insider Writing Assignments

Two areas examined below, classical studies and service learning, are representative of the burgeoning literature on writing across the curriculum, as addressed in John Bean's *Engaging Ideas* and Art Young's *Teaching Writing Across the Curriculum*. Many of their suggested writing assignments ("microthemes," peer reviews, assessment of evidence or issues in learning) can be adapted to specific disciplines, and further refined to employ an insider's perspective.

Dramatizations of Classical Works

Classical studies professors Christy Friend and Mark C. Carnes created classroom experiences comparable to my own. Desperate to liven up classes full of passive, tuned-out students, each teacher devised classroom dramatizations of classical works in which students played insider roles in the cultures they were learning about. In each course, as in mine, the students, well informed, wrote more sophisticated and longer papers analyzing the issues addressed. Friend's students reenacted the *controversiae* on affirmative action from Quintilian's *Institutio Oratoria,* openly "questioning assumptions about merit and equality, and examining the political, historical and cultural factors" influencing these (9–12). In Carnes's "Liminal Classroom" students enacted scenes from their reading, such as Plato's account of the trial of Socrates in *The Republic* and Confucius's resolution of disputes in *The Analects,* examining the classical works within "the contexts of the impassioned debates and dramas from which they had emerged." Because the students in both teachers' classes became so thoroughly invested in their subjects that they not only "spent countless hours outside of class meeting in factions and cajoling the undecided [,] they worked harder on papers and submitted more of them," even though the assignments were "far more demanding" than they had been earlier, when students merely read the texts (Carnes B6–B8).

Real-World Writing: Insider Writing in Service-Learning Courses

Service-learning courses in all disciplines put students into real-world writing situations where it is impossible to plagiarize. The students serve as aides or interns in nonprofit organizations, public schools, hospitals, prisons, homeless shelters, and other community service endeavors (see Deans, *Writing Partnerships,* appendix B; Grobman 129; Cushman, "Service Learning"). From their "insider" perspective, albeit one with limited authority, they write either in, about, or for that context. Often they cross "cultural and class boundaries by collaborating" both in writing and in "pragmatic civic action" with "community partners" who may be very different from themselves (Deans, *Writing Partnerships,* 9–10). Their writings are thus specific to both context and situation: reports, bulletins, brochures, operating manuals, position statements, case studies, reflections on programs and the student's participation therein are among the plethora of possibilities (see Flower; Deans, *Writing Partnerships;* Cushman, "Sustainable Programs"). Service learning owes much to Freire's liberation pedagogy of "social dreaming," which assumes "that if students perform ideological analysis and critical literacy in the classroom, they will parlay that critical consciousness into concrete civic action later in their lives" (qtd. in Deans, *Writing Partnerships,* 109).

Space considerations allow only a single characteristic service-learning assignment to represent the philosophical and pedagogical rationale for such writing. Deans's textbook, *Writing and Community Action,* offers two alternative forms: either a "Community-Based Research Essay" that explores "A Social Concern or Local Problem" or an "Agency Profile Report." Both incorporate experience and comparable research methods, requiring students to interview agency personnel and community members and to do fieldwork through writing field notes and journal entries, evaluating sources, and synthesizing material from agency documents, library, and Web sources. The student's investigation might be a "prelude to community service," helping newcomers—new tutors, for instance—"understand social issues and engage in community work." Or students could use community service to "explore complex problems, and spur critical reflection" through analyzing their fieldwork in its social context. For instance, a student working in a homeless shelter could progress from the fairly literal, "How do I make sense of what I saw today?" to the broader, "What options for job training are available?" to considering the most general and most difficult, the influence of "local, national, and global economic forces" on homelessness. In addition, community-based research can be "a form of social action in its own right," if students, as they work with community members, can actually produce position papers or reports that "can help social change organizations do their work." In all assignments, students examine ethical issues: What is the project's purpose? Does it respect everyone's "rights and dignity"? Who might it benefit, and how? Might there be any "potentially problematic consequences"? (*Writing and Community Action,* 273–76).

As this assignment illustrates, writing in service-learning courses involves so many separate components, each embedded in the students' ongoing experiences, that it would be impossible to fake. Although these writings are not without problems, including what Cushman describes as the "liberal do-gooder stance" of the newly socially conscious ("Public Intellectual," 132), or the "hit it and quit it" superficiality of a single semester's involvement ("Sustainable Programs," 40), all are perforce original. Claims that exceed the authority of the students' limited experience can usually be tempered by judicious questions, to be addressed in the requisite revision, on the order of: How do you know? What's your evidence—and from what sources? Is what you say always true? Applicable in all instances?

Insider Assignments: They're Really Not about Plagiarism

In the final analysis, avoiding plagiarism is fundamentally a secondary concern for teachers, whose efforts are better spent inventing writing assignments that are original, intellectually demanding, participatory—the essence of insider writing. As we have seen, such assignments can open up new ways of responding to the student's world, to the world of ideas, to issues that are relevant to contemporary life. These writing assignments promise to be exhilarating, creative, fun. Best of all, they inspire the passion that comes from investment in one's work, pride of authorship of writing one owns and loves.

APPENDIX: WRITING IN THE MANNER OF THOREAU
AND OTHER NATURE WRITERS
Thoreau set the style and pace for 150 years of American nature writers who continue to follow in his footsteps. Among the major characteristics are the following:

- First-person perspective. "It is, after all, always the first person that is speaking" (107).
- Unassuming authorial persona.
- Desire for simplicity. "My purpose in going to Walden Pond was . . . to transact some private business with the fewest obstacles" (119).
- Self-reliant and resourceful. "I lived alone . . . a mile from any neighbor, in a house which I had built myself. . . and earned my living by the labor of my hands only" (107).
- Philosophical. "To be a philosopher . . . [is] so to love wisdom as to live according to its dictates, a life of simplicity, independence, magnanimity, and trust" (116) [e.g., a natural philosopher].
- Curious.—intellectually, philosophically, existentially—about everything.

- Love of solitude. "I find it wholesome to be alone the greater part of the time." (See "Solitude" chapter.)
- Compulsion to march to a different drummer. "The greater part of what my neighbors call good I believe in my soul to be bad, and if I repent of any thing, it is very likely to be my good behavior" (113).
- Sensitivity to the natural world, all things under the sun, great and small. "For many years I was self-appointed inspector of snow storms and rain storms" (118).
- Cosmic awareness, a vision of infinity, eternity. "Walden has become situated not only in Massachusetts but in the heart of America and in the center of the universe" (116).
- A desire to live fully in the moment. "In any weather, at any hour of the day or night, I have been anxious to improve the nick of time . . . have been anxious . . . to stand on the meeting of two eternities, the past and future, which is precisely the present moment" (117).
- Sense of moral superiority and physical well-being. Uses the natural setting as the basis for providing a critique of society (including the entire world), and sets up his corner of the universe as a model for the world to follow.

This is a partial list, to which we can add. (See also Lawrence Buell, *The Environmental Imagination: Thoreau, Nature Writing, and the Formation of American Culture* (Harvard University Press, 1995.) Your Thoreauvian notebooks should exhibit some of these characteristics in each entry; try in some entries to imitate Thoreau's style of writing, as well. Feel free to disagree with Thoreau's opinions, as you wish.

Works Cited

Adler-Kassner, Linda, Robert Crooks, and Ann Watters, eds. *Writing the Community: Concepts and Models for Service-Learning in Composition.* Washington, DC: American Association for Higher Education, 1997.

Bean, John C. *Engaging Ideas: The Professor's Guide to Integrating Writing, Critical Thinking, and Active Learning in the Classroom.* San Francisco: Jossey-Bass, 1996.

Bloom, Lynn Z. "Living to Tell the Tale: The Complicated Ethics of Creative Nonfiction." *College English* 65, no. 3 (2003): 276–89.

Buell, Lawrence. *The Environmental Imagination: Thoreau, Nature Writing, and the Formation of American Culture.* Cambridge: Harvard University Press, 1995.

Carnes, Mark. "The Liminal Classroom." *Chronicle of Higher Education,* October 8, 2004, B6–B8.

Cushman, Ellen. "The Public Intellectual, Service Learning, and Activist Research." *College English* 61 (1999): 328–36.

Cushman, Ellen. "Service Learning as the New English Studies." In *Beyond English, Inc.: Curricular Reform in a Global Economy,* ed. David B. Downing, Claude Mark Hurlbert, and Paula Mathieu, 204–18. Portsmouth, NH: Boynton, 2002.

Cushman, Ellen. "Sustainable Service Learning Programs." *College Composition and Communication* 54 (September 2002): 40–65.

Deans, Thomas. *Writing and Community Action: A Service-Learning Rhetoric with Readings.* New York: Longman, 2003.

Deans, Thomas. *Writing Partnerships: Service-Learning in Composition.* Urbana, IL: National Council of Teachers of English, 2000.

Downing, David B., Claude Mark Hurlbert, and Paula Mathieu, eds. *Beyond English, Inc.: Curricular Reform in a Global Economy.* Portsmouth, NH: Boynton, 2002.

Flower, Linda. *The Construction of Negotiated Meaning: A Social Cognitive Theory of Writing.* Carbondale: Southern Illinois University Press, 1994.

Friend, Christy. "Imitations of Battle: Quintilian on the Classroom and the Public Sphere." *Composition Forum* 14, no. 1 (2003): 1–16.

Grobman, Laurie. "Is There a Place for Service Learning in Literary Studies?" In *Profession 2005,* 125–40. New York: Modern Language Association, 2005.

Howard, Rebecca Moore. *Standing in the Shadow of Giants: Plagiarists, Authors, Collaborators.* Stamford, CT: Ablex, 1999.

Scholes, Robert. *Textual Power: Literary Theory and the Teaching of English.* New Haven: Yale University Press, 1985.

Young, Art. *Teaching Writing Across the Curriculum.* 3rd ed. Saddle River, NJ: Prentice Hall, 1999.

Plagiarism across Cultures

Is There a Difference?

Joel Bloch

The first part of my title, "Plagiarism across Cultures," raises a question that has been fiercely debated for many years in the field of second-language (L2) composition, particularly in what is called contrastive or intercultural rhetoric (Connor). Research in this area has examined how a student's first language and home culture may affect his second language writing. The second part of my title, "Is There a Difference?" raises another question, of how great are these differences and what is their significance for the teaching of L2 composition. This issue of cultural difference in attitudes toward plagiarism has always been strongly contested, with charges and counter-charges about racism and about "essentialism," and whether Western attitudes toward English-language teaching denigrates the cultural values of English-language learners (e.g., Kubota and Lerner).The sharpest division of opinion has been about how cultural differences affect the attitudes these English-language learners have toward plagiarism (Bloch; Matalene; Pennycook; Chandrasoma, Thompson, and Pennycook; Stanley). Much of the research has examined possible cross-cultural differences among English-language learners whose first language is Chinese. Teachers have often jumped on this view of cultural difference to justify their views of plagiarism in Chinese society (Matalene). Many Western educators believe that Chinese students neither understand Western concepts nor feel that such plagiarism is an unacceptable practice. And sometimes this view is true, especially when we define plagiarism in absolute terms.

While China has a long tradition of literacy, the importance it places on collectivism is often seen as dichotomous to the Western concept of individualism. It is often assumed that this collectivistic nature devalues the Romantic concept of authorship prevalent in the West and places a greater value on imitation. Because it has been thought that China is more of a collective society, it has been assumed that there is less concern for how intellectual property is appropriated or attributed. Therefore, a greater degree of imitation in the creation of new intellectual property is both encouraged and valued. These assumptions underlie the belief that all English-language learners bring to the classroom a different value system in regard to plagiarism than the one prevalent in the West (Howard "Standing"; Chandrasoma, Thompson, and Pennycook). Chandrasoma, Thompson, and Pennycook argue that some forms of plagiarism can be acts of resistance to the dominant forms of rhetoric, especially where these forms contradict the students' own epistemological traditions (189).

These problems can be especially true in Chinese cultures where imitation has long been highly valued. The link between originality and ownership, which often shapes the moral metaphors regarding "theft" related to discussions of plagiarism in the West, may not be as clear-cut in Chinese culture. This essay will examine the nature of this relationship between imitation and originality and how a different perspective on this relationship can affect both our attitudes toward plagiarism and how we teach our L2 students about plagiarism.

I became interested in this topic because of two incidents I experienced many years ago when I was teaching in China. I was teaching at a time when there were still few materials available to my students about current trends in composition pedagogy. My aunt had forwarded a copy of *College English* that contained Carolyn Matalene's often cited and highly controversial article on contrastive rhetoric, which was based on her teaching experiences in China. I gave copies of this article to my students to read and respond to. That evening there was a knock on our door from a group of very agitated students, who were upset at what Matalene had said, particularly about how Chinese students do not seem to share a negative attitude toward plagiarism that she would expect to find. I would later tell this story to Alton Becker, who has written extensively on intercultural linguistics. His response was that when you tell someone they are different, they think you mean they are inferior, a topic that I will return to later.

The second incident I encountered illustrates how the basis of this controversy over plagiarism has its roots in the concepts of imitation and originality. During a visit to my father-in-law, who is a well-known professor of Western art in Guangzhou, I told him about an exhibit of a thousand years of Chinese art and how impressed I was with the continuity of the artworks across such a long period of time. He glared at me across the dining room table and said, "There is nothing similar about them." What was imitation to me was highly original to him. My encounters with my students and my father-in-law have helped shape my view today that the answer to the question, "Is there a dichotomy between these two cultures in how they view imitation, originality, and plagiarism?" is always "maybe."

The Dichotomy and English-Language Learners

How we answer this question shapes how we view our students and their problems in negotiating the boundaries of plagiarism. Pennycook, for instance, raises a concern about whether the application of such concepts as plagiarism, which are deeply rooted in American economic life, might reflect a desire to impose Western values in contexts where they may not apply. Therefore, he argues that plagiarism can be seen as an act of resistance against the imposition of alien rules. In other cases, it may be seen as an act of survival where the risk of having the wrong idea outweighs the reward of having an original one. I have told the story of a Chinese student who admits to having plagiarized during the Cultural Revolution in order to be sure to have the correct political line, from which any deviation could result in severe penalties. His acts of imitation and plagiarism may be thought of as acts of political survival and therefore something to be admired (Bloch 218).

As most advocates of contrastive rhetoric would argue, differences in languages and attitudes do not normally imply a "deficit." However, resistance to the idea of a deficit, both in rhetorical and moral terms, seems to fade away when discussing plagiarism. Kubota, for example, has argued that focusing on cultural differences can cause students to feel negative about their own language and practices, as my students in China seemed to show. The consequences of this essentialism can be seen in how some teachers in the United States condescend to international students by assuming that they should not be held to the same standards as native speakers since they simply do not seem to "get it" in regard to plagiarism.

At the heart of these misunderstandings has been the assumption that originality and imitation are opposites in the same way that individualism and collectivism are. A Romantic view of artistic creation has led some to denigrate the value of imitation. In fact, Westerners memorize, imitate, and plagiarize all the time. Imitation in the form of using other peoples' ideas is seen in the West as intertextuality. Memory pervades everything we say and write. As Alton Becker put it, "The history of our particular interactions, oral and written, builds each of us a domain of discourse, a constantly changing-drifting-domain of discourse in which we live and have an identity" (230). The recall of these memories can also be seen as an integral part of what it means to be literate. The precise ways in which such memories are used can vary greatly both across and within different genres of writing. In postmodern views of academic writing, we memorize the writings of the "giants" and use them in our papers to show that we have read them (ethos), that they agree with us (logos), and if they disagree, they either must be wrong or discussing something different (Latour).

Yet imitation continues to be associated primarily with so-called collectivistic cultures, such as China, which values the imitation of previous knowledge as an expression of the connection between past and present. This dichotomy between individualism and collectivity has been strongly challenged by many researchers in Chinese thought. Hall and Ames argue that individualism and collectivism are not mutually exclusive, but are both deeply integrated in Chinese culture. An individual in Chinese society can be concerned with herself as an individual and with the society at the same time. We can see the same in the Chinese rhetorical tradition. There is no question that Chinese learning emphasizes the imitation of traditional forms of intellectual property. Learning is shaped at an early age by the importance given in literacy instruction to memorizing characters and imitating the classic writings of the sages. Achieving literacy requires the rote memorization of characters. Chinese children are taught that it is not enough to learn to write; one must also imitate the traditional stroke order for every character. From this perspective, how Chinese writers appropriate texts is deeply inherent in Chinese culture.

The imitation of a common canon of texts, which is thought to be the source of much of the problem with plagiarism, may be culturally crucial, but it does not obviate the importance of critical thinking or personal expression. This same viewpoint has been found in Chinese rhetoric for the last three thousand years. For example, when Chinese children learn ancient T'ang poetry, they begin by memorizing the poetry. The Chinese believe that such memorization is a good exercise for the brain. By memorizing the rhymes, they can better understand their beauty. However, as my early encounter with my father-in-law showed me, the importance placed on imitation does not obviate the importance of originality. But what is meant by originality still may not be the same as it is in the West, and therefore what is meant by plagiarism may also not be the same.

The Chinese have often reflected on this question of imitation and originality. There is a Chinese saying, perhaps somewhat sarcastic, that goes

> Memorizing three hundred poems from the Tang dynasty,
> Even if you don't know how to write,
> You can steal the pieces to write a poem.

How do we view creations such as these? An act of theft? An act of learning? An act of creation? Regardless of the answers, we can recognize in this saying our own Western concept of intertextuality. This saying also recognizes the value imitation has on the production of original knowledge. The rhetoric of imitation is also part of the Chinese form of epistemology, which can be seen in another saying, *Wen gu ru xin* (Review the old materials to gain a new perspective) that demonstrates how imitation can lead to originality rather than be a hindrance. We can see this traditional Chinese way of thinking reappear in contemporary thinking about intellectual property. The term *remixing,* which Lawrence Lessig has applied to how new forms of intellectual property are created from old forms, suggests the thought that all texts "remix" prior texts to create something new. Perhaps the Chinese approach to memorization and originality is not dramatically different from what is found in the West. Therefore, the importance given today to this intertextuality in all forms of writing has made it necessary to rethink attitudes toward plagiarism, especially as it applied to non-Western cultures.

Historicizing Cultural Differences

Scholars have shown that current ideas and practices related to intellectual property and plagiarism are socially constructed and therefore can change as social and economic factors change. We can see in historical studies of Chinese rhetoric that imitation is only one form of epistemology that Chinese thinkers could draw upon (Blinn and Garrett; Garrett). A study of traditional Chinese texts, even those written hundreds of years ago, can reveal how Chinese writers would imitate the classics, but at the same time extend their meaning and add their own voice (Henricks). Although textual attribution might be quite different, Chinese attitudes toward intertextuality and remixing have never been monolithic but have greatly varied across different periods and between different rhetoricians and philosophers.

The importance given to imitation has carried over into some, but not all, of the rhetorical systems traditionally found in Chinese literacy. The examination system for over a thousand years stressed the importance of memorizing and imitating classic texts, although this approach to education was never the only one that existed. Confucius's famous dictum, "I transmit rather than create," has often been cited, perhaps in an oversimplified manner, as referring to the appropriation of texts with no need for additional interpretation. Memorization and imitation, however, were not viewed as simply the recapitulation of ideas but rather as a fusion between the learner's process of thinking and that of the sages, as is any form of intertextuality. An individual in Chinese society can be concerned with herself as an individual and with the society at the same time, in the same way any writer can be concerned with both.

The complexity of this relationship between imitation and originality can be seen in the difficulty students can have in judging what constitutes plagiarism. The question a lawyer might ask about how much a piece of intellectual property has to be transformed before it is considered "original" is similar to the question the student might ask about whether a piece of text is considered plagiarized. Answers to students' questions about how much they can imitate before their writing is considered to be plagiarism or whether common knowledge must be cited revolve around attitudes toward intellectual property and plagiarism, which, in both China and the West, have been shaped by cultural, economic, and historical factors (Alford; Jaszi; Lunsford and Ede; Vaidhyanathan).

This connection between concepts of plagiarism and concepts of intellectual property can give researchers an important perspective for overcoming the often simplistic way cultural differences in plagiarism have been viewed. To Westerners, China appears to lack a sophisticated system for protecting intellectual property, which is then seen to be a cause of the apparent proclivity of Chinese students to commit plagiarism. If English-language learners do not agree that plagiarism is the same as the theft of real property (as the etymology of the word *plagiarism* as "kidnapping" suggests), then societies such as China will inevitably be viewed as "a nation of pirates." Should teachers feel, then, that Chinese culture encourages plagiarism in the same way the record and motion picture companies seem to feel Chinese culture encourages the theft of their songs and movies?

Looking at these issues in a historical context will show that these differences are not as wide as is often thought. As Alford points out, attempts to impose Western forms of intellectual property law in China were problematic because they did not attempt to account for "the character of Chinese political culture" (2). The idea of protecting the intellectual property of a "creative genius" has been considered at odds with the "collectivist" nature of Chinese society. Despite differences, there has been a recognition, as there has been in the West, of the author's ownership of her intellectual property.

However, there are differences as well, which may be related to the greater emphasis placed on the community. Chinese intellectual property law has long been as concerned with the control of property as much as with the rights of individual authors (Alford 57). As is shown by the deals the Chinese government has cut with Yahoo and Google to limit access to online materials, the government has more often focused on the control of private property than on granting private property rights. The relationship between the individual and the society has never appeared to be as dichotomized as it is sometimes seen in the West (Mao).

Therefore, it can be said that neither intellectual property law nor attitudes toward plagiarism have developed in the same way in China as they have in the West. Bloch and Chi found that traditionally Chinese writers did not place as much importance on the attribution of source texts as their Western counterparts, although, as will be discussed below, the situation has recently been changing. The differences in such practices may cause some Chinese texts to be considered plagiarized by Western standards. Yet Bloch and Chi also found much similarity in the rhetorical purposes these citations were used for, indicating that these differences are not as pervasive as is often thought.

As Vaidhyanathan demonstrates, nineteenth-century America, which imported much of its intellectual property from England, had lax attitudes toward plagiarism, and the wholesale theft of intellectual property occurred, creating what we sometimes refer to, in regard to present-day China, as a "culture of plagiarism." While we speak today, sometimes sarcastically, of a "plagiarism epidemic" among today's students, research shows that plagiarism was extensive in the nineteenth-century American university (Berlin; Russell; Vecsey). Vaidhyanathan argues that new forms of intellectual property, such as the development of motion pictures and the domination of the United States in the world market, helped change attitudes toward the protection of intellectual property. At the same time, universities became more research oriented, and students were expected to emulate the intellectual work of their professors (Vecsey), which may have contributed to new attitudes toward plagiarism.

However, as the history of intellectual property and plagiarism indicates, these attitudes can change dramatically as the social and historical context changes. A historical study challenges the concept that attitudes toward plagiarism are somehow intrinsic to specific cultures. We can expect that attitudes toward plagiarism in both China and the West will shift as historical factors converge and become more homogenized, even as these factors may have diverged at other times. Therefore, as Howard argues, we should change our attitudes and policies toward plagiarism as we have changed our approaches toward teaching composition, especially in the age of the Internet, when new forms of online texts require new approaches to thinking about plagiarism (Howard, "Understanding," 11).

There have been similar changes in how plagiarism is viewed in China. In modern times, Chinese thinkers, perhaps influenced by the West or by changing contexts inside China, have become more reflective about this concept. Liang Shiqiu, a Western-educated Chinese academic, comments ironically about that Chinese perspective on the relationship between imitation, originality, and plagiarism:

> Copying from a book is called "Plagiarism";
> Writing a book based on ten is called "Reference";
> Writing a book based on a hundred is called "Creation."

There have been obvious changes today in how plagiarism is viewed in Chinese academic society. While the pirating of intellectual property is still widespread, those segments of Chinese academia who wish to integrate themselves into Western cultural traditions are changing their attitudes toward plagiarism. For example, *Science* magazine, the official journal of the American Academy of Sciences, has reported a number of cases in the past decade of Chinese scientists caught plagiarizing (Li and Xiong). Over the same time, many American academics and journalists have also been caught. Therefore, it can be argued that neither society is more a culture of plagiarism than the other.

What is more interesting about these stories is how differently the accused have responded in each country. Li and Xiong report on a case of a scientific article considered to be plagiarized that had been submitted to a Western academic journal. The authors were not accused of stealing data but only the words of the English-language papers. Unlike Americans, who usually claim carelessness or memory lapses when accused of plagiarism, these Chinese academics, when confronted by their colleagues, readily admitted that they had copied parts of the literature review but felt that "the charge of plagiarism is not valid because we have all the data" (Li and Xiong 337). They argued that they had not falsified or stolen data, which occurs frequently in scientific research; rather, because of their limited English, they had had to resort to copying to make their paper suitable for publication. It could be argued that because this paper had been published, the fresh data was sufficient to provide a new meaning for the text that was allegedly plagiarized.

The surprise that these Chinese academics felt toward these accusations of plagiarism can be seen as a reflection of changes in attitudes toward plagiarism, as well as changes in the goals of those Chinese academics who wish to move to the center of Western academic societies. To achieve these goals, Chinese academic may have to devalue previously held views about the relationship between imitation and originality. Neither the Chinese authorities who reported the incident nor the Western journal editor valued this process of "remixing" through which new meaning was created. In essence, despite the relevance of the authors' findings, their process of memory and imitation was not valued, which put the authors in the same situation as if they had falsified or stolen their data.

It could be argued these scientists were guilty only of patch writing; that is, imitating the ideas of those who came before and then mixing in their own ideas as a means to become accepted as academic writers. However, they were not viewed in that way by their colleagues. This conflict over the relationship between imitation and originality also revealed changes in attitudes by the Chinese academics who blew the whistle on their colleagues. They seemed to feel that their own work would not be accepted in the West unless they adhered to Western standards regarding plagiarism. There have been parallel changes in the enforcement of Western forms of intellectual property law in China because of the government's desire to enter the World Trade Organization.

We can see in the "crackdown" on academic plagiarism, like the "crackdown" on pirating software and DVDs, how attitudes are changing in China. Chinese academics, like Chinese government officials, seem to realize that if they want to play in the game, they have to play by the already established rules. Speaking of the Chinese molecular biologist who led the inquiry into the accusations of plagiarism of the scientific article, Robert Schilperoot, the editor of the journal *Plant Molecular Biology* where it was published, said, "I think he's part of the new generation that is pushing hard to adapt Western standards" (Li and Xiong 337). Clearly, traditional

Chinese rhetorical standards, including the relationship between imitation and originality, were not thought good enough to be valued in the West.

As we come to recognize the contingent nature of plagiarism, we need to reframe the discussion on attitudes toward plagiarism across cultures. Chinese academics want to be accepted in Western academic communities, to be able to move from the periphery to the center (Lave and Wegner), which today means primarily publishing in English-language journals regardless of the writer's English-language ability. This tension between how Westerners view Chinese culture and how Chinese view their own culture is not new; it has existed for hundreds of years.

In conclusion, there is not today, nor ever has been, a single Chinese perspective on imitation, originality, and plagiarism, but, as I learned from my father-in-law, there is a different sense in how these concepts interact. Studying this relationship in a cross-cultural perspective reminds us of the danger of dichotomizing these concepts across cultures, so that only one culture is viewed as the "other." The result has often been an oversimplification of many aspects of the learning process—how students interact, how students think logically and critically, and even how they organize their papers, but the potentially most damaging effect can be found in how we understand the literacy practices of our students. At best, there has been a condescending attitude toward international students: that they should be treated differently because they don't know better. At worst, we have lost the opportunity to understand the complex learning strategies our students bring to the classroom.

If we place notions of intertextuality and remixing at the center of our teaching of writing, we can shift the debate away from moralistic approaches to plagiarism and toward a pedagogical one. Nonnative English speakers may still have problems negotiating the rules of plagiarism, but the problem is one of understanding the rules about how intertextuality is treated, not of obeying moral precepts. Moreover, when their process of imitation does not yield the desired result, their problems can be seen more as a language issue than a moral one. As Becker puts it, the process of entering into a new culture is one of confronting the "silences" of the new culture with the memories one brings along.

Plagiarism is similarly a problem of language. After all, these rules that govern plagiarism, like any set of rules, are never monolithic or static. They can vary across different genres and different writing contexts, but most importantly, the more complex the rule, the more it needs to be taught so that everyone can play on a level playing field. This perspective can help both researchers and teachers develop a framework for discussing plagiarism and developing pedagogies for teaching about plagiarism that helps our L2 students understand its subtleties and contradictions, as well as the reasons why the rules exist in the first place, in the same way they learn about any other aspect of literacy.

Works Cited

Alford, William P. *To Steal a Book Is Elegant: Intellectual Property Law in Chinese Civilization.* Stanford, CA: Stanford University Press, 1995.

Angélil-Carter, Shelley. *Stolen Language? Plagiarism in Writing.* Harlow, England: Longman, 2000.

Becker, Alton. L. "A Short Essay on Languaging." In *Method and Reflexivity: Knowing as a Systemic Social Construction,* ed. Frederich Steier, 226–34. London: Sage, 1991.

Berlin, James. A. "Rhetoric and Ideology in the Writing Class." *College English* 50 (1988): 477–94.

Blinn, Sharon B. and Mary M. Garrett. "Aristotelian *Topoi* as a Cross-Cultural Tool." *Philosophy and Rhetoric* 26 (1993): 93–112.

Bloch, Joel. "Plagiarism and the ESL Student: From Printed to Electronic Texts." In *Linking Literacies: Perspectives on L2 Reading-Writing Connections,* ed. Diane Belcher and Alan Hirvela, 209–28. Ann Arbor: University of Michigan Press, 2001.

Bloch, Joel, and Lan Chi. "A Comparison of the Use of Citations in Chinese and English Academic Discourse." In *Academic Writing in a Second Language,* ed. by Diane Belcher and George Braine, 231–74. Norwood, NJ: Ablex, 1995.

Chandrasoma, Ranamukalage, Celia. M. Thompson, and Alistair Pennycook, "Beyond Plagiarizing: Transgressive and Nontransgressive Intertextuality." *Journal of Language, Identity, and Education* 3 (2004): 171–93.

Connor, Ulla. "Intercultural Rhetoric Research: Beyond Texts." *Journal of English for Academic Purposes* 3 (2004): 291–304.

Fox, Helen. *Listening to the World: Cultural Issues in Academic Writing.* Urbana, IL: National Council of Teachers of English, 1994.

Garrett, Mary. "The Asian Challenge." In *Contemporary Perspectives on Rhetoric,* 2nd ed., ed. Sonja K. Foss, Karen A. Foss, and Robert Trapp, 295–314. Prospect Heights, IL: Waveland Press, 1991.

Hall, David, and Roger Ames. *Thinking through Confucius.* Albany: State University of New York Press, 1987.

Henricks, Robert G. *Philosophy and Argumentation in Third-Century China: The Essays of His K'ang.* Princeton: Princeton University Press, 1983.

Howard, Rebecca Moore. *Standing in the Shadow of Giants: Plagiarists, Authors, Collaborators.* Stamford, CT: Ablex, 1999.

Howard, Rebecca Moore. "Understanding 'Internet Plagiarism'." *Computers and Composition* 24 (2007): 3–15.

Hull, Glynda, and Mike Rose. "Rethinking Remediation: Toward a Social-Cognitive

Understanding of Problematic Reading And Writing." *Written Communication* 6 (1989): 139–54.

Jaszi, Peter. "On the Author Effect: Contemporary Copyright and Collective Creativity." In *The Construction of Authorship: Textual Appropriation in Law and Literature,* ed. Martha Woodmansee and Peter Jaszi, 29–56. Durham, NC: Duke University Press, 1994.

Kubota, Ryuko. "An Investigation of L1–L2 Transfer in Writing among Japanese University Students: Implications for Contrastive Rhetoric." *Journal of Second Language Writing* 7 (1998): 69–100.

Kubota, Ryuka, and Alan Lehner. "Toward Critical Contrastive Rhetoric." *Journal of Second Language Writing* 13 (2004): 7–27.

Latour, Bruno. *Science in Action.* Cambridge: Harvard University Press, 1988.

Lave, Jean, and Etienne Wegner. *Situated Learning: Legitimate Peripheral Participation.* Cambridge: Cambridge University Press, 1991.

Li, Xiguang, and Lei Xiong. "Chinese Researchers Debate Rash of Plagiarism Cases." *Science* 274 (1996): 337–38.

Lunsford, Andrea A., and Lisa Ede. "Collaborative Authorship and the Teaching of Writing." In *The Construction of Authorship: Textual Appropriation in Law and Literature,* ed. Martha Woodmansee and Peter Jaszi, 417–38. Durham, NC: Duke University Press, 1994.

Mao, Luming. "Persuasion, Cooperation, and Diversity of Rhetorics." *Rhetoric Society Quarterly* 19 (1990): 131–42.

Marsh, Bill. "Turnitin.com and the Scriptural Enterprise of Plagiarism Detection." *Computers and Composition* 21 (2004): 427–38.

Matalene, Carolyn. "Contrastive Rhetoric: An American Writing Teacher in China." *College English* 47 (1985): 789–808.

Pecorari, Diane. "Good and Original: Plagiarism and Patchwriting in Academic Second-Language Writing." *Journal of Second Language Writing* 12 (2003): 317–45.

Pennycook, Alastair. "Borrowing Others' Words: Text, Ownership, Memory, and Plagiarism." *TESOL Quarterly* 30 (1996): 201–30.

Rose, Mark. *Authors and Owners: The Invention of Copyright.* Cambridge: Harvard University Press, 1993.

Russell, David. R. *Writing in the Academic Disciplines, 1870–1990: A Curricular History.* Carbondale: Southern Illinois University Press, 1991.

Stanley, Karen, ed. "Perspectives on Plagiarism in the ESL/EFL Classroom." *TESL-EJ* 6, no. 3 (2002). http://www-writing.berkeley.edu/TESL-EJ/ej23/f1.html, consulted August 15, 2004.

Vaidhyanathan, Siva. *Copyrights and Copywrongs: The Rise of Intellectual Property and How it Threatens Creativity.* New York: New York University Press, 2001.

Vecsey, Lawrence R. *The Emergence of the American University.* Chicago: University of Chicago Press, 1965.

Woodmansee, Martha. "On the Author Effect: Recovering Collectivity." In *The Construction of Authorship: Textual Appropriation in Law and Literature,* ed. Martha Woodmansee and Peter Jaszi, 15–28. Durham, NC: Duke University Press, 1994.

Framing Plagiarism

Linda Adler-Kassner, Chris M. Anson,
and Rebecca Moore Howard

> *The analysis of common sense, as opposed to the exercise of it, must . . .*
> *begin by redrawing [the] erased distinction between the mere matter-of-fact*
> *apprehension of reality—or whatever it is you want to call what we appre-*
> *hend merely and matter-of-factly—and down-to-earth, colloquial wisdom,*
> *judgments or assessments of it.*
>
> —Clifford Geertz, *Local Knowledge*

On any given day, it's easy to find media coverage of plagiarism. A search in the Lexis-Nexis Academic database reveals hundreds of stories published in the last six months alone. A Google search with the words *plagiarism and college students*—which, admittedly, pulls up a range of items *about* college students and plagiarism, resources to address the issue of plagiarism, and other items related to the keywords—results in a staggering 1,690,000 hits. Plagiarism is *hot*. Nor is that heat limited to the popular media; colleges, faculty, and students are equally consumed by the notion that plagiarism is widespread and uncontrollable. Writing for the *New York Sun*, Lauren Mechling worries that originality itself is endangered by rampant plagiarism. And she quotes statistics offered by a university-sponsored consortium: "According to a recent article in *The New York Times*, Duke University's Center for Academic Integrity says 40% of college students admit to plagiarizing off the Internet, up from 10% in 1999." The *BBC News*, meanwhile, alludes to an "epidemic" of plagiarism, invoking the metaphor of disease—disease spreading uncontrollably—as a frame for understanding plagiarism. A volatile mix is brewing here: the fear that plagiarism is not only rising but attaining the status of a pandemic; that the core values of our society (such as its reverence for originality) are threatened by this virus; that students are duplicitous cheats or naive innocents; that technology functions as a medium for facilitating plagiarism; that technology can likewise be used to curb plagiarism; and that teachers' function is to thwart or catch plagiarists.

As faculty members in composition and rhetoric and as writing program administrators, we share in the concerns about plagiarism that are voiced by colleagues in our programs and institutions, by administrators, and by members of the public. Yet as scholars of student authorship, we have come to realize that this attention to plagiarism represents students and technology in ways that undermine not only good writing instruction, but the values of a liberal education.

News media reflect and perpetuate these problematic representations by describing student plagiarists as Web-savvy cheaters or as naive innocents.[1] This binary sensationalizes and simplifies the issue while "naturalizing" its own assumptions, impeding a critical understanding of intertextuality that can be applied in educational settings. Pedagogical possibilities are similarly constrained, deriving from a model of honorable or dishonorable, knowledgeable or ignorant students. As a counteractive, we advocate using the concept of "plagiarism" as a starting point for teaching students to recognize and adapt to the wide variations in the values informing the creation, use, and representation of text in the academy and the larger culture. This approach, we argue, is vital for students' development and for the educational enterprise itself. In 2003 all three of us contributed to a best-practices document about plagiarism that was commissioned and published by the Council of Writing Program Administrators (CWPA, "Defining"). That document promotes not only academic ideals of source citation but also academic ideals of writing instruction. Although teachers and administrators can and do draw on elements of that document, representations of plagiarism in news media (especially definitions of the problem and its one-step, technological solution in programs like Turnitin.com) demonstrate the power of the "plagiarism narrative" and the challenge of moving the conversation beyond a moral dualism, reductionism, and oversimplification.

Cultural theorists such as Stuart Hall explain the cultural process whereby definitions associated with "events" (such as plagiarism) are "constructed into a seamless narrative." Because they reflect and perpetuate the worldview of those participating in the narrative, these definitions become naturalized so that it is impossible to raise new questions or consider alternatives (Hall 4). This narrative is encompassed by what cognitive theorists, most notably George Lakoff, call "frames"—"unconscious cognitive models" that shape humans' understandings of the metaphors through which we construct our worlds (Lakoff, *Moral Politics* (1996) 159). Naturalized frames powerfully shape current understandings and future actions. The frames around "plagiarism" shape a narrative about how the roles of students, technologies, and writing instruction are dictated either by deceitful or ignorant students whose (intentional or unintentional) disregard for conventions of academic ownership are undermining the educational system. These actions that are taken (by educators and policymakers, especially) have significant consequences for students and for the broader culture that defines "education" (and particularly "college education") as a virtual requirement for participation in the nation's civic dialogue (e.g., Butler).

Naturalized Representations of Plagiarism

Representations of students, technology, and the purpose of writing instruction in the news stories analyzed here contribute to a conception of education that involves not teaching, but "catching" students. Students were described as duplicitous cheats in twelve of twenty-two (or about 54 percent) of the stories examined. Typical of this narrative is a statement by a philosophy professor from Eureka College: "When I was young, they were copying out of the encyclopedia. Now, they're copying stuff off the Internet" (Steinbacher). The representation of students as naive innocents who "don't necessarily know what plagiarism is" and "don't know that copying a few lines is plagiarism" appears in eight of twenty-two (or about 36 percent) of the stories in the sample (Diamond). Our sample was also dominated by two portrayals of technology. In fourteen stories (or 63 percent), technology was a medium facilitating plagiarism; this was coupled with the intimation that duplicitous students knew well how to use technology to their advantage and to undermine good teacherly intentions. Phil Anderson, director of the Honors System at Kansas State University, "credits" student ingenuity in a story from *Community College Week*. "The technology is certainly an enemy of academic integrity, and we have to figure out how to address those issues. The students are on the cutting edge" (Finkel).

The Internet is also portrayed as the weapon that can prevent this perceived abuse when it is used by qualified professionals. Of the fourteen stories in which technology was a medium facilitating plagiarism, ten stories also described technology—specifically, Turnitin.com—as a tool that could be turned against cheaters. A statement such as this could have come from any of these stories:

> The Internet constitutes a school. It is offering a course of direct and specific instruction to plagiarize. Students are learning lessons in cheating, but no one in a position of responsibility knows anything about them, because students are much tech-savvier than they are.

But it didn't. The "quotation" above actually comes from a 1910 article entitled "The Moving Picture: A Primary School for Criminals" and reads this way:

> These moving picture shows constitute a school. They are offering a course of specific and direct instruction. . . . The boys and girls of the land are learning . . . lessons in wrongdoing, but no one in a position of responsibility knows anything . . . about [them]. (McKeever 184)

Internet frames for discussing plagiarism reprise long-playing themes about the perils of technology, especially for children. Finding stories about the threat of one communication form or another to students or children in 2005, or 1954, or 1904 is an easy job (see, for example, McKeever's article, or Fredric Wertham's *The Seduction of the Innocent* for earlier examples; for scholarly analyses see Gilbert, May, or Douglas). It also doesn't take much digging to find discussions of the role of schooling in transmitting (or communicating, or teaching) "traditional American values," particularly the idea that a democratic society is perpetuated through the participation of virtuous citizens who understand the values of that democracy (see, for example, Dewey's *Democracy and Education,* or the language in the No Child Left Behind Act [United States Department of Education]).

But implied in the news stories about plagiarism is an additional complication: students are now using technology *in schools* to thwart the purpose *of* education. The level of threat is therefore more severe because one of the institutions charged with protecting "higher moral principles" and ensuring their perpetuation is being undermined by the very technologies that are doing the undermining outside of school. Thus, these news stories also fulfill a paradoxical role often played by mainstream media: stabilizing the threat posed by other media to those values. In this case, stabilization occurs in part through the framing of students and "antiplagiarism" technology discussed earlier, and in part through the framing of the teaching of writing. In the few stories here that mention writing instruction, the primary purpose of that instruction was not to foster good writing and good writers, but to prevent duplicitous students from cheating.

Certainly, good teaching prevents or at least deters plagiarism. Certainly, instructors in *all* fields should create original assignments, work with students on multiple drafts, and engage with students in the work of a classroom. But all too often stories frame this good work as important not because it helps to develop good writing or good writers, but because it *prevents* students from fulfilling the role of Web-savvy, duplicitous cheats. An interview with Greg Van Belle, a composition instructor at Edmonds Community College, illustrates how language that invokes best practices in writing instruction is framed by the idea that the purpose of good instruction is to stop bad students. "Detection services only inspire more ingenious cheaters," the story reports. "[Instructors] argue that carefully crafted assignments and more creative teaching is a *better* deterrent to plagiarism. . . . Van Belle said assigning an essay on the same topic year after year invites cheating. Better to vary assignments, link classic texts to current events, or ask students to write about how a work of literature relates to their lives, he said" (Thompson; emphasis added).

Van Belle's remarks capture an additional dilemma posed by the current frames surrounding writing instruction, technology, and writers: negating a frame—insisting, for example, that students are *not* looking to cheat—only serves to perpetuate the frame (Lakoff, *Elephant,* 3). The takeaway message from this story, for instance, is not that carefully crafted and more creative teaching will lead to good writers and good writing, but that such pedagogy will prevent students from cheating. Invoking "better ways to prevent plagiarism" serves only to strengthen the assumption that students are looking to plagiarize.

In the frame that dominates news media representation of plagiarism, students are undermining foundational principles of education associated with ownership and credibility; if they are smart, they are doing so intentionally, and if they are naive, they are doing it unintentionally. Teachers are either being duped or are playing catch-up to their more sophisticated students, often with the aid of ostensibly even more sophisticated technological aids.

Media representations create an objective for educators—the prevention of plagiarism and the detection and punishment of transgressors. This representation competes with and even detracts from the objectives that educators themselves hold—objectives such as helping students understand and participate in complex cycles of credit and credibility, write effectively, take responsibility for their writing, and participate in civic dialogue. Pursuing such objectives requires that we shift the use and meaning of "plagiarism" and the representations of students, technology, and education that accompany it.

Reclaiming the Frame: Citation Practices

Reclaiming education entails teaching students to recognize and adapt to wide variations in the values that determine how a text is created, used, and represented in specific social, academic, and occupational contexts— values often connected to cycles of credit and credibility that obtain in the academy and the larger culture. Consider one such textual domain, broadly characterized by "public information" and increasingly accessed over the Internet. If you happen to be searching for information about safe food handling in your kitchen, you might stumble on a fact sheet at the USDA's substantial Food Safety and Inspection website. This fact sheet contains the following information about defrosting frozen foods:

> Never defrost foods in a garage, basement, car, dishwasher or plastic garbage bag; out on the kitchen counter, outdoors or on the porch. These methods can leave your foods unsafe to eat. (USDA)

Although much boilerplate fills the pages of the Web, this statement, with its odd use of a semicolon and its journalism-style omission of the comma before the last element in a series, can be considered a piece of "original" text. In fact, it is unusual enough to have prompted the following exchange between two members of the Internet forum Insanetrain.com:

> BANANA: I just read this on a food safety site. "Never defrost foods in a garage, basement, car, dishwasher or plastic garbage bag." Has anyone ever defrosted food in the frickin dishwasher?!?!?!
> DEVIOUS: Or in your car?

As original as the fact sheet excerpt is, we find it repeated verbatim—idiosyncrasies of content and punctuation preserved—at a site promoting the preparation and consumption of curries (CurryCooking.com). In the absence of any citation, visitors to this site must assume that the text was authored by someone at this organization, whose Web page includes the global statement, "Copyright © 2005 CurryCooking.com and its licensors. All rights reserved." The text is also replicated in an article, "Focus on Freezing Foods," at a site promoting Filipino recipes and cuisine (lutongbahay.com). Along with other unacknowledged information from the FDA source, the article is authored "by Lutongbahay" and later is said to be "brought to you," the consumer, by the site's sponsoring organization, with a 2001 copyright. A bit of searching yields many more cases in which material from the FDA document, including this excerpt, is provided verbatim and without attribution—at cooking and recipe sites, at state and municipal agencies, and at business sites selling food products.

Curiously, however, a slightly altered version of the excerpt appears at the website of the Johnson County, Kansas, Environmental Department, where the odd semicolon has disappeared, replaced by a period and followed by three newly inserted words before the original text is taken up again verbatim:

> Never defrost foods in a garage, basement, car, dishwasher or plastic garbage bag. Never defrost foods out on the kitchen counter, outdoors or on the porch. These methods can leave your foods unsafe to eat. (Johnson County Environmental Department)

The website does acknowledge a source (the Food Safety Inspection Service) and includes a page of disclaimers, among them that users of the site "are responsible for checking the accuracy, completeness, content, currency, suitability, and timeliness of all information." A search for this slightly altered version yields several other sites where it appears verbatim, with the longer string of locations and the absence of the odd semicolon, but again without attribution. At one site, Colorado State University's Cooperative Extension page, an article titled "Foods in the Freezer: Are They Safe?" authored by Margaret Miller, who works for the university, includes the altered line verbatim; the page itself looks like a conventional article, with a title in a larger font centered at the top, then Miller's name, then the text (Miller).

At this point, several interesting and puzzling phenomena concerning the food-handling text have emerged. The USDA site seems to be the "source" of the text, but it is impossible to know from the site where it came from and who wrote it (since many public-service government documents are not individually attributed). Other sites—CurryCooking.com, people at the University of Georgia and the University of Colorado, the Filipino cooking organization, and companies like Corex.com, a manufacturer of Italian pastas—also could be the likely authors of this text, but they variously claim or disclaim ownership, fiddle with the text or leave it as is, and in all cases embed it within the rhetorical, informational, and pragmatic goals of their organization. Reflected in the many sites where one or another version of this excerpt appears is a kind of open-source attitude toward textuality, a free sharing of and even a willingness to slightly edit information with some trappings of ownership and intellectual property rights layered thinly over it all. The free-floating use of text repeats itself throughout the civic or public world. Explorations of other information domains—what do to when a tornado is approaching, the myths and facts of lightning, how to avoid being harmed in a flood or hurricane—yield hundreds of cases in which source text is replicated verbatim, cut and pasted without attribution, and in many cases so embedded in the organization's Web-presented material that it appears to have been created from scratch. Were these websites written by students and submitted in a college class, they would doubtless reinforce the argument advanced in the news stories analyzed above. Filtered through the dominant news media frame for representing plagiarism, these sites would most likely be called the work of plagiarists. Yet if we step outside the binary frames provided by the news media, we can apply alternative frames to interpret these issues of text ownership, and thereby situate our concerns and admonitions about plagiarism in the broader world of words and ideas.

One such frame comes from sociologists of knowledge Bruno Latour and Steven Woolgar, who have studied the ways in which science and scientists operate, and the values that drive their profession and give them individual and collective incentive. In their analysis, academics who want to rise in their professions become caught in a cycle of credit and credibility that is based in research and publication. As this credibility accrues, authorized by a complex system of professional checks and balances (for example, by reviewers who themselves have earned sufficient credibility to be appointed judges and evaluators), scientists earn credit—material rewards such as increased income and marketability, promotion and tenure, royalties, grants, assistants, equipment, and honorariums. Latour and Woolgar explain that this increased credit in turn produces additional credibility that enables further publication, public appearances, grants, prestige—and the cycle continues.

For many academics, the desire for credit and credibility provides a powerful motivation to research and write.[2] That desire is continually reified through the system of rewards and punishments practiced in academic institutions—a system that, in recent years, has found its way into educational institutions whose previous missions focused primarily on teaching, such as two-year schools and smaller liberal arts colleges (the administrative motivation presumably being to advance credibility at an institutional level). As opportunities for publication have become increasingly constrained, the competition for credibility is only heightened, fortifying the ideology of "intellectual property." For academics, it is difficult to imagine doing research for an institution, writing it up, and not wanting to "own" it.

Seen through this frame, the rampant replication of documents written in public contexts for the public good, such as the information about safe food handling, may seem reprehensible, misguided, and unethical. Outside the academic frame, however, such practices look quite different. If credibility is not earned through the production of public documents, credit does not become a motivating force, and giving or getting credit for a text hardly matters. The goal of text produced in civic contexts is not to garner credit and credibility in the ways academics understand these concepts. Government offices even encourage the adoption and circulation of public texts. If anything, credit in public contexts comes from the appropriation and replication of important information; success in the production of a leaflet on AIDS awareness, for example, is measured not by the fact of its publication and its contribution to the author's curriculum vitae, but by the massive reproduction and circulation of its contents, with or without attribution.

In fact, academic institutions are themselves constituted of multiple activity systems and discursive communities and thus reflect varying ways to earn credit and credibility and various means by which certain outputs are or are not rewarded. Many cases of so-called plagiarism occur at the borders where one set of (typically academic) values and practices blurs into another (typically public) set of values and practices. For example, cases exist in which one university reproduces the plagiarism policy statement of another university without attribution, placing it on its website for public consumption (see Morgan and Reynolds). In such cases, a period of recantation, apology, and shame follows the discovery of the ironic borrowing, reflecting the conflict of two institutionally inscribed value systems (one that argues fiercely for intellectual property rights, and another that argues for the free use of existing documents when there is no sense in creating unnecessary labor). In other settings at these same institutions, faculty no doubt exchange and use syllabi, teaching strategies, outcomes statements, administrative procedures, and other texts without citing their original source. Because the value system does not reward the production of such texts—

despite the fact that they involve deep commitments of creativity, energy, and time to produce—their ownership and attribution are not important.

In spite of the nearly universal academic mantra for giving credit, few scholars and educators acknowledge the rhetorical and pragmatic forces that also work *against* attribution. For example, educational institutions do not want to create a public persona in which it appears that they are too lazy or unproductive to write their own plagiarism statements. Finding a perfectly acceptable plagiarism statement at another institution may be an attractive alternative to writing their own, but the desire to create a persona of industry and originality acts as a disincentive to crediting the other institution. Similarly, many business contexts operate with *selective* proprietary interests in their own texts. Internet travel brokers will replicate descriptions of resort properties verbatim from the resort's site, preferring to use the resort's descriptions instead of risking misrepresentation with their own; yet they rarely cite the resort itself as the source of the text. They want consumers to *believe* that they are representing the property themselves in order to create trust and gain their loyalty. The resort hardly cares whether the PR material it commissioned is being co-opted by the broker, as long as it helps to fill rooms. But if a competing resort were to use the same text without permission, litigation would certainly result. Here, the value system driving the selective application of copyright provisions is almost purely economic, the "credit" connected not to individual authorship but to corporate profit. In many cases, the text itself only partly reflects corporate identity and ownership since portions are often replicated from site to site, blurring the lines between intellectual property and boilerplate (e.g., *"Ideally situated close to shopping and major attractions,* the [El Corazon Resort and Spa features a series of Mexican-style villas, each appointed with] . . . "[El Corazon]).

Acknowledging the existence of different discursive communities with different practices and activities allows us to imagine that in no community is the textual value system unitary or stable (see Russell). With this more nuanced understanding of textuality, teachers can help novice writers to make ethically and rhetorically sound choices specific to the various textual situations in which they find themselves.

Aligning Representation with Practice

The divergences between frames surrounding representations of authorial practice and the realities of that practice constitute what linguist Michael

Agar has called a rich point, a moment when different interpretations of a metaphor, shaped by different frames, come into contact (and often clash) with one another. This rich point has fueled a sense of emergency that informs public and academic discourse on the topic of plagiarism. Alarmed by the latest technology that seems to threaten literacy and ethics, and working within frames that portray students as duplicitous cheats or naive innocents, educational efforts too often fail to recognize that the goal of writing instruction is to help develop good writers who, among other things, understand that textual practices (including those of source use and attribution) exist within rhetorical contexts and know how to analyze and meet the expectations in those contexts. Instead, these efforts strive to remediate individuals or systems in order to prevent students from fulfilling the role of duplicitous cheats.

The remediation of individuals occurs in institutional documents like the student handbook, which typically includes a definition of plagiarism, together with institutional regulations against the practice of plagiarism. Individuals are also remediated in writing from sources through classroom instruction that is focused on transmitting textual conventions (practices of quotation, citation, and documentation). Both of these efforts work within the frame of the student as naive innocent: If students are informed of the institution's policies and are taught the rules of citation, they will have the information needed for avoiding plagiarism. But behind them— in the judicial boards or deans' offices where plagiarism cases are sent—lies the frame of duplicitous cheats, as well.

These remediations work from what Paolo Freire has called a "banking" model of education (77), in which education consists of transmitting information. In this model, individuals are machines that act seamlessly as a result of being programmed with the necessary information. Failure to do so derives from a conscious choice to transgress; it constitutes an ethical lapse in the subject.

Not only individuals but also social systems are remediated within the frame of students as duplicitous cheats or naive innocents. Systemic remediations may take place in the classroom or the larger institution. Rewriting plagiarism policy, instituting an honor code, and redefining the term *plagiarism* are three types of systemic reform.

A fourth type of system reform—and one that dominates media coverage of plagiarism—is the use of automated plagiarism-checking programs, especially Turnitin.com. In this remediation, the purpose of systemic reform is not education but control—control of the duplicitous cheater.

This control can be instigated through dire warnings in institutional policies about the punishment for plagiarism, striking fear into the hearts of the would-be plagiarists. It can then be enforced by compelling students to "submit"—and here the dual meaning of that word is significant—to *submit* their work to an online plagiarism-checking service. McGill University in 2003 went so far as to require that all students in all classes submit all their papers to Turnitin.com before they would be graded. Writing in the journal *Computers and Composition,* Bill Marsh describes some of the implications:

> [I]n remediating submitted papers, Turnitin.com introduces, as ethical technology, an ethical drug test to which all participants are subjected. Whether guilty or innocent under prevailing ethical codes and textual ownership laws, writers who undergo the test see their writing produced in particular ways by the Turnitin.com remediation machine. In submitting their papers, writers submit to the color-coded reconstruction of their texts and, more profoundly, their identities as writers, insofar as the originality report frames every submission in terms of its program-driven assessment of similarity. (434)

The presence of Turnitin.com as the for-profit consequence of the "duplicitous cheat" frame is repeatedly reinforced in news stories, which directly or indirectly refer to the product as a "cure" (and use its founder as a source) for the problems caused by plagiarism; yet its prescription is to strip from students not only their "identity," but also their agency as individual authors, actually undermining the very education that those concerned about plagiarism are trying to "protect."

We endorse the need for institutions to establish clear, fair policies on plagiarism. However, we also understand that these policies must derive from nuanced frames for understanding plagiarism, students, the purpose of writing instruction, and education itself. As our analysis of the appropriations from the USDA fact sheet illustrates, textual practices always exist within specific contexts and reflect the values of those contexts. Textual education needs to draw on the rhetorical savvy and analytic skills that our students have developed from their interactions with a variety of on- and offline genres and rhetorical communities. To be sure, these genres and communities may diverge from the dominant academic model of textual ownership and attribution; nevertheless, analyzing and appreciating their textual conventions can contribute to a greater respect for and more successful participation in the textual values that the academy valorizes.

These textual values inform "Defining and Avoiding Plagiarism," the

2003 best-practices document to which we referred earlier (see CWPA, "Defining"). That statement says that one responsibility of administrators is "publicizing policies and expectations for conducting ethical research, as well as procedures for investigating possible cases of academic dishonesty and its penalties." The document also calls on instructors to teach "the conventions for citing documents and acknowledging sources in their field, and allowing students to practice these skills."

At the same time, the CWPA document urges caution in the adoption and use of automated plagiarism-checking programs: "Although such services may be tempting, they are not always reliable. Furthermore, their availability should never be used to justify the avoidance of responsible teaching methods such as those described in this document." The word *temptation* here is significant. The temptation of automated plagiarism-checking programs to teachers parallels the temptation of paper mills to students. Both are typically driven by panic. Students may resort to purchased term papers when they are confused or disengaged. Instructors may turn to Turnitin for similar reasons, when they have given a generic assignment or when they don't work with their students during the writing process. And just as students' use of term paper sites positions them to prevent the learning that the assignment was designed to foster, so the use of automated plagiarism-checking programs typically positions instructors to sidestep the instruction in writing that students need if they are to make nuanced, ethical decisions in the wide range of textual situations in which they will find themselves. The use of automated plagiarism-checking programs perpetuates a frame that reduces the objective of instruction to preventing, detecting, and punishing plagiarism instead of helping students analyze and participate in the practices of writing for the various contexts in which they write. The use of automated plagiarism-checking programs elides analysis of textual practices in specific contexts—the very study that should be at the core of instruction in written communication.

All writers are always in a developmental trajectory; writing is always intertextual; a variety of rhetorical and pragmatic forces work *against* attribution of sources; the use of texts is a complex act that is steeped in the conventions (disciplinary, behavioral, and otherwise) of academe; and the sanctioned academic expectations for attribution are often applied unevenly, even by experienced, ethical writers. Most urgently needed are educational efforts that give students experience in applying the skills and practices they need in order to do their own work in a wide range of situations.

The challenge, then, is to escape the limitations reflected and perpetuated by the frames surrounding media representations of students, technology, and plagiarism, and reframe the ways that educators—and writing instructors specifically—talk about conventions of textual practice. We recommend the CWPA's "Defining and Avoiding Plagiarism" document as a starting point for instructors and institutions. It describes educational practices within the frames of the developing student writer and the variability of writing situations and textual expectations.

Institutions that act upon this reframing would not just reform institutional policy but also pedagogical methods. This would involve faculty development workshops that are focused not on detecting or preventing plagiarism but on creating a classroom environment in which students feel able to and motivated to do the assigned work. It also could involve public events—public within the classroom, the writing program, the institution, or the community—that celebrate outstanding student writing.

Teaching citation conventions is a largely technical enterprise; one either has or has not correctly cited a source. Reforming institutional policy is largely procedural, regardless of how contested that procedure may be. But reframing the discussion of plagiarism to focus on pedagogy that engages students in a study of genres and texts in specific contexts is central to real change both in the frame around, and the incidence of, plagiarism in academic settings. To be sure, this is a messy, open-ended enterprise and as a result is often neglected as a response to concerns about plagiarism. Yet if educators can successfully teach critical reading and citation conventions, revise our institutional policies so that they don't include misuse of sources in the definition of *plagiarism*, and create pedagogies of mentored engagement in course materials, the need for control mechanisms such as Turnitin.com will shrink to insignificance.

Notes

1. Stories selected for this analysis were published between February and July 2005 and indexed in the Lexis-Nexis Academic database. Using the search terms *plagiarism and students*, we selected the first two screens' worth of stories excluding international and business-oriented publications.

2. Sociologists of knowledge such as David Hull go so far as to propose that this motivation is the primary engine of intellectual progress.

Works Cited

Agar, Michael. *Language Shock: Understanding the Culture of Conversation.* New York: Wm. Morrow, 1995.

Butler, Johnnella E. "Democracy, Diversity, and Civic Engagement." *Academe* 86, no. 4 (July–August 2000). http://www.aaup.org/publications/Academe/2000/00ja/JA00Butl.htm, consulted July 23, 2007.

Center for Academic Integrity. Kenan Institute for Ethics, Duke University. http://www.academicintegrity.org/, consulted September 26, 2005.

Council of Writing Program Administrators (CWPA). "Defining and Avoiding Plagiarism: WPA Statement on Best Policies." Council of Writing Program Administrators, January 2003. http://www.wpacouncil.org/positions/index.html, consulted January 10, 2006.

CurryCooking.com. "Focus on Freezing." 2005. http://www.currycooking.com/freezersafety.html, consulted January 11, 2006.

Dewey, John. *Democracy and Education*. New York: Macmillan, 1916.

Diamond, Laura. "Curriculum Will Address Plagiarism." *Atlanta Journal Constitution*, April 24, 2005, 1JJ. Lexis-Nexis, June 2005.

Douglas, Susan. *Where the Girls Are: Growing Up Female with the Mass Media*. New York: Random House, 1994.

El Corazon. http://www.elcorazondesantafe.com/about.jsp, consulted July 23, 2007.

"'Epidemic' of Student Cheating?" *BBC News*, June 30, 2004. http://news.bbc.co.uk/2/hi/uk_news/education/3854465.stm, consulted June 30, 2004.

Finkel, Ed. "Sticky Fingers on the Information Superhighway." *Community College Week*, February 28, 2005, 7–8. Lexis-Nexis, June 2005.

Freire, Paulo. *Pedagogy of the Oppressed*. Trans. M. B. Rames. New York: Continuum, 1970.

Geertz, Clifford. *Local Knowledge*. New York: Basic, 1983.

Gilbert, James. *A Cycle of Outrage*. New York: Oxford University Press, 1986.

Hall, Stuart. "The Narrative Construction of Reality: An Interview with Stuart Hall." *Southern Review* 17 (March 1984): 1–17.

Hull, David. *Science as a Process*. Chicago: University of Chicago Press, 1988.

Johnson County Environmental Department. 2005. http://jced.jocogov.org/food_protection/faq/faq_freezer.htm, consulted January 11, 2006.

Lakoff, George. *Don't Think of an Elephant: Know Your Values and Frame the Debate*. White River Junction, VT: Chelsea Green, 2004.

Lakoff, George. *Moral Politics: How Liberals and Conservatives Think*. Chicago: University of Chicago Press, 1996.

Lakoff, George, and Mark Johnson. *Metaphors We Live By*. Chicago: University of Chicago Press, 1980.

Latour, Bruno, and Steven Woolgar. *Laboratory Life: The Construction of Scientific Facts*. Princeton, NJ: Princeton University Press, 1979.

Lutongbahay.com. "Focus on Freezing Foods." 2001. http://lutongbahay.com/index.cfm?pagename=articles&opn=1&ArticleID=80, consulted January 11, 2006.

Marsh, Bill. "Turnitin.com and the Scriptural Enterprise of Plagiarism Detection." *Computers and Composition* 21 (2004): 427–38.

May, Elaine Tyler. *Homeward Bound: American Families in the Cold War Era*. New York: Harper, 1999.

McKeever, William. "The Moving Picture: A Primary School for Criminals." *Good Housekeeping*, August 1910, 184–86.

Mechling, Lauren. "Plagiarism Is the Sin du Jour." *New York Sun,* September 29, 2004. http://www.nysun.com/article/2386, consulted September 30, 2004.

Miller, Margaret. "Foods in the Freezer: Are they Safe?" Colorado State University Cooperative Extension. October 30, 1998. http://www.ext.colostate.edu/PUBS/columncc/cc981030.html, consulted January 11, 2006.

Morgan, Peter W., and Glenn H. Reynolds. *The Appearance of Impropriety: How the Ethics Wars Have Undermined American Government, Business, and Society.* New York: Free Press, 1997.

Steinbacher, Michele. "Clicking Away at Cheating." *The Pantagraph* (Bloomington, IL), April 10, 2005: A1. Lexis-Nexis, June 2005.

Thompson, Lynn. "Educators Blame Internet for Rise in Student Cheating." *Seattle Times,* January 16, 2005, B1. Lexis-Nexis, June 2005.

Russell, David. "Activity Theory and Its Implications for Writing Instruction." In *Reconceiving Writing, Rethinking Writing Instruction,* ed. Joseph Petraglia, 51–78. Mahwah, NJ: Lawrence Erlbaum, 1995.

United States Department of Agriculture (USDA). Food Safety and Inspection Service. "Fact Sheets: Safe Food Handling." October 2005. http://www.fsis.usda.gov/Fact_Sheets/Focus_On_Freezing/index.asp, consulted January 11, 2006.

United States Department of Education. "Overview: Executive Summary." February 10, 2004. http://www.ed.gov/nclb/overview/intro/execsumm.html, consulted January 11, 2006. .

Wertham, Fredric. *The Seduction of the Innocent.* New York: Rinehart, 1954.

Selected Bibliography

Aarseth, Espen J. *Cybertexts*. Baltimore: Johns Hopkins University Press, 1997.

Across the Disciplines: Academic Perspectives on Language, Learning and Academic Writing, 2005. http://wac.colostate.edu/atd/articles/hall2005.cfm.

Adler-Kassner, Linda, Robert Crooks, and Ann Watters, eds. *Writing the Community: Concepts and Models for Service-Learning in Composition*. Washington, DC: Amer. Assn. for Higher Education, 1997.

Agar, Michael. *Language Shock: Understanding the Culture of Conversation*. New York: Wm. Morrow, 1995.

Alford, William P. *To Steal a Book Is Elegant: Intellectual Property Law in Chinese Civilization*. Stanford: Stanford University Press, 1995.

Angélil-Carter, Shelley. *Stolen Language? Plagiarism in Writing Elegant: Intellectual Property Law in Chinese Civilization*. Harlow, England: Longman, 2000.

Arias, Arturo, ed. *The Rigoberta Menchú Controversy*. Minneapolis: University of Minnesota Press, 2001.

Bakhtin, M. M. *Speech Genres and Other Late Essays*. Trans. V. W. McKee. Austin: University of Texas Press, 1986.

Barnstone, Willis. *The Poetics of Translation*. New Haven: Yale University Press, 1993.

Barthes, Roland. "The Death of the Author." *Image Music Text*. Trans. Stephen Heath. New York: Hill and Wang, 1978. 142–48.

Bartow, Ann. "Educational Fair Use in Copyright: Reclaiming the Right to Photocopy Freely." *University of Pittsburgh Law Review* 60 (1998): 149–230. http://ssrn.com/abstract=506983.

Basic Books, Inc. v. Kinko's Graphic Corp., 758 F. Supp. 1522, 1528–29 (S.D.N.Y. 1991).

Bawarshi, Anis. *Genre and the Invention of the Writer: Reconsidering the Place of Invention in Composition*. Logan: Utah State University Press, 2003.

Bean, John C. *Engaging Ideas: The Professor's Guide to Integrating Writing, Critical Thinking, and Active Learning in the Classroom*. San Francisco: Jossey-Bass, 1996.

Beckett, Samuel. *Texts for Nothing*. Trans. Samuel Beckett. London: Calder and Boyers, 1974.

Bell, Tom W. "*Fared Use v. Fair Use:* The Impact of Automated Rights Management on Copyright's Fair Use Doctrine." *North Carolina Law Review* 76 (1998): 557–619.

Benjamin, Walter. "The Work of Art in the Age of its Technological Reproducibility Second Version." *Selected Writings* 3. Cambridge: Belknap Press of Harvard University Press, 1996. 101–33.

Berlin, James. A. "Rhetoric and Ideology in the Writing Class." *College English* 50 (1988): 477–94.

Berlin, James A. *Writing Instruction in Nineteenth-Century American Colleges.* Carbondale: Southern Illinois University Press, 1984.

Beverley, John. *Testimonio: On the Politics of Truth.* Minneapolis: University of Minnesota Press, 2004.

Biagioli, Mario, and Peter Galison, eds. *Scientific Authorship—Credit and Intellectual Property in Science.* New York: Routledge/Taylor and Francis Books, Inc., 2003.

Blackmore, Susan. *The Meme Machine.* Oxford: Oxford University Press, 1999.

Bloom, Lynn Z. "Living to Tell the Tale: The Complicated Ethics of Creative Nonfiction." *College English* 65 (Jan. 2003): 276–89.

Buranen, Lise, and Alice M. Roy, eds. *Perspectives on Plagiarism and Intellectual Property in a Postmodern World.* Buffalo: SUNY Press, 1999.

Callahan, Daniel. *The Cheating Culture: Why More Americans Are Doing Wrong to Get Ahead.* Orlando: Harcourt, 2004.

Carey-Webb, Allen. "Transformative Voices." In *Teaching and Testimony: Rigoberta Menchú and the North American Classroom,* edited by Allen Carey-Webb and Stephen Connely Benz, 3–18. New York: State University of New York Press, 1996.

Carroll, Jude, *A Handbook for Deterring Plagiarism in Higher Education,* Oxford: Oxford Centre for Staff and Learning Development, 2002.

Chandrasoma, Ranamukalage, Celia. M. Thompson, and Alistair Pennycook, "Beyond Plagiarizing: Transgressive and Nontransgressive Intertextuality." *Journal of Language, Identity, and Education* 3 (2004) 171–93.

Claxton, Larry D. "Scientific Authorship." *Mutation Research* 589 (2005): 17–30.

Coe, Richard, Lorelei Lingard, and Tatiana Teslenko, eds. *The Rhetoric and Ideology of Genre.* Cresskill, NJ: Hampton Press, 2002.

Cohen, Julie E. *Copyright in a Global Information Economy.* New York: Aspen Law & Business, 2002.

Connor, Ulla. "Intercultural Rhetoric Research: Beyond Texts." *Journal of English for Academic Purposes* 3 (2004): 291–304.

Coombe, Rosemary J. "Fear, Hope, and Longing for the Future of Authorship and a Revitalized Public Domain in Global Regimes of Intellectual Property." *DePaul Law Review* 52 (Summer 2003): 1171–91.

Corbett, Edward P. J. "The Theory and Practice of Imitation in Classical Rhetoric," *College Composition and Communication,* 22, no. 3 (October 1971): 243–50.

Creative Commons. 7 June 2006. http://www.creativecommons.org.

Day, Michael, and Carol Lipson, eds. *Technical Communication and the World Wide Web in the New Millennium.* Mahway, NJ: Erlbaum, 2005.

Deahl, Jasper Newton. *Imitation in Education: Its Nature, Scope, and Significance* (New York: The Macmillan, 1900).

Deans, Thomas. *Writing and Community Action: A Service-Learning Rhetoric with Readings.* New York: Longman, 2003.

Deans, Thomas. *Writing Partnerships: Service-Learning in Composition.* Urbana: NCTE, 2000.

Delbanco, Nicholas. *The Sincerest Form.* Boston: McGraw Hill, 2004.

Dixon, Nancy. *Common Knowledge: How Companies Thrive by Sharing What They Know.* Boston: Harvard Business School, 2000.

Downing, David B., Claude Mark Hurlbert, and Paula Mathieu, eds. *Beyond English, Inc.: Curricular Reform in a Global Economy.* Portsmouth, NH: Boynton, 2002.

Eakin, Paul John. *The Ethics of Life Writing.* Ithaca: Cornell University Press, 2004.

Elbow, Peter. "Reflections on Academic Discourse: How It Relates to Freshmen and Colleagues." *College English* 53, no. 2 (1991): 135–55.

Elkin-Koren, Niva, and Neil W. Netanel, eds. *The Commodification of Information.* The Hague: Kluwer Law International, 2002.

Flower, Linda. *The Construction of Negotiated Meaning: A Social Cognitive Theory of Writing.* Carbondale: Southern Illinois University Press, 1994.

Foucault, Michel. "What Is an Author?" *Textual Strategies.* Trans. and ed. Josué Harari. London: Methuen, 1978. 141–60.

Fox, Helen. *Listening to the World: Cultural Issues in Academic Writing.* Urbana, IL: NCTE, 1994.

Frank, Martin. "Access to the scientific literature." *New Engl J Med* 354 (2006): 1552–55.

Freire, Paulo. *Pedagogy of the Oppressed.* Trans. M. B. Rames. New York: Continuum, 1970.

Galison, Peter, and Mario Biagoli, eds. *Scientific Authorship: Credit and Intellectual Property in Science.* New York: Routledge, 2003.

Geertz, Clifford. *Local Knowledge.* New York: Basic, 1983.

Giltrow, Janet. *Academic Writing.* 3rd ed. Peterborough, ON: Broadview, 2002.

Ginsburg, Jane C. "Authors and Users in Copyright," *Journal of the Copyright Society of the USA* 45 (1997): 1–20.

Gladwell, Malcolm. "Something Borrowed: Should a Charge of Plagiarism Ruin Your Life?" *New Yorker.* November 22, 2004. 40–48.

Green, Stuart P. "Plagiarism, Norms, and the Limits of Theft Law: Some Observations on the Use of Criminal Sanctions in Enforcing Intellectual Property Rights." *Hastings Law Journal,* 54 (2002): 167–242.

Grossberg, Michael. "Plagiarism and Professional Ethics—A Journal Editor's View," *Journal of American History,* 90 (2004): 1333–40.

Hacker, Diana. *Rules for Writers.* 5th ed. New York: Bedford St. Martin's, 2004.

Hansen, Hugh, ed. *U.S. Intellectual Property: Law* and *Policy.* London: Sweet and Maxwell, 2000.

Harris, Robert. *The Plagiarism Handbook: Strategies for Preventing, Detecting, and Dealing with Plagiarism.* Los Angeles: Pyrczak Publishing, 2001.

Heilker, Paul. *The Essay: Theory and Pedagogy for an Active Form.* Urbana, Illinois: National Council of Teachers of English, 1996.

Hoffer, Peter Charles. *Past Imperfect, Facts, Fictions, Fraud—American History from Bancroft and Parkman to Ambrose, Bellesiles, Ellis, and Goodwin.* New York: Public Affairs, 2004.

Howard, Rebecca Moore. "Plagiarisms, Authorships, and the Academic Death Penalty." *College English* 577 (November 1995): 788–806.

Howard, Rebecca Moore. *Standing in the Shadow of Giants: Plagiarists, Authors, Collaborators.* Stamford, CT: Ablex, 1999.

Johns, Ann M. *Text, Role, and Context: Developing Academic Literacies.* New York: Cambridge University Press, 1997.

Johnson, Andrew, and Rosemary Clerehan, "A Rheme of One's Own: How 'Original' Do We Expect Students to be?" *Journal of University Teaching and Learning Practice,* 2, 3a, (2005): 37–47.

Kostouli, Fillia, ed. *Writing in Context(s):Textual Practices and Learning Processes in Sociocultural Settings.* Amsterdam: Kluwer Academic Publishers, 2004.

Koutsantoni, Dimitra. "Attitude, Certainty and Allusions to Common Knowledge." *Journal of English for Academic Purposes* 3 (2004): 163–82.

Lakoff, George. *Don't Think of an Elephant: Know Your Values and Frame the Debate.* White River Junction, VT: Chelsea Green, 2004.

Lakoff, George, and Mark Johnson. *Metaphors We Live By.* Chicago: University of Chicago Press, 1980.

Larkham, P. J., and S. Manns, "Plagiarism and Its Treatment in Higher Education." *Journal of Further and Higher Education,* 26, no. 4, (2002): 341–49.

Latour, Bruno, and Steven Woolgar. *Laboratory Life: The Construction of Scientific Facts.* Princeton: Princeton University Press, 1979.

Lessig, Lawrence. "Dear Starbucks, Say It Ain't True?" *Lawrence Lessig.* 23 May 2003. http://www.lessig.org/blog/archives/2003_05.shtml#001223. 2 May 2005.

Lessig, Lawrence. *Free Culture: How Big Media Uses Technology and the Law to Lock Down Culture and Control Creativity.* New York: Penguin Press, 2004.

Lipson, Charles. *Doing Honest Work in College.* Chicago: University of Chicago Press, 2004.

Litman, Jessica. "Copyright and Information Policy," *Law & Contemporary Problems* 55 (1992): 189–209.

Litman, Jessica. *Digital Copyright: Protecting Intellectual Property on the Internet.* Amherst, N.Y.: Prometheus Books, 2001.

Litman, Jessica. "The Public Domain," *Emory Law Journal* 39 (1990): 965–1023.

Mallon, Thomas. *Stolen Words: Forays into the Origins and Ravages of Plagiarism.* New York: Ticknor and Fields, 1989.

McCullough, Malcolm. *Abstracting Craft: The Practiced Digital Hand.* Cambridge: MIT Press, 1998.

McKeever, Lucy, "Online Plagiarism Detection Services—Saviour or Scourge?" *Assessment and Evaluation in Higher Education,* 31, no. 2 (2006): 155–66.

McSherry, Corynne. *Who Owns Academic Work? Battling for Control of Intellectual Property.* Cambridge: Harvard University Press, 2001.

Menchú, Rigoberta. *I, Rigoberta Menchú.* Ed. Elizabeth Burgos-Debray. Trans. Anne Wright. New York: Verso, 1996.

Meyer, Michael, ed. *Thinking and Writing about Literature: A Text and Anthology.* 2nd ed. Boston: Bedford-St. Martin's, 2001.

Nelson, Cary. "Murder in the Cathedral: Editing a Comprehensive Anthology of Modern American Poetry." *American Literary History* 14 (2002): 311–27.

"Precautions or Prohibitions on Publishing." Editorial. *Nature,* May 19 , 2005.

Price, Margaret, "Beyond 'Gotcha!': Situating plagiarism in policy and pedagogy." *College Composition and Communication* 54, no. 1, (2002): 88–114.

Princeton University Press v. Michigan Document Servs., Inc. 1996 FED App. 0357P (6th Cir.) 17 April 2005 http://fairuse.stanford.edu/primary_materials/cases/ michigan_document_services/110896cofadec.html.

Robin, Ron. *Scandals and Scoundrels: Seven Cases That Shook the Academy.* Berkeley and Los Angeles: University of California Press, 2004.

Roig, Miguel. *Avoiding Plagiarism, Self-plagiarism, and Other Questionable Writing Practices: A Guide to Ethical Writing.* Office of Research Integrity, Dept of Health and Human Services, http://ori.hhs.gov/education/products/roig_st_johns/

Russell, David, and David Foster, eds. *Writing and Learning in Crossnational Perspective.* Urbana, Ill.: National Council of Teachers of English Press, 2002.

Sommers, Nancy, and Laura Saltz. "The Novice as Expert: Writing the Freshman Year." *College Composition and Communication* 56, no. 1 (2004): 124–49.

Steneck, Nicholas H. "Fostering Integrity in Research: Definitions, Current Knowledge, and Future Directions." *Science and Engineering Ethics* 12 (2006): 53–74.

Steneck, Nicholas H. "Institutional and Individual Responsibilities for Integrity in Research." *American Journal of Bioethics* 2 (2002): 51–53.

Steneck, Nicholas H. *Office of Research Integrity Introduction to the Responsible Conduct of Research.* Washington, DC: Department of Health and Human Services, 2004.

United States Patent and Trademark Office. "Trademark, Copyright or Patent?" 2004. http://www.uspto.gov/web/offices/tac/doc/basic/trade_defin.htm.

Vaidhyanathan, Siva. *Copyrights and Copywrongs: The Rise of Intellectual Property and How It Threatens Creativity.* New York: New York University Press, 2001.

Weiner, Jon. *Historians in Trouble: Plagiarism, Fraud, and Politics in the Ivory Tower.* New York: New Press, 2005.

Weinreb, Lloyd. "Commentary: Fair's Fair: A Comment on the Fair Use Doctrine." *Harvard Law Review* 105 (1990): 1137–61.

Winter, Richard, Alyson Buck, and Paula Sobiechowska. *Professional Experience and the Investigative Imagination: The Art of Reflective Writing.* London: Routledge, 1999.

Witte, Stephen, Neil Nakadate, and Roger Cherry, eds. *A Rhetoric of Doing: Essays on Written Discourse in Honor of James L. Kinneavy.* Carbondale: Southern Illinois University Press, 1992.

Woodmansee, Martha. *The Author, Art, and the Market.* New York: Columbia University Press, 1994.

Woodmansee, Martha, and Peter Jaszi, eds. *The Construction of Authorship: Textual Appropriation in Law and Literature.* Durham, N.C.: Duke University Press., 1994.

Yu, Peter K. "The Escalating Copyright Wars." *Hofstra Law Review* 32 (2004): 907–51.

Contributors

Linda Adler-Kassner is Associate Professor of English and Director of First-Year Writing at Eastern Michigan University. Recently, her work has focused on how writing and writers are framed in media and public policy documents. Her most recent book examines these conceptions in broader sociocultural contexts and explores how writing instructors can adapt strategies from community organizers and media strategists to affect frames and the actions extending from them.

Chris M. Anson is University Distinguished Professor and Director of the Campus Writing and Speaking Program at North Carolina State University. He has published widely in rhetoric and composition, literacy, and writing across the curriculum. He has just finished a book on digital literacies in the classroom, coauthored with Richard Beach, Lee-Ann Breuch, and Thom Swiss.

Anis Bawarshi, Associate Professor of English and Director of the Expository Writing Program at the University of Washington, Seattle, is the author of books and articles on rhetorical genre theory, rhetorical invention, and composition studies. He is currently working on the influence of prior genres on genre acquisition, as well as on the rhetoric of the Israel-Palestine conflict.

Anne Berggren, Lecturer at the Sweetland Writing Center, is the author of "Reading Like a Woman" in the anthology *Reading Sites.* She is currently expanding her earlier study of women readers and the novel.

Joel Bloch teaches ESL composition at Ohio State University. He has published articles on technology, plagiarism, and academic writing. He is currently completing a book on technology in the second-language composition classroom.

Lynn Z. Bloom, Board of Trustees Distinguished Professor and Aetna Chair of Writing at the University of Connecticut, is the author of biography (*Doctor Spock,* 1972), autobiography (*The Seven Deadly Virtues and Other Lively Essays,* forthcoming 2008), composition studies research (*Composition Studies in the 21st Century,* 2003), textbooks (*The Essay Connection,* 9th ed., 2010), and numerous creative nonfiction essays. Her current research focuses on ethics, essays (canonical and otherwise), and food writing.

Christiane Donahue, Associate Professor and Director of the Composition Program at the University of Maine-Farmington, is a member of the THEODILE research group (Théorie et Didactique de la Lecture-Ecriture) at the Université de Lille III, and is the author of a book, articles, and book chapters on using cross-cultural and cross-disciplinary discourse analysis to study textual construction in student writing. She is currently directing a longitudinal study in the United States and participating in three international research projects studying writing in the disciplines in other countries.

Caroline Eisner was the Associate Director of the Sweetland Writing Center at the University of Michigan from 2001–2007, where she taught courses on peer tutoring, composition pedagogy, and advanced academic writing. In 2007, she became the Academic Dean at Landmark College in Putney, Vermont. Since 1998, Caroline has been the director of BreadNet, a national K–12 teacher network at Middlebury College's Bread Loaf School of English.

Lisa Emerson, Associate Professor at Massey University, New Zealand, is the author of numerous papers on plagiarism, writing in the sciences, action research and writing, and online learning as it relates to writing skills. She is currently working on a project relating to i-maps and science writing, and another that compares stress and achievement levels of students working with online and paper-based learning resources.

Amy England is Assistant Professor of Rhetoric and Composition at the Center for Access and Transition at the University of Cincinnati. She has presented several conference papers on issues associated with plagiarism and patch writing and is currently researching how students sort and select electronic resources for their research assignments.

Erhardt Graeff, a graduate of Rochester Institute of Technology's programs in information technology and international studies, is a postgraduate student and researcher of social computing phenomena. He is currently study-ing recent experiments in e-government and e-democracy from a sociolog-ical perspective.

Michael Grossberg is the Sally M. Reahard Professor of History and a Pro-fessor of Law at Indiana University. He has written a number of books and articles on American legal and social history and is currently working on a history of child protection in the United States. He edited the *American His-torical Review* from 1995 to 2005 and has published several articles on schol-arly editing.

Rebecca Moore Howard, Associate Professor of Writing and Rhetoric at Syracuse University, is the author of books, essays, and articles on author-ship studies and composition and rhetoric. She is currently conducting text-based research on students' uses of cited sources.

Gordon Kane, Director of the Michigan Center for Theoretical Physics and Victor Weisskopf Collegiate Professor of Physics at the University of Michi-gan, Ann Arbor, is the author of papers and technical and general books on elementary particle physics and cosmology. He works on the phenomenol-ogy of string theory, supersymmetry, Higgs physics, collider physics, dark matter, dark energy, and inflation.

Christopher M. Kuipers, Assistant Professor of English and member of the graduate faculty of literature and criticism at Indiana University of Penn-sylvania, is the author of articles and case studies on the dynamics of anthology making and canon formation. His current projects include a conceptual history of "the canon," an edited collection of essays on the HBO series *The Wire,* and a postmodern anthology addressing 9/11.

Jessica Litman teaches copyright law, Internet law, and trademarks and unfair competition law at the University of Michigan Law School. She is the author of *Digital Copyright* (Prometheus, 2001) and the coauthor with Jane Ginsburg and Mary Lou Kevlin of *Trademarks and Unfair Competition Law: Cases and Materials* (4th ed., Foundation, 2007). Litman is a Trustee of the Copyright Society of the USA, a member of the Intellectual Property and Internet Committee of the ACLU, and the Chair of the Association of American Law Schools Section on Intellectual Property Law.

Laura J. Murray teaches American literature, the history of the book, and the cultural practices of copyright law at Queen's University, Kingston, Canada. She is the founder of www.faircopyright.ca, a public interest resource on Canadian copyright. She is currently researching a comparative study of the rhetoric of copyright in Canada and the United States.

Gilbert S. Omenn, Professor of Internal Medicine, Human Genetics, and Public Health and Director of the Center for Computational Medicine and Biology at the University of Michigan, is the author or editor of eighteen books and more than four hundred articles on genetics, public health, cancer prevention, proteomics, health policy, and science policy. He was President of the American Association for the Advancement of Science and is a member of the Institute of Medicine of the National Academy of Sciences and of the American Academy for Arts and Sciences.

Alan Peacock is Subject Leader: Screen Cultures and Interactive Media in the School of Film, Music and Media at the University of Hertfordshire, UK. As practitioner, theorist, and educator, his teaching, research, and creative artworks are based in an examination of the emergence of a digital culture. He is Project Leader of the Matrix of Information Handling Skills enquiry funded through the University's Learning and Teaching Fund, and its Blended Learning initiative.

Christina Pugh, Assistant Professor of English at the University of Illinois at Chicago, is the author of two books of poems: *Rotary* (Word Press, 2004) and the chapbook *Gardening at Dusk* (Wells College Press, 2002), as well as articles on contemporary poetry. She is currently working on a book of poems inspired by sonnets and an article about Emily Dickinson's metrical choices.

Amit Ray, Associate Professor in the Department of English at the Rochester Institute of Technology, is the author of *Negotiating the Modern: Orientalism and Indianness in the Anglophone World* (Routledge, 2007). He is currently, and not without irony, crafting a scholarly monograph on wikis and authorship.

Martine Courant Rife is a Michigan licensed attorney and a faculty member in the writing program at Lansing Community College. She is the author of several articles and book chapters on issues of copyright, the law of digital writing, international intellectual property, and fair use as it influences writing processes. She is currently working on a doctoral dissertation in the Rhetoric & Writing Program at Michigan State University: "Is There a Chilling of Digital Communication: Knowledge and Understanding of Fair Use in Digital Composing Environments."

Stefan Senders, a cultural anthropologist, is a Visiting Fellow in Peace Studies at Cornell University; he formally taught writing at Hobart and William Smith Colleges. He publishes on immigration, legal anthropology, anthropological epistemology, and issues in rhetoric, including plagiarism, narrativity, and legibility. His most recent book (with Allison Truitt) is *Money: Ethnographic Encounters* (Berg, 2007).

Martha Vicinus, Director of the Sweetland Writing Center and Eliza M. Mosher Professor of English and Women's Studies at the University of Michigan, Ann Arbor, is the author of books and essays on Victorian women, nineteenth-century popular culture, and the history of sexuality. She is currently working on a study of contemporary attitudes toward plagiarism.

Kim Walden, Senior Lecturer in Digital Discourse and Culture at the School of Film, Music and Media in the Faculty for Creative and Cultural Industries at the University of Hertfordshire, UK, has research interests in the fields of film, new media and media education and has published widely in the field. The i-map is part of an educational research project called Matrix of Information Handling Skills (MIHS), which is funded by the University's Learning and Teaching development fund and BLU-Sky initiative.

Jeff Ward, Ph.D. candidate in rhetoric at the University of Minnesota, Twin Cities, specializes in visual rhetoric with a particular emphasis on the photography. He is currently researching late-nineteenth-century rhetorics of place.

Index